WASHINGTON
WILDFLOWER HIKES

WASHINGTON
WILDFLOWER
HIKES

50 DESTINATIONS

NATHAN BARNES & JEREMY BARNES

**MOUNTAINEERS
BOOKS**

MOUNTAINEERS BOOKS is dedicated to
the exploration, preservation, and enjoyment of
outdoor and wilderness areas.

1001 SW Klickitat Way, Suite 201, Seattle, WA 98134
800-553-4453, www.mountaineersbooks.org

Printed in China
Distributed in the United Kingdom by Cordee, www.cordee.co.uk
First edition, 2021

Copyeditor: Erin Cusick
Cover design and layout: Jen Grable and Kate Basart/Union Pageworks
Cartographer: Lohnes+Wright
Illustration: Anna-Lisa Notter
All photographs by the authors, except for bottom photo on page 119 by Laura Shauger
Cover photograph: *Blue stickseed at Windy Pass (Hike 15)*
Frontispiece: *Approaching the summit of Bald Mountain on the Walt Bailey Trail (Hike 21)*
Back cover photographs: *Mount Baker from the Chain Lakes loop (Hike 11); subalpine mariposa lily; orange hawkweed; wildflower-filled meadows of Tiffany Mountain (Hike 17)*

The background maps for this book were produced using the online map viewer CalTopo. For more information, visit caltopo.com.

Library of Congress Cataloging-in-Publication Data is on file for this title at https://lccn.loc.gov/2020032362. The ebook record is available at https://lccn.loc.gov/2020032363.

Mountaineers Books titles may be purchased for corporate, educational, or other promotional sales, and our authors are available for a wide range of events. For information on special discounts or booking an author, contact our customer service at 800-553-4453 or mbooks@mountaineersbooks.org.

Printed on FSC® certified materials

ISBN (paperback): 978-1-68051-095-9
ISBN (ebook): 978-1-68051-096-6

An independent nonprofit publisher since 1960

CONTENTS

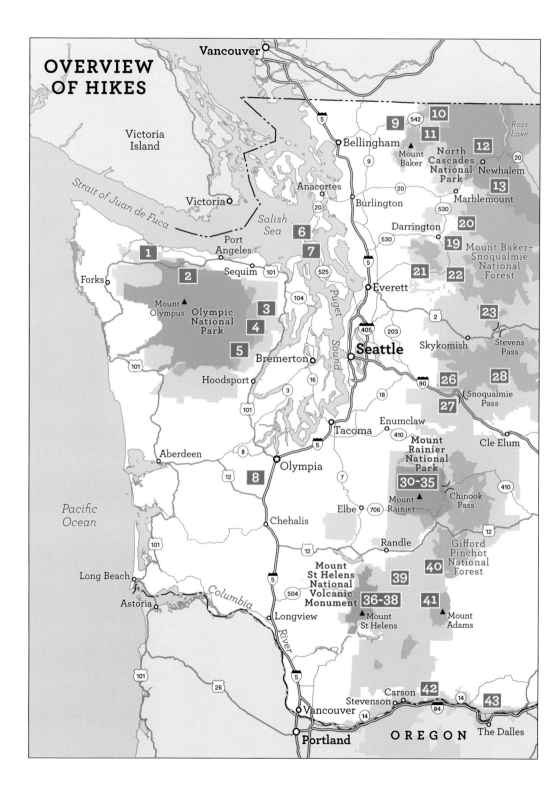

OVERVIEW OF HIKES

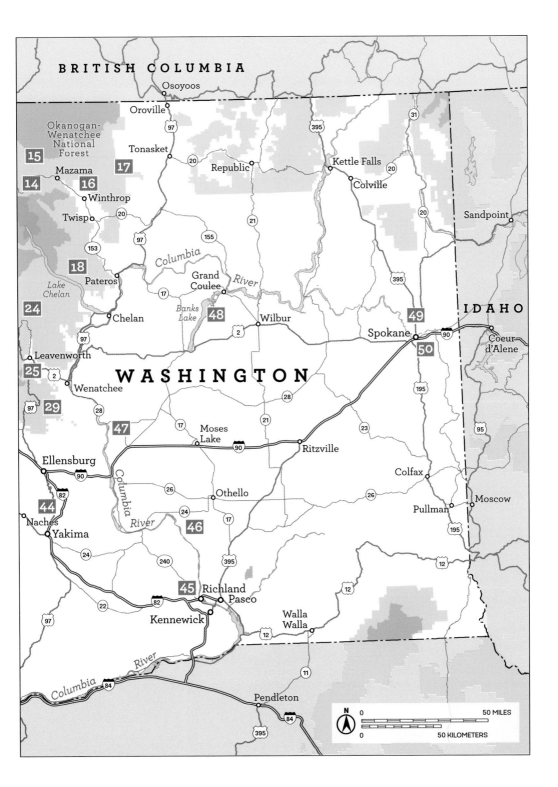

BRITISH COLUMBIA

Osoyoos

Oroville

97

Okanogan-
Wenatchee
National
Forest

15

Mazama

14   16

Winthrop

Twisp

20

97

153

18

Pateros

Lake
Chelan

24

Chelan

97

Leavenworth

25

2

Wenatchee

WASHINGTON

97 29

28

47

17

Ellensburg

90

82

44

Naches

Yakima

24

22

97

Tonasket

20

Republic

21

155

Columbia

Grand
Coulee

River

17

Banks
Lake

48

2

Wilbur

Moses
Lake

90

26

Othello

24

17

46

240

395

45 Richland

Pasco

82

Kennewick

12

Walla
Walla

Columbia

River

84

Pendleton

395

84

Ritzville

21

23

28

395

49

Spokane

90

50

195

23

Colfax

26

Pullman

195

Kettle Falls

20

Colville

20

31

395

IDAHO

Sandpoint

Coeur
d'Alene

95

Moscow

12

11

N

0   50 MILES

0   50 KILOMETERS

7

HIKES AT A GLANCE

HIKE	DISTANCE (MILES)	ELEVATION GAIN (FEET)	HIGH POINT (FEET)	DIFFICULTY	BEST SEASON FOR FLOWERS	TRAIL TRAFFIC	VIEWS	OVER-NIGHT
OLYMPIC PENINSULA & PUGET SOUND								
1. Mount Muller	8.4	2700/450	3748	Moderate	Late spring to early summer	Light	•	
2. Klahhane Ridge	6.4	1300/700	5900	Moderate	Late spring to summer	Heavy to moderate	•	
3. Mount Zion	4.4	1300	4274	Moderate	Late spring to early summer	Moderate	•	
4. Marmot Pass	10.4	3500	6000	Moderate	Summer	Moderate to heavy	•	•
5. Lake of the Angels	7	3400	4950	Hard	Summer	Light	•	•
6. Goose Rock	2.7	400	480	Easy	Late spring to early summer	Heavy	•	
7. Ebey's Landing	3.7	250	250	Easy	Early spring to midsummer	Moderate	•	
8. Mima Mounds	3.3	Negligible	240	Easy	Early spring to midsummer	Moderate		
NORTH CASCADES								
9. Skyline Divide	8.8	2400/200	6500	Moderate	Summer; good fall color	Heavy	•	
10. Yellow Aster Butte	7.6	2500	6200	Hard	Late spring to midsummer; excellent fall color	Heavy	•	•
11. Chain Lakes Loop	6	1700	5400	Moderate	Summer; good fall color	Heavy	•	•
12. Sourdough Mountain	9	5000	5985	Hard	Late spring to early summer	Light to moderate	•	•
13. Cascade Pass and Sahale Arm	11.2	4000	7600	Hard	Mid to late summer	Heavy to moderate	•	•
14. Maple Pass Loop	6.6	2100	6950	Moderate	Mid to late summer; golden larches enhance fall color	Heavy	•	
15. Windy Pass	7.8	Negligible/700	7000	Easy	Summer	Light to moderate	•	•

OPPOSITE: *Cloud-clad Mount Rainier rises above the Naches Loop Trail (Hike 33).*

HIKE	DISTANCE (MILES)	ELEVATION GAIN (FEET)	HIGH POINT (FEET)	DIFFICULTY	BEST SEASON FOR FLOWERS	TRAIL TRAFFIC	VIEWS	OVER-NIGHT
16. Lewis Butte	5.4	1100	3340	Moderate	Spring to early summer	Light	•	
17. Tiffany Mountain	4.2	1700	8245	Moderate	Summer; larches glow in fall	Moderate	•	•
18. Summer Blossom Trail	4	1500	7850	Moderate	Early to midsummer	Light	•	
CENTRAL CASCADES								
19. Old Sauk Trail	6	100	800	Easy	Late spring to early summer	Moderate		
20. Green Mountain Lookout	7.6	3000	6500	Hard	Late spring to summer; excellent fall color	Moderate	•	•
21. Walt Bailey Trail	9	2100	4800	Hard	Spring to summer	Light	•	•
22. Glacier Basin	13	2200	4400	Hard	Summer	Heavy to light		•
23. Scorpion Mountain	8	2300/300	5540	Hard	Late spring to early summer; excellent fall color	Light	•	•
24. Alpine Lookout	9.6	2400/200	6235	Moderate	Summer; good fall color	Moderate	•	
25. Icicle Ridge	4.6	1800	3000	Moderate	Spring to early summer	Heavy	•	
26. Mount Defiance	10.4	3400	5584	Hard	Late spring to early summer	Heavy to moderate	•	•
27. Lodge Lake	4	450/350	3500	Easy	Summer	Light to moderate	•	•
28. Esmeralda Basin	6.8	1700	6000	Moderate	Summer	Moderate	•	
29. Tronsen Ridge	4.6	800/300	4850	Easy	Late spring to early summer; golden larches in fall	Moderate	•	
MOUNT RAINIER & SOUTH CASCADES								
30. Spray Park and Spray Falls	8.2	1600	6400	Moderate	Late spring to late summer	Moderate to heavy	•	•
31. Grand Park	8.5	1100	5600	Moderate	Spring to late summer	Moderate	•	•
32. Fremont Lookout	5.8	800	7200	Easy	Summer	Heavy	•	
33. Tipsoo Lake and Naches Peak Loop	3.5	500	5900	Easy	Summer to early fall	Heavy	•	
34. Van Trump Park	6	2900	6500	Hard	Summer	Moderate	•	
35. Paradise Meadows Loop	4.8	1400	6800	Moderate	Summer	Heavy	•	
36. South Coldwater Trail	6.6	1300/100	3900	Moderate	Late spring to early summer	Light	•	

HIKE	DISTANCE (MILES)	ELEVATION GAIN (FEET)	HIGH POINT (FEET)	DIFFICULTY	BEST SEASON FOR FLOWERS	TRAIL TRAFFIC	VIEWS	OVER-NIGHT
37. Johnston Ridge	7.4	700/400	4600	Moderate	Summer to early fall	Heavy to moderate	•	
38. Norway Pass and Mount Margaret	11	2200/100	5800	Moderate	Late spring to summer	Light	•	
39. Tongue Mountain	3	1000	4600	Moderate	Late spring to early summer	Light	•	
40. Snowgrass Flat	10.2	1800	6400	Moderate	Summer	Heavy	•	•
41. Killen Creek Meadow	8	2300	6900	Moderate	Summer	Moderate to heavy	•	•
42. Dog Mountain	6.6	2800	2900	Moderate	Late spring to summer	Heavy	•	
43. Columbia Hills	6.4	800/100	1200	Easy	Spring to early summer	Heavy	•	
EASTERN WASHINGTON								
44. Umtanum Creek Canyon	3.6	200	1600	Easy	Spring to early summer	Moderate		•
45. Rattlesnake Slope	5	700	1100	Easy	Spring to summer	Light	•	
46. Hanford Reach and White Bluffs	6	200	1000	Easy	Spring to late summer	Light	•	
47. Ancient Lakes and Potholes Coulee	5	200	1000	Easy	Spring to late summer	Moderate to heavy		•
48. Steamboat Rock	3.9	700	2300	Easy	Early spring to early summer	Moderate	•	
49. Little Spokane River Natural Area	7.7	1000	2450	Moderate	Spring to early summer	Moderate	•	
50. Dishman Hills Conservation Area	5	1200	3600	Moderate	Spring to early summer	Moderate	•	

Beargrass-lined trail on the shoulders of Mount Defiance (Hike 26)

INTRODUCTION

Wildflowers are the jewels of the trail, a splash of decorative color that pops against spring-green underbrush or sandy desert scrubland. These trailside beauties attract interested hikers and back-packers as easily as they do bees, birds, and other pollinators. Wildflowers offer you a great reason to pause, catch your breath, and deepen your connection with nature. Learning to identify plants and flowers was part of our hiking experience growing up and continues to enhance our trips to this day.

Hikers seeking a trail through fields of wild-flowers are fortunate when hiking in Washington State, as our diverse environments are home to a wide variety of wildflowers that bloom at different times throughout the year. From Puget Sound lowlands to alpine passes to rolling desert scrublands, hikers can find flowers blooming from early spring to fall. Different ecological environments are home to different plants, and some hikes travel through multiple areas, which means that hikers can, for example, find water-loving calypso orchids

in the lowland forests of a hike, then climb up into rocky alpine zones covered in phlox and heather.

While we've spent a great deal of time learning a lot about plants and flowers we've come across while exploring trails across the state, we are not experts. We are not botanists or biologists, and we have no formal training in these areas. Instead, we consider ourselves wildflower enthusiasts who enjoy the color and variety of the many, many wildflowers and flowering shrubs found in Washington. As a result, this

Wildflowers brighten the trail up to Windy Pass (Hike 15).

Western Labrador tea thrives on rocky slopes along the Summer Blossom Trail (Hike 18).

book is not a technical manual for serious flower-hounds: You will not find extremely detailed specifications of wildflowers, plant descriptions filled with dense botanical terminology, or strict parsing of whether a particular flower is a weed, a wildflower, or a shrub. We leave that level of detail and assessment to more serious guides authored by experts in their field.

Instead, this book is intended as a guide for casual observers who enjoy taking in the bright colors on the trail and have a passing curiosity as to the name of the flower. Each entry includes a featured wildflower that grows along the trail as well as a checkbox that allows you to keep track of the flowers you have found. It's a fun way to add something extra to your hiking experience and begin learning about the many wonderful wildflowers growing throughout Washington. Photographs of the featured wildflowers and many of the other wildflowers are grouped by color in the identification guide (see page 30). This book is not a comprehensive

guide to wildflowers but rather seeks to be both a starting point for those who may want to get more serious down the line, as well as an excellent resource for those who enjoy keeping their wildflower appreciation on the lighter side.

While keeping the technical aspects light, we have included scientific (Latin) names for every featured wildflower. Many plants have multiple common names, and sometimes trying to identify a flower with only a common name can cause some confusion. Having the Latin name makes searching for more information in a flower guidebook or online much easier. In addition, sometimes the scientific name helps explain a particular common name or provides a little background on the flower's history.

We hope that this guide sets you down a path of many wildflower-filled hikes and excellent experiences on the trail. The goal is to point you toward the wildflowers and provide everything you need to get the most out of your hike and, above all, have fun on the trail. Adventure awaits!

HIKING BEST PRACTICES

Hiking is perhaps the most approachable of outdoor activities. You do not need special equipment or training. The surroundings in which you undertake a walking journey from one destination to another distinguish a hike from merely a stroll. Your morning walk to your office, bus stop, or school and the daily trip down two flights of stairs to the office coffee machine are all walking journeys, but they are not hikes. Where the journey takes you and your reason for undertaking the journey are what make it a hike. Perhaps because hiking appears so easy, many hikers do not take the trail's location and characteristics into consideration before they start barreling down it. Where you're hiking matters—not all trails are the same.

The hikes described in this book vary from short jaunts relatively close to civilization to longer forays into the wilderness, and hikers need to prepare accordingly. This guide assumes that readers have some hiking experience and know they should approach trails with an abundance of caution. We cannot warn of every hazard that a hiker may encounter on any given trail, as trail conditions change frequently. If you are new to hiking, round up some more experienced friends to bring along. These broad guidelines—not intended as a primer on *how* to hike—offer some topics to consider as you plan.

Be Aware

Although most hikers return from their trips without incident, hiking is filled with potential hazards. Loose trail surfaces, rotten snow, rockfall, lightning strikes, falling trees, fast-running icy creeks, snakebites, charging goats, and much more can be found along the trails in this book. At the same time, prepared hikers who pay attention to their surroundings can usually avoid these dangers. In short, do not assume that trails are safe. Be aware that trail routes and conditions may have changed significantly since the time of this writing.

If a route ever seems unsafe, listen to your instincts. Always exercise caution and do not be afraid to turn around and hike another day, even when the rest of your group disagrees with your assessment. As beautiful and enjoyable as nature is, it is also indifferent and unforgiving.

Bring the Right Gear

Pages upon pages could be filled with discussions about the best equipment for any given hike, what is a must-have and what is superfluous. Some backpackers and hikers spend endless hours arguing that the gear they use, the way they pack, and the methods they use on the trail are superior. But the truth is that the gear you bring along on a hike depends on the destination and the people involved, as well as the weather conditions. However, there is one requirement: always pack the Ten Essentials. If you do not know what the Ten Essentials are, consider finding a more experienced hiker to accompany you on your first trails into more rugged country.

The Ten Essentials

The point of the Ten Essentials, originated by The Mountaineers, has always been to answer two basic questions: Can you prevent emergencies and respond positively should one occur (items 1–5)? And can you safely spend a night—or more—outside (items 6–10)? Use this list as a guide and tailor it to the needs of your outing.

1. **Navigation:** The five fundamentals are a map, altimeter, compass, GPS device, and a personal locator beacon or other device to contact emergency first responders.
2. **Headlamp:** Include spare batteries.
3. **Sun protection:** Wear sunglasses, sun-protective clothes, and broad-spectrum sunscreen rated at least SPF 30.
4. **First aid:** Basics include bandages; skin closures; gauze pads and dressings; roller bandage or wrap; tape; antiseptic; blister prevention and treatment supplies; nitrile gloves; tweezers; needle; nonprescription painkillers; anti-inflammatory, antidiarrheal, and antihistamine tablets; topical

antibiotic; and any important personal prescriptions, including an EpiPen if you are allergic to bee or hornet venom.

5. **Knife:** Also consider a multitool, strong tape, some cordage, and gear repair supplies.

6. **Firestarter:** Carry at least one butane lighter (or waterproof matches) and fire-starter, such as chemical heat tabs, cotton balls soaked in petroleum jelly, or com-mercially prepared firestarter.

7. **Shelter:** In addition to a rain shell, carry a single-use bivy sack, plastic tube tent, or jumbo plastic trash bag.

8. **Extra food:** For shorter trips a one-day supply is reasonable.

9. **Extra water:** Carry sufficient water and have the skills and tools required to obtain and purify additional water.

10. **Extra clothes:** Pack additional layers needed to survive the night in the worst conditions that your party may realisti-cally encounter.

While there are few right answers to the ques-tion of exactly what gear to bring, there are cer-tainly wrong answers. Here are a few general gear and supply suggestions to help you avoid some common pitfalls:

- **Do not wear sandals or lightweight tennis shoes:** These footwear choices unnecessarily increase the risk of foot injury and make it harder to navigate the trail. Wear lugged-sole hiking sneakers or, for rugged trails, water-proof or water-resistant hiking boots for ankle protection and traction on rocky terrain.

- **Do not wear clothing that is restrictive, dif-ficult to move in, or not functional.** Avoid wearing something that will make it more difficult to survive a night in the wilderness.

- **Do not carry food on overnight trips with-out a way to secure it from scavengers and bears.** Always bring a bear can or a sturdy sack and a length of rope to tie up your food.

Leave No Trace and Have Zero Impact

Many of the hikes in this book visit mountain meadows brimming with wildflowers that may be tempting to explore. Most hikers know not to pick the flowers so that others can enjoy the color they bring to a hike. But many hik-ers may not realize that these meadows are extremely fragile and easily damaged, espe-cially at higher alpine elevations. Errant feet can cause damage that will take the landscape many years to recover from. With so many peo-ple exploring many of these trails every year, it is critical to treat these areas respectfully, lest they be loved and enjoyed right into oblivion. It takes only a brief visit to popular destina-tions like Mount Rainier's Paradise Meadows to see how easily the flowers can be trampled out of existence.

Attempt a zero-impact approach when hik-ing through sensitive and fragile areas. Hike in small groups, stick to the trail and rocks, and use backcountry toilets where available. Camp only at existing sites, and practice Leave No Trace (LNT) principles.

If you are not familiar with LNT principles, take some time to review this philosophy on the Leave No Trace Center for Outdoor Ethics website, https://lnt.org/learn/7-principles. The goal is to leave no physical evidence of your time on these trails, which is particularly import-ant in wilderness areas.

Two particularly important points related to minimizing your impact on trails involve switchbacks and the landscape itself. Do not cut switchbacks. This practice destabilizes the slope and makes it more likely that large sec-tions of trail will be destroyed. There is never a need to take a shortcut; after all, spending time in the wild is the whole reason for hiking!

Do not alter the landscape. Leave it like you found it and pack out what you bring in. Don't carve your initials into logs, draw on rocks, cut down trees, pick wildflowers, or otherwise mar the environment.

OPPOSITE: *Glaciated Mount Rainier looms large above Paradise Meadows (Hike 35).*

Wilderness Guidelines

Some of the hikes in this book venture into wilderness areas or other specially regulated areas. The US Forest Service provides helpful pamphlets on wilderness regulations and guidelines that can be found on their website (see Appendix: Managing Agencies). Each forest has its own set of pages with information specific to that area.

The wilderness regulations and permit requirements change frequently enough that it is not prudent to reproduce them here. Bad information can ruin a carefully planned backpacking trip. Instead, hikers and backpackers should review the regulations and permit requirements every season to keep up with any changes.

It's also a good practice to check road and trail conditions before getting in the car to drive to the trailhead. Current road and trail conditions can be found on the Forest Service websites (see Appendix). The Washington Trails Association (www.wta.org) is also an excellent resource on trail conditions, as members of the organization often post trip reports that offer insight into the current conditions of a trail.

Follow Trail Etiquette

Hiking culture has its own etiquette and norms, which include certain practices that other hikers will assume you know, understand, and follow. Following this etiquette will help you better share the trail.

- **Hikers headed downhill yield to hikers climbing uphill.** Hikers working their way uphill are focused on that effort, while those going down are better positioned to step aside for those headed up.
- **Slower hikers yield to faster hikers.** There is no wrong pace for a hike, but hikers taking the slow approach need to be aware of those coming up behind them to avoid creating a traffic jam on narrow trails.

- **It is customary to give a simple greeting to other hikers you encounter on the trail,** as long as a trail isn't flooded with people.
- **Be aware that your voice could cover a great distance and disturb wildlife and people you may not be able to see.** Sound can carry a long way in forests and wild areas, especially across lakes. You don't need to speak only in hushed, reverent whispers—speaking at normal tones and volume levels is just fine. Avoid shouting, especially around lakes or open areas where there are fewer trees to muffle the sound.

For those venturing out on their first few hikes, these simple guidelines will quickly become second nature as you encounter other hikers on the trail. If for some reason you find that you've forgotten what you're supposed to do, just be courteous—hikers are a friendly and forgiving bunch. You'll get the hang of it in no time.

ABOVE: *Calypso orchid (Hike 42)*
OPPOSITE: *A pika huddles in the talus near Glacier Basin (Hike 22).*

HOW TO USE THIS GUIDE

This guide highlights fifty hiking destinations across Washington State that offer wildflower-viewing opportunities. The hikes are grouped by geographic proximity, from the rain-soaked Olympic Peninsula to the arid scrublands of Eastern Washington. For each hike, we provide data and descriptions outlining what to expect on the trail, how to get there, what you're likely to see, and the history of the area.

KEY HIKE INFORMATION

Each hike profile begins with basic information about the hike, including key trail data, such as distance and elevation gain, which topographic map covers the area, and what—if any—permits are required.

Distance: All hike distances are given in miles, roundtrip from the trailhead to the destination and back. They were calculated by comparing and cross-checking several different sources of information so as to be as accurate as possible. The given mileages can, and often do, vary from the mileages seen on signs along the trail or in other sources. In many cases, this is due to trail routes changing over time, coupled with varying methods for measuring trail distances. The result is that posted distances are rounded into the nice, clean tenths of a mile that trail-goers expect but are not always correct.

Elevation Gain: The approximate amount of elevation hikers can expect to climb to the destination is given in feet, rounded to the nearest ten. If there is significant elevation gain on the return hike to the trailhead, that figure is also provided. In most cases, the gain is simply the difference between the starting elevation and the highest point on the trail. We do not account for situations in which elevation is lost and then regained farther down the trail. If hikers want to know that information, the recommended topographic map will lend insight into a trail's ups and downs.

High Point: The highest point of elevation is provided in feet, to let hikers know how high they will be climbing. This approximate figure is useful in assessing whether a trail is above the snow line or likely has lingering snow in spring or even summer. If a hike ends at the top of an officially measured summit, that summit elevation is used.

Difficulty: Each hike is rated for difficulty: easy, moderate, or hard. These subjective ratings are intended to give hikers a rough idea of how much effort a given hike requires for the average hiker. Although the total elevation gain is a good indicator of how much climbing is involved, on some hikes that amount is spread evenly along the trail, and on others it is bunched up in tight, steep bursts. Beyond elevation gain, other factors rolled into the difficulty rating include the quality of the trail, the difficulty of navigating obstacles, and the extent to which the trail is maintained. Depending on your fitness level and what you consider a reasonable amount of effort on a given hike, you may find that, for example, a hike rated "hard" is closer to "moderate" for you.

Hiking Time: The approximate number of hours it will take the average hiker to complete the hike is given, almost always in a range. It is possible that some focused hikers will complete the hikes in less time and just as likely that some hikers will take more time. This entry gives a general idea of the amount of time to set aside for enjoying the hike at a reasonable pace. Hikes that are suitable for overnight trips are called out on the at-a-glance chart.

Best Season: In general, the best season to hike to enjoy the wildflowers along a trail is late spring to early summer. For each hike, a range of seasons is given for when flowers are most likely to be in bloom, not necessarily aligned with the featured wildflower for that hike. These general guidelines may not hold from year to year: Some years the snow melts weeks earlier than expected, and the flowers are not far behind. Other years wildflowers bloom late. Always check the current trail conditions before heading to the trailhead. As a bonus, we mention when a hike has particularly beautiful fall color.

Trail Traffic: This entry is based on typical weekend traffic on the trail during summer and includes foot traffic and livestock traffic (mostly

A NOTE ABOUT SAFETY

Safety is an important concern in all outdoor activities. No guidebook can alert you to every hazard or anticipate the limitations of every reader. Therefore, the descriptions of roads, trails, routes, and natural features in this book are not representations that a particular place or excursion will be safe for your party. When you follow any of the routes described in this book, you assume responsibility for your own safety. Under normal conditions, such excursions require the usual attention to traffic, road and trail conditions, weather, terrain, the capabilities of your party, and other factors. Keeping informed on current conditions and exercising common sense are the keys to a safe, enjoyable outing.

—*Mountaineers Books*

OPPOSITE: *Wildflower meadows on the trek up to Lake of the Angels (Hike 5)*

From the Wild Goose Trail (Hike 11), admire the Bagley Lakes in a rugged bowl.

equestrian) as well as mechanized traffic. These subjective ratings, measured as light, moderate, or heavy, give hikers an idea of a trail's popularity with hikers as well as other users.

Managing Agency: This is the group or entity in charge of managing the forest, national park, or wild area that the hike is located in. This is provided for readers that may have questions or need additional information not otherwise provided in the guide. The entries correspond to contact information listed in Appendix: Managing Agencies.

Permit: The permit or permits required to park at the trailhead are listed here. In most cases this will be either a Northwest Forest Pass, issued by the Forest Service, or a Discover Pass, issued by the State of Washington. Hikes in national parks often require a daily, weekly, or annual parks pass; if you plan to visit more than one national park (or one park multiple times) in a given year, the annual pass may be a good option. Some hikes may require day-use permits, instructions for which will be included in the hike description.

Maps: United States Geological Survey (USGS) and Green Trails maps are listed for each hike where possible. USGS maps are excellent for hiking off-trail and orienting by compass, while Green Trails maps are a better resource for hiking on trails.

Trailhead GPS: The GPS coordinates (in decimal degrees) for the trailhead are intended to allow drivers with navigation systems to plug in the coordinates and have an easier time finding their way to the trailhead. Of course, consult the accompanying driving directions to make sure they generally align with where your navigation device is directing you. The coordinates were calculated based on the WGS 84 datum.

Note: Some trails have significant obstacles or difficulties that hikers must be aware of before embarking on them. A common example might be pet restrictions for certain trails in national parks. Other considerations mentioned in this entry include crowded parking conditions, special permits, or road conditions that require a high-clearance vehicle or four-wheel drive.

FEATURED WILDFLOWER PROFILE

Each hike highlights a flower found along the trail, along with a checkbox that you can tick off once you've found that flower. The profile features a picture of the flower, a description of the plant, and interesting background information when available.

Other Wildflowers on the Trail: At the end of each flower profile is a list of wildflowers we encountered or reliably verified that others have encountered along the trail. We list them this way, instead of in the hike description, to allow for significantly longer, more detailed lists. That said, it is by no means an attempt at a comprehensive list, which would be a task well beyond the scope of this guide. In addition, different wildflowers bloom at different times of year, which means that a particular listed flower may not be blooming when you set out on a particular trail. This list is meant as a resource to help narrow your search of what to look out for on the trail. And if you miss a wildflower or two that you had hoped to see, you have a great reason to revisit that hike another time.

GETTING THERE

Driving directions to the trailhead start from a nearby city or town, generally along a major highway, such as Interstate 90 or State Route 20. Because trailheads can be approached from more than one direction, the driving directions are written to take this into account. In order to be as accurate as possible, every effort has been made to provide directions that match the actual signage posted at critical junctions on the driving route. Occasionally, online mapping and GPS systems will show information that does not match the posted signs. Where there is a discrepancy, the directions refer to the signs we saw on our way to the trailhead.

HIKE DESCRIPTION

This main section of each hike covers the step-by-step hiking directions. They tell you what to do at each junction you encounter and help you reach your destination. Use these directions along with the hike map to find your way.

HISTORY

Every trail has a story to tell, a reason the trail was cut through the forest, blasted out of rock, or carved into a mountainside. Sometimes that reason is simply to get to a delightful alpine lake, but more often than not the trail follows in the footsteps of prospectors, lumberjacks, and fisherfolk. The mountain ranges of Washington have drawn people for generations, and where there are people, there are stories. This section provides a window into that history and helps to connect trail users to the trail and the land. Humans are full of curiosity, and knowing what came before can enhance your appreciation of a hike.

MAP LEGEND

WILDFLOWER BASICS

Identifying a wildflower along the trail is a skill that requires dedication and time to cultivate. Not only are there a staggering number of different wildflowers in Washington, but plants of the same species can vary a great deal. It takes time, practice, and access to reliable field guides to become skilled at plant identification. This book is designed to get hikers started on that journey. People who catch the wildflower bug will want to invest in a few field guides and wildflower identification resources to supplement this book.

At more advanced levels, wildflower identification can become quite technical, sometimes involving nearly imperceptible variations in obscure parts of the plant best left to botanists and plant experts. This book focuses on the fundamentals of plant identification, which at its most basic level is an exercise in narrowing down the field of possibilities—best done by observing different plant characteristics and zeroing in on the plant that matches your observations. Over time, you will begin to recognize a familiar set of characteristics and be able to observe, for example, "This looks like a type of vetch" or "This is definitely some type of larkspur." Knowing what to look for is the first step. Consider the following attributes when attempting to identify a wildflower.

PLANT TYPE

The vast majority of the flowers in this book are herbaceous plants that grow each spring and summer and die back in the winter. However, some woody shrubs and trees are included as well. There's even a cactus or two! Knowing whether the plant you're looking at is woody or not will quickly exclude quite a number of options. As the term implies, woody shrubs and trees are made of wood that splinters when broken. They do not die back to their roots in the winter.

LEAVES

It's tempting to focus first on the flower, but sometimes blooms are damaged, past their prime, or otherwise do not match the photos of ideal specimens in wildflower guides. Instead, start with the leaves.

Arrangement: There are four basic types of leaf arrangement: alternating, opposite, whorl, and basal. Alternating leaves alternate on the plant stem, whereas opposite leaves grow in pairs opposite each other. Whorls are simply three or more leaves attached at the same point; basal leaves are confined to the base of the plant.

Type: Leaves can be simple or compound. Simple leaves are composed of one discrete leaf on a stem, while compound leaves have multiple leaves on a single stem. Common examples of these leaf types can be found on balsamroot, which has simple leaves, and lupine, which sports compound leaves.

Margin: The margin is more or less the edge of the leaf. It's often helpful in identifying a specific plant. There are quite a few very specific names for leaf margin types that quickly wade into technical waters. Beginners can simply note whether the leaf edge is smooth or toothed and whether it has distinct lobes.

Color: While most leaves are of course green, there is a surprising amount of variation.

PARTS OF A WILDFLOWER

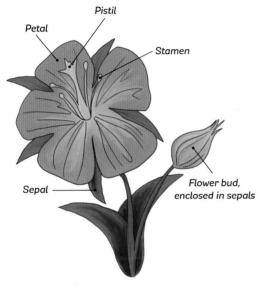

Petal

Pistil

Stamen

Sepal

Flower bud, enclosed in sepals

LEAF ARRANGEMENTS

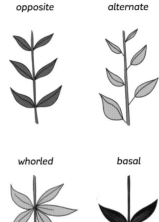

opposite

alternate

whorled

basal

TYPES OF LEAVES

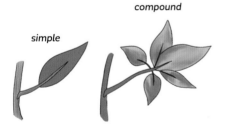

simple

compound

compound

doubly compound

LEAF MARGINS

toothed

toothless

lobed

Whether leaves are pale green, dark green, or tend toward another color should be noted.

Texture: Note whether the leaves are thick and fleshy or thin and flimsy. Do they have prominent veins, or are they smooth and shiny? It's also helpful to note whether they are covered in fine hairs. All these qualities can help determine what wildflower you're looking at.

FLOWERS

When first looking at a wildflower, we naturally focus on the color. Successful identification requires more than simply noting the color of the bloom, though the color is an important starting point.

Color: Most wildflower guides are organized by color for ease of identification. However, keep in mind that many wildflower species vary in color. Blooms can also change color as the flower matures. Avoid the trap of relying too heavily on flower color to narrow down your search. Reds can become pinks; purples can fade to blues. If you think you've identified the plant but the flower color is off, you've likely got the right plant. Do some further research to see if the plant you think it might be varies in flower color. Quite often you will find it does.

Size: Bloom size can vary from extremely tiny to several inches across. Knowing how big a flower tends to be can help narrow the list of potential candidates.

Petals: The number of petals can be important, but only up to about six. Flowers with more than six petals generally do not have a set number of petals, so the exact number is unlikely to be helpful. The shape of the petals can also be helpful, so note whether edges are smooth, lobed, or ragged.

Stamens and Pistils: Stamens produce the plant's pollen, while the pistil produces the plant's seed. There is generally one central pistil that extends beyond multiple stamens, though two major exceptions are members of the pea and sunflower families, which do not follow this general guideline. Noting the number, shape, and prominence of these structures is sometimes helpful in the identification process.

Sepals and Tepals: The sepal is the generally greenish portion of the flower that supports the petals. It is occasionally colorful, as anyone who has ever hiked past a flowering paintbrush has observed. *Tepal* is just another name for both petals and sepals. While these flower parts are nearly too much detail for this book, a few featured wildflowers are identified by these characteristics. In most cases for our purposes, being able to discern sepals and tepals is not necessary to identify a wildflower.

ENVIRONMENT

Where you find a flower is also an important consideration. Different wildflowers prefer different soils and environments, so note where the flower is growing.

Elevation: This value need not be exact. But generally knowing whether you're in a lowland forest, on a forested mountainside, or in an alpine meadow will help narrow the possibilities.

Soil Moisture: Essentially, you'll want to note whether the flower is clinging to a streamside or is eking out an existence in the arid scrublands. Rocky, dry soil conditions are home to different wildflowers than snowmelt-soaked mountain meadows.

Location: The specific geographic location where you've come across a wildflower can also be helpful in identifying a particular plant. Like all living things, wildflowers are commonly found within a defined range, which can sometimes aid you in identification.

CLIMATE

Similar to the wildflower's environment, knowing the general climate the wildflower is found in can quickly point you in the right direction.

OPPOSITE: *Scarlet paintbrush brightens the slopes of Johnston Ridge (Hike 37) with cloud-covered Mount St. Helens on the horizon.*

Broadly speaking, there are four distinct wildflower climates in Washington.

Coastal: Wildflowers in this environment thrive in moist but sandy soils at low elevation. They are often in more exposed environments and are therefore lower to the ground and tend to rely more often on wind pollination.

Subalpine Forest: The most common wildflower climate in Washington is the subalpine forest, which for purposes of this book encompasses all forests up to the alpine tree line. Wildflowers in this environment enjoy soils that are generally moister and benefit from the sheltering trees. Flowers tend to be vibrant as they attract a variety of insects and other pollinators.

Alpine: Climates above the tree line, the elevation above which trees do not grow, are prone to increased exposure to wind, and snows linger long. Wildflowers in this zone grow low to the ground and thrive in thin, rocky soils. With access to fewer pollinators, blooms tend to be less vibrant than flowers at lower elevations.

Scrubland: Much of the eastern portion of the state is essentially scrubland or desert prairie. Harsh winters and hot summers sweep through this region annually, so wildflowers in this habitat are built to withstand more extreme swings in temperature and are drought resistant. Blooms vary widely, with some wildflowers putting on brilliant floral displays, while others prefer a more sedate presentation. These flowers depend on a wide range of pollinators, from bees to bats.

Finally, the most important tip might be to take a couple of pictures of each plant you want to identify, making sure you get a good shot of both the flower and the leaves. Good luck, and remember to have fun!

PHOTOGRAPHING WILDFLOWERS

Many hikers are eager to take beautiful photographs of the wildflowers they find on the trail. Whether the photos are destined to be shared with friends or merely used to later identify the flower, here are some tips for taking the best photographs without trampling the flowers.

- **Use a macro lens** (105 mm recommended) **or a telephoto lens** so you can shoot your flower subject from a distance, or walk on

rocks to get closer to the wildflowers you're shooting without trampling vegetation.

- **If you use a cell phone to take photos, a selfie stick can get your camera closer** to the flower while you stay on the trail.
- **Plan your shot** before you take it by getting close to the ground without looking through the viewfinder. This way you can pay attention and avoid damaging your surroundings.
- **Consider using a camera with a live-view display that can articulate 90 degrees.** This feature allows you to put your camera close to the ground without having to lie on the ground. Alternatively, many DSLRs have viewfinder attachments so you can look down at the camera versus being on the ground.
- **Carry a tripod** so you can be more careful about what you're doing. If you're serious about doing close-up photos of flowers, a tripod is all but required, as the high f-stop (f-10 or above) necessary to get a reasonable depth of field lowers shutter speed and makes it more likely that small camera shakes will blur the images.

- **Plan to crop your image.** The resolution on most modern cameras is very high, which allows you to take flower pictures from a distance, then crop them later while keeping very good image quality.
- **Consider skipping flowers that are difficult to get to.** There is a good chance you'll see the same species farther down the trail in a spot where it's easier to photograph—if not, there are always more hikes to do!

We also have a few tips on technique:
- **Use a macro lens** for up-close work **and a wide angle** for landscapes.
- **Practice!** The more shots you take, the better you will become at knowing which photographs are worth your time.
- **Get low to the ground.** Be eye-level with the blooms, or use a right-angle viewfinder.
- **Be patient.** Often the breeze will work against you, or people on the trail will be in your shot, so wait for a calm moment.
- **Take multiple shots from different angles.** Often the third or fourth shot will turn out to be the best one.
- **Avoid harsh lighting.** While high contrast can sometimes produce interesting images, flower petals are often somewhat reflective, which can spoil the photograph. Consider underexposing your photos in bright lighting and correcting them later.
- **If you're using a cell phone camera with HDR (high-dynamic range), try out that feature to boost the contrast in your images.** Portrait mode can blur the background in an appealing way. Remember that many cell phones have a panorama mode that is excellent for big landscapes. Avoid using zoom and cropping images, which can degrade the quality.
- **Avoid selfies.** Have someone else take a picture of you so you can stay safe and avoid damaging the vegetation.

ABOVE: *A ground squirrel peeks up from the ground in the midst of phlox near Windy Pass (Hike 15).*
OPPOSITE: *Mount Townsend seen from summit of Mount Zion (Hike 3)*

WILDFLOWER IDENTIFICATION GUIDE

Washington State is home to thousands of different wildflowers and flowering plants, with some sub-species unique to a small area of the state. With such a broad range of plants to try and identify, serious flower-hounds often end up collecting multiple books and pamphlets on plant identification as they become more proficient at recognizing different species. For hikers just getting started, we've included this short flower identification guide curated from the more than 300 species we reference within these pages. We found and photographed each of the 120 flowers listed here on our treks down these trails, which makes it likely you will encounter them as well.

The wildflowers are organized by bloom color and then listed alphabetically to help you quickly narrow down your search. Featured wildflowers are indicated by a bright green box displaying the hike number; refer to that hike for more detailed information about and background on that flower. With regard to common names, some species are known locally by a variety of them; we chose common names based on their prevalence and our familiarity with them. You may know some of these wildflowers by other names. This guide will broaden your understanding and knowledge.

WHITE

| Alpine buckwheat | Alpine pennycress | American bistort 13 | Avalanche lily 31 |
| Beargrass 26 | Bunchberry | Chickweed | Columbia milkvetch |

Columbia windflower	False Solomon's seal	Indian pipe 19	Large-flower triteleia
Lyall's mariposa lily	Mountain death camas 4	Pearly everlasting	Red elderberry
Scalloped onion 2	Serviceberry	Sickletop lousewort	Smooth woodland star
Spotted saxifrage 9	Spring beauty	Starflower	Starry false lily of the valley
Subalpine mariposa lily 38	Subalpine sulphur flower 14	Thimbleberry	Trillium

Tweedy's lewisia 29

Twinflower

Utah honeysuckle

Virginia strawberry

Western Labrador tea 18

Western pasqueflower 20

White campion

Yarrow

YELLOW & ORANGE

Arrowleaf balsamroot 16

Barestem biscuitroot

Birdsfoot trefoil

Bitterbrush

Bracted lousewort

Broadleaf stonecrop 6

California poppy

Carey's balsamroot

Common monkeyflower

Dalmatian toad-flax

Desert yellow fleabane

Fan-leaf cinquefoil 41

Glacier lily 23	Jim Hill mustard	Meadow hawkweed	Nineleaf biscuitroot
Orange hawkweed 1	Oregon grape	Oregon sunshine	Pale agoseris
Pioneer violet	Rock buckwheat	Scotch broom	Spring gold
Tiger lily 21	Western wallflower	Yellow flag iris 49	Yellow salsify 44

PINK & RED

Bitterroot 24

Bush penstemon

Calypso orchid 42

Elephant's head 11

Fireweed 12	Foxglove 36	Lewis's monkeyflower 22	Longleaf phlox
Pacific rhododendron 3	Pink mountain-heather 35	Pink wintergreen	Red campion
Scarlet paintbrush	Sea blush	Showy phlox	Small-flowered paintbrush 30
Snow dwarf primrose	Sticky geranium	Subalpine spirea 27	Veiny dock 46
Western columbine 39	Wood's rose		

BLUE & PURPLE

Ballhead waterleaf

Blue stickseed 15

Cardwell's penstemon 37

Cascade aster

Columbia Gorge broadleaf lupine 43

Common bugloss

Common butterwort

Common camas 8

Cusick's speedwell 10

Hookedspur violet

Hooker's onion 47

Hound's tongue

Howell's triteleia 45

Jeffrey's shooting star 28

Kittentails

Menzies' larkspur 33

Milk thistle 5

Northern bog violet

Purple cushion fleabane

Purple deadnettle

Purple sage

Rocky Mountain iris

Sagebrush violet 48

Showy Jacob's-ladder 50

Showy penstemon

Small-flowered penstemon 17

Spreading phlox 32

Tall bluebells 34

Threadleaf phacelia

Upland larkspur

Wandering fleabane 40

Woolly vetch 25

BROWN

Chocolate lily 7

Fernleaf biscuitroot

OPPOSITE: *Lake Crescent in the distance from the upper reaches of Mount Muller (Hike 1)*

OLYMPIC PENINSULA & PUGET SOUND

1 MOUNT MULLER

DISTANCE: 8.4 miles
ELEVATION GAIN: 2700 feet in; 450 feet out
HIGH POINT: 3748 feet
DIFFICULTY: Moderate
HIKING TIME: 4 to 6 hours
BEST SEASON: Late spring to early summer
TRAIL TRAFFIC: Light foot, mountain bike, and equestrian traffic
MANAGING AGENCY: Olympic National Forest

PERMIT: Northwest Forest Pass
MAPS: USGS Mount Muller, USGS Snider Peak
TRAILHEAD GPS: 48.07610°N, 124.01310°W
NOTE: More than half of the route is along the Mount Muller Trail #882, a multiuse trail frequented by mountain bikers and horseback riders. Be prepared to share the trail and yield when appropriate.

This shortened version of a classic loop ascends the steep forested shoulders of Snider Ridge to reach wildflower-filled meadows along the ridgeline. While the wooded summit of Mount Muller skimps on views, trailside vistas showcase the surrounding landscape. On clear days you can see the greens of the Sol Duc Valley below with Mount Olympus and Mount Baker rising above and the waters of Lake Crescent and the Strait of Juan de Fuca sparkling in the distance.

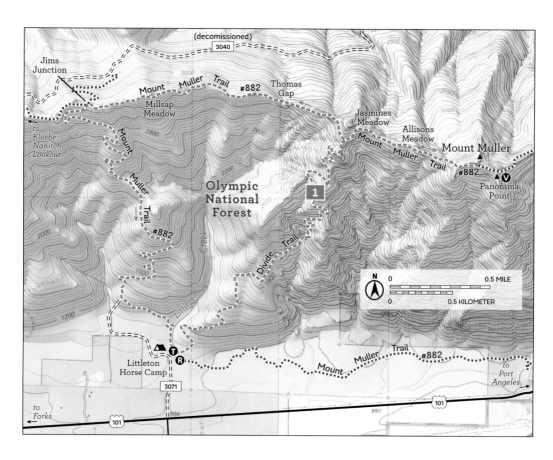

FEATURED WILDFLOWER

ORANGE HAWKWEED
Hieracium aurantiacum

Easy to identify by its stunning starburst blooms and leafless stem, orange hawkweed was imported from Europe to the US in the mid-1800s, and it has aggressively proliferated throughout the country, often crowding out native flora. The flower also goes by the name devil's paintbrush and is considered a noxious weed in all but a few counties in Washington.

The sun-loving plant is often found on roadsides and in forest clearings, growing from 6 to 24 inches tall. Brilliant yellow-and-orange flowers bloom from late spring to late summer in clusters of five or more near the top of the plant, which eventually give way to a dandelion-like bunch of seeds designed to catch the wind. Leaves, stem, and bracts are all covered in long hairs. Note that damage to the plant will result in leakage of a milky white liquid.

Other Wildflowers on the Trail: Alpine strawberry, avalanche lily, beargrass, bleeding heart, broad-leaf lupine, bunchberry, calypso orchid, chocolate lily, crevice alumroot, harsh paintbrush, Indian thistle, larkspur, milk thistle, Oregon bedstraw, oxeye daisy, pink wintergreen, pipsissewa, queen's cup, scarlet paintbrush, Scouler's valerian, selfheal, spreading phlox, spreading stonecrop, starflower, thread-leaf sandwort, tiger lily, trillium, twinflower, western columbine, woodland pinedrops, woolly vetch

GETTING THERE: From Port Angeles, follow US Highway 101 west for 32 miles. West of milepost 217, keep an eye out for a sign pointing right toward the Olympic Discovery Trail and another for "FS Rd 2918." Turn at the next right after the second sign onto unmarked Forest Road 3071.

From Forks, follow Highway 101 east for 25 miles. Just after milepost 216, pass a sign indicating that the Mount Muller–Littleton Loop Trailhead is the next left, followed by a sign for "FS Rd 2918," which is on your right. Turn at the next left after this sign onto unmarked FR 3071.

Whichever direction you came from, once you're on gravel FR 3071, follow it about 0.3 mile to the Mount Muller Trailhead and Littleton Horse Camp. Privy available.

From the parking area, two ends of the Mount Muller Trail #882 lead into a mixed second-growth forest. While you can follow the trail in either direction to eventually reach vistas and flower-filled meadows, we recommend heading to the right for a few hundred feet to a junction, where a small, hard-to-find sign marks a former logging road now known as the Divide Trail. Completed in 2012, this newest hiker-only addition to the Mount Muller loop is steeper and rougher than other boot-worn sections, but it cuts out a few trail miles and delivers you to the top of Snider Ridge quickly. The path to your left at this junction is your return trail.

The former roadbed soon yields to an increasingly steep and narrow trail. Tight switchbacks and sharp inclines snake up through stands of alder and then pines and firs.

This more challenging approach sees fewer hikers and is more prone to blowdowns, so come prepared for a little extra work early in the season. Continue to climb. And climb. Climb the nearly 2500 feet up to the ridgeline, reconnecting with the Mount Muller Trail at 2.5 miles. Head right and climb up to Jasmine's Meadow in 0.1 mile, the first of a handful of signed wildflower meadows along the route. Leave the trees and stroll past brightly colored columbine and orange hawkweed while taking in the valley below. Work your way over some small ups and downs to reach a junction pointing you up to Mount Muller's summit at the 3.2-mile mark. It's a short jaunt up to the top through meadows full of flowers and greenery. While most of the summit is covered with trees, the meadows just below offer a glimpse of Lake Crescent and Mount Olympus.

Once you've taken a few moments to explore the peak, head back down to the main trail. From here, most hikers will want to opt for heading right to begin the loop back to the trailhead. However, those looking for a longer day can continue left along the Mount Muller Trail to see a few more flowers, some fantastic views at Panorama Point, a stop at Fouts Rock House (a cavelike formation), and a long trek through lush forests near the valley floor to the trailhead, roughly 8 miles from here. Even if you're opting for the shorter route, take a few moments to visit Panorama Point, a rocky prominence just off the trail that is arguably the hike's best viewpoint, accessed via a boot path a little over 0.1 mile down the trail. From the point, Lake Crescent and Mount Storm King are seen to the east, with snowcapped Mount Baker and Glacier Peak in the distance. To the south find Aurora Ridge and Mount Olympus with the whole of the Sol Duc Valley spreading out below and to the west.

Whether you visit Panorama Point or not, to return to these challenges, head right from the summit junction, retracing your steps back past the Divide Trail and continuing along the ridgeline on the Mount Muller Trail. Beyond the Divide Trail junction, work your way down and back up Thomas Gap before reaching Millsap Meadow and its resident wildflowers at the 5.3-mile mark. Continue onward, and at 5.6 miles reach Jim's Junction and the trail out to Kloshe Nanitch, the site of a former fire lookout, 3.7 miles distant. Today, only an observation platform built on the old lookout foundation marks the site.

At Jim's Junction, turn left to stay on the Mount Muller Trail and soon begin your descent. It's less steep than the Divide Trail, but expect plenty of switchbacks and downhill stretches as you descend through the trees, with lusher undergrowth as you approach the valley floor. The grade eases as you enter the final stretch of the hike, crossing Littleton Creek before closing the loop near the parking area at 8.4 miles.

HISTORY

Back around the turn of the last century, the Muller family made their living near Lake Crescent. While clearing some land in 1907, the ranching family started a brush fire that quickly got out of control and burned more than 12,000 acres, including some slopes on Mount Muller. Most likely, the distinctive scars from that fire lingered for years and were easy to see for miles, quickly making it a landmark that was later named after the family.

Perhaps in response to the 1907 fire, the Kloshe Nanitch fire lookout was built in 1917 (the name is somewhat literal; it's Chinook Jargon for "look out"). For decades most of the people headed up the mountain visited the lookout or what remained of it.

Today's expanded trail system exists largely thanks to the US Forest Service's Molly Erickson, who spearheaded the project with the help of trail builders like Stan Fouts, for whom Fouts Rock House is named. Formalized in the 1990s, the trail features mile markers and quite a few signs marking various meadows and points of interest along the way.

OPPOSITE: *Meadowlands near the summit of Mount Muller*

2 KLAHHANE RIDGE

DISTANCE: 6.4 miles
ELEVATION GAIN: 1300 feet in; 700 feet out
HIGH POINT: 5900 feet
DIFFICULTY: Moderate
HIKING TIME: 4 to 5 hours
BEST SEASON: Late spring to summer
TRAIL TRAFFIC: Heavy foot traffic near visitor center; moderate on Klahhane Ridge

MANAGING AGENCY: Olympic National Park
PERMIT: National Park Pass
MAPS: USGS Mount Angeles; Green Trails Hurricane Ridge No. 134S
TRAILHEAD GPS: 47.97010°N, 123.49510°W
NOTE: Wait times for a parking space can be long in peak summer months. Arrive early to get a spot. Pets are prohibited on this trail.

With easy-to-reach panoramic views of the Puget Sound and the Olympic Mountains, this area is perennially popular. The trek out to Klahhane Ridge takes you beyond the paved interpretive trails, where the crowds quickly thin. Enjoy a long traverse across the exposed shoulders of Sunrise Ridge, with big views and abundant wildflowers along the way.

Wildflower meadows below the Hurricane Ridge Visitors Center

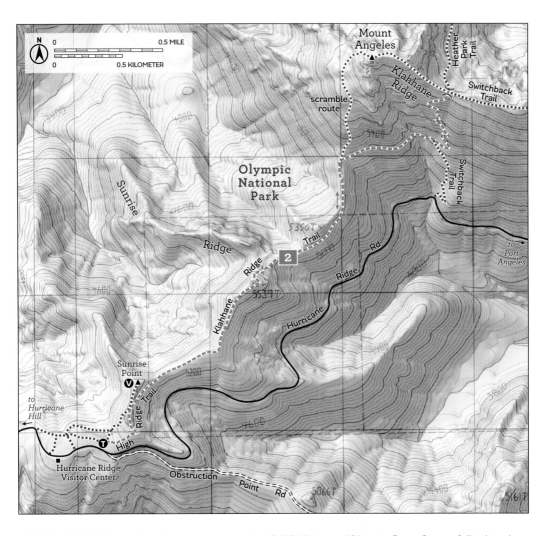

GETTING THERE: From Port Angeles, turn south off US Highway 101 onto Race Street, following signs directing you toward Olympic National Park and Hurricane Ridge. Continue on Race Street for 1.1 miles as it briefly changes to Mount Angeles Road. After the Olympic National Park Visitor Center, the road splits. Keep right as the road becomes Hurricane Ridge Road (also known as Heart o' the Hills Parkway). Continue 17.7 miles up to the Hurricane Ridge Visitor Center and parking area. Privy available at visitor center.

From the east end of the parking lot, begin by following the paved Cirque Rim Trail, soon passing the Big Meadow Trail, to reach the High Ridge Trail in a few hundred feet. Veer right and climb the ridgeline for 0.3 mile to the end of the pavement and, not far beyond, a trail intersection. Here the High Ridge Trail loops back toward the parking area to the left.

Continuing straight ahead is a short 0.1-mile spur trail up to Sunrise Point and its popular views. Those same views can also be found by heading to the right along the Klahhane Ridge Trail (aka Hurricane Ridge to Klahhane Ridge Trail) to begin the hike in earnest.

From here the trail drops slightly as you traverse under Sunrise Point, soon leaving

FEATURED WILDFLOWER

SCALLOPED ONION
Allium crenulatum

A member of the onion family, the bulb-producing scalloped onion, or Olympic onion, shares many trademark features of the *Allium* genus: an umbel of flowers, flat leaves, and leafless flowering stems. The tepals are pink to white with darker pink veins. Growing in clusters, the bell-shaped flowers bloom from mid-spring to midsummer and have prominent stamens that produce bright yellow pollen. This variety is native to the Pacific Northwest.

Other Wildflowers on the Trail: American bistort, avalanche lily, broadleaf lupine, Cascade wallflower, cow parsnip, Cusick's speedwell, fan-leaf cinquefoil, Fendler's waterleaf, glacier lily, harebell, harsh paintbrush, magenta paintbrush, nineleaf biscuitroot, Olympic larkspur, orange agoseris, scarlet paintbrush, Scouler's valerian, small-flowered penstemon, spreading phlox, spreading stonecrop, threadleaf sandwort, wandering fleabane, western sweetvetch, western wormwood, woolly sunflower, yarrow

the crowds behind. Wildlife is common in the area, especially during the cooler parts of the day, when you may spy deer wandering the grassy slopes, hear marmots whistle, or spot a ground squirrel darting across the rocks. Soon find yourself walking the ridgeline and catching your first glimpses of the sparkling Strait of Juan de Fuca to the north and the snow-topped Olympic Mountains to the south. Ahead, the craggy summit of Mount Angeles dominates the skyline.

Push onward, passing through small stands of trees and patches of meadow filled with wildflowers. The views continue to captivate as the trail drops off the ridge and continues its march toward Mount Angeles. As you near the base of the mountain, pass a junction with a climber's route up to the summit at 2.1 miles. Keep to the right and enter slightly denser forest. At the 2.6-mile mark the trail intersects the signed Switchback Trail, which switchbacks steeply down to Hurricane Ridge Road and a

small parking area. Many hikers opt for this short-and-steep approach to Klahhane Ridge as the 1.5-mile climb saves time and avoids the hassle of parking at the visitor center.

To continue, follow the Switchback Trail up the flanks of Klahhane Ridge to a saddle between Mount Angeles and the upper reaches of Klahhane Ridge, 3.2 miles from the trailhead. On clear days, you will have singularly spectacular views from this vantage point above a long glacial valley leading out to the sea. You may even see Mount Baker off in the distance to the northeast. To the southwest, Mount Olympus presides over a kingdom of craggy peaks, rocky ridges, and forested hills. Settle in and soak up the views from this quiet viewpoint, far from the bustling parking lot.

While this saddle is a great turnaround point, there's plenty more exploring left for those still hungry for more trail time. To the left a path leads up the mountainside for a challenging scramble to the summit of Mount

Angeles, which should be reserved for those with scrambling experience. To the right, the Switchback Trail continues upward and follows the Klahhane ridgeline for more views and adventure. Ahead, the Heather Park Trail drops into the valley to cut across Mount Angeles on a long climb out to Heather Park, an alpine parkland below Wildcat Mountain.

HISTORY

The area's spectacular vistas have long enticed adventurers to make the climb up from the coastal lowlands. In July 1885, Lieutenant Joseph O'Neil and Norman Smith clambered up to the top of what we now call Hurricane Ridge. They were the first recorded Europeans to visit the area, and they spent a chilly night in the mountains. Lieutenant O'Neil soon returned with more members of his 1885 army expedition to explore the interior of the Olympic Peninsula. They established a base camp on the ridge for their expeditions, and explorers, prospectors, trappers, and hikers soon followed.

In 1897 on an extremely windy day, one of those early prospectors, W. A. Hall, climbed to the top of what settlers had been calling "Old Hurricane." He dubbed it Hurricane Hill, overriding the short-lived Mount Eldridge moniker that the Seattle Press Expedition had given it in 1889. The name was apt; gales of up to 100 miles per hour can whip through this area as storms are pushed inland from the ocean and crash into the mountains. Klahhane Ridge was named by locals around this time as well. The Chinook Jargon name refers to the outdoors, meaning roughly "good times out of doors" or simply "outdoors." Decades later in 1961, the name made its way onto official maps.

Mining in the area remained exploratory and was largely cost prohibitive until World War I, when the need for manganese for munition production prompted miners to tunnel into the area around Mount Angeles, with operations eventually growing to twenty-six claims by the 1930s. However, access remained limited to trail and packhorse, and Washington State could not justify the cost to build a road that would support the burgeoning business, so the mines were slowly abandoned. It wasn't until the 1950s that Hurricane Ridge Road and the former Hurricane Ridge Lodge were built to help increase park visitation, a problem that the road seems to have handily solved in the intervening years.

Traversing Sunrise Ridge with Klahhane Ridge in the distance

3 MOUNT ZION

DISTANCE: 4.4 miles
ELEVATION GAIN: 1300 feet
HIGH POINT: 4274 feet
DIFFICULTY: Moderate
HIKING TIME: 3 to 4 hours
BEST SEASON: Late spring to early summer
TRAIL TRAFFIC: Moderate foot traffic; light equestrian and mountain bike traffic

MANAGING AGENCY: Olympic National Forest
PERMIT: Northwest Forest Pass
MAPS: USGS Mount Zion; Green Trails Olympic Mountains East No. 168SX
TRAILHEAD GPS: 47.92280°N, 123.02580°W
NOTE: Expect bike and equestrian traffic on this multiuse trail. Use caution at the summit as there are steep drop-offs close to the trail.

Climb up slopes covered in dense evergreen forest and rhododendrons on your way to big views from rocky outcroppings and a former lookout site. Located in the Olympic Peninsula's rain shadow, this lower-elevation hike offers shoulder-season hiking, as well as an impressive display of pink rhododendron blooms in the spring and early summer. With the best flowers at lower elevations, hikers of all ages can enjoy the floral show, even if they do not trek all the way to the summit for its vistas.

Mount Townsend rises from the forest as seen from the slopes of Mount Zion.

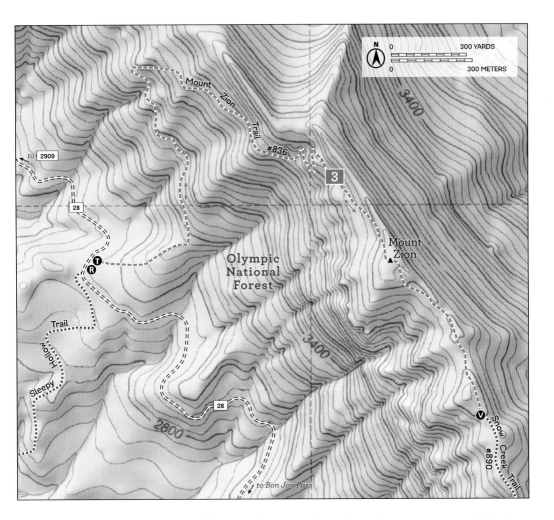

GETTING THERE: Take US Highway 101 to Lords Lake Loop Road, located on the west side of the high-way 2.4 miles north of the Quilcene Ranger Station and 7.8 miles south of the junction with State Route 104. Follow Lords Lake Loop Road 3.4 miles to Forest Road 28 (Little Quilcene Road) on the left just before the lakeshore. Veer onto FR 28, keeping right when the road splits and turns to gravel in 0.8 mile. Continue on FR 28 for 4.7 miles, passing FR 27 shortly before reaching a three-way intersection, labeled Bon Jon Pass on most maps. Head right onto unmarked FR 28, continuing 1.9 miles to the Mount Zion/Sleepy Hollow Trailhead. Privy available.

From the parking area, cross FR 28 to reach the well-signed trailhead, and quickly enter the mature second-growth forest, immediately beginning your climb up the slopes on the Mount Zion Trail #836. Find a fern-lined path as you pass trunks of hemlock and fir beneath an evergreen canopy dripping with lichen. Not far from the trailhead, reach a dense stand of Pacific rhododendron lining both sides of the trail and overarching the trail in places. Between early spring and early summer, the spindly shrubs burst with big bunches of light-pink flowers, adding a bright pop of color against the forest's greens and dark browns.

FEATURED WILDFLOWER

PACIFIC RHODODENDRON
Rhododendron macrophyllum
A staple of backyards across the Pacific Northwest, this familiar flowering shrub produces large clusters of bell-shaped flowers, often brightly colored against thick deep green leaves. Affectionately referred to as "rhodies" by gardeners, these hardy plants remain green year-round. While the domesticated varieties produce blooms in a wide range of different colors on densely leaved shrubs, in the wild they are quite spindly, with a few leaves on the tufted ends of the branches, and they sport flowers from early spring to early summer that are almost exclusively a shade of pink. Pacific rhododendrons can grow quite tall, up to 24 feet.

Other Wildflowers on the Trail: Broadleaf lupine, broadleaf penstemon, coralroot orchid, Davidson's penstemon, fireweed, harsh paintbrush, oceanspray, pink wintergreen, queen's cup, small-flowered penstemon, spreading stonecrop, twinflower, western columbine, woodland pinedrops, yarrow

Continue to work your way up the mountainside, alternating between sections of flat grade and somewhat steeper trail. As you approach the ridgeline, exposed rock and stone begin to emerge from the forest floor. At about 1.2 miles, find the first hints of the views to come, with breaks in the trees allowing some tantalizing glimpses of Gold Creek valley below.

Push onward and upward, following the trail as it gains the ridge and trades solid tread for a rocky path along the mountain's jagged crest. At the 1.7-mile mark, reach the old lookout site at the summit, in a large clearing surrounded by view-obscuring trees and a few rhododendrons. Continue following the well-trodden boot path as it extends south along the rocks for roughly 0.5 mile to the end of the hike, where you can find big views of Bon Jon Peak, looming Mount Townsend, and the Olympic Range. To the south, the Snow Creek Trail #890 begins its long 2.2-mile descent down the shoulders of the mountain, with viewpoints showcasing the Puget Sound, Mount Baker, and even Mount Shuksan on a good day.

Turn around here for a short and approachable hike suitable for families with young children. People looking for a longer hike can add miles by exploring the Snow Creek Trail, with the opportunity to make a large loop by heading all the way down the mountain, passing a junction with the Deadfall Trail #849 along the way. Once at the bottom, it's 3.6 miles of hiking along FR 28 to make it back to the trailhead.

HISTORY
Much of Mount Zion's past is wrapped up in wildfires. Fires repeatedly ravaged the slopes between 1850 and 1930 and cleared the summit of trees, providing sweeping views of the surrounding valleys. Around 1935, the Forest Service decided to make the most of this new 360-degree vantage point and built a simple lookout structure on the mountaintop. During World War II a cabin was added, and the outpost operated as an Aircraft Warning Service station. After the war, the lookout continued to be used for decades before it was dismantled in 1970.

4 MARMOT PASS

DISTANCE: 10.4 miles
ELEVATION GAIN: 3500 feet
HIGH POINT: 6000 feet
DIFFICULTY: Moderate
HIKING TIME: 6 to 7 hours
BEST SEASON: Summer
TRAIL TRAFFIC: Moderate to heavy foot traffic; light equestrian traffic
MANAGING AGENCY: Olympic National Forest

PERMIT: Northwest Forest Pass
MAPS: USGS Mount Townsend, USGS Mount Deception; Green Trails Olympic Mountains East No. 168SX
TRAILHEAD GPS: 47.82780°N, 123.04100°W
NOTE: Wilderness regulations apply in Buckhorn Wilderness; see Wilderness Guidelines in Hiking Best Practices.

Follow the Big Quilcene River through miles of mountainside greenery, brimming with wildflowers in the summer and aglow with autumnal reds and oranges in the fall, to reach alpine highlands and magnificent vistas showcasing some of the most rugged peaks of the Olympic Range.

GETTING THERE: Take US Highway 101 to Penny Creek Road, approximately 2 miles south of Quilcene. Turn west onto Penny Creek Road, following it 1.4 miles to a junction with Big Quilcene River Road (Forest Road 27) and the end of the pavement. Veer left onto gravel and stay on FR 27 as it crosses the national forest boundary, becomes paved again, and reaches FR 2750 in 9.2 miles. Veer left onto gravel for another 4.7 miles to the Upper Big Quilcene Trailhead. Privy available.

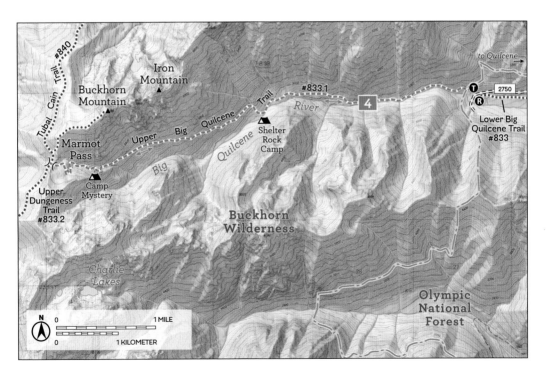

FEATURED WILDFLOWER

MOUNTAIN DEATH CAMAS
Anticlea elegans

As its name suggests, mountain death camas is highly poisonous due to the high levels of alkaloids found in all parts of the plant. One of a variety of death camas species, the plant grows between 1 and 3 feet tall, with grasslike leaves surrounding a tall flower stalk, which sports a branched flower cluster known as a *raceme*. The six-petaled white flower blooms in summer and has a distinctive yellow-green, heart-shaped mark on each petal. Look for mountain death camas in moist soils at higher elevations.

Other Wildflowers on the Trail: Alpine leafybract aster, broadleaf lupine, bunchberry, Cascade wallflower, chocolate lily, cliff dwarf-primrose, Columbia lewisia, coralroot orchid, Cusick's speedwell, Drummond's cinquefoil, foamflower, harsh paintbrush, Indian thistle, milkvetch, monkeyflower, mountain owl's clover, orange agoseris, Pacific rhododendron, pale agoseris, Parry's catchfly, partridgefoot, pearly everlasting, queen's cup, Scouler's valerian, selfheal, sickletop lousewort, small-flowered penstemon, spreading phlox, sticky goldenrod, threadleaf sandwort, wandering fleabane, western globeflower, western meadow-rue, white aster, woolly sunflower, yarrow

From the trailhead, the Upper Big Quilcene Trail #833.1 enters a dense, mossy forest and soon crosses into the Buckhorn Wilderness in 0.1 mile where it saddles up alongside the Big Quilcene River. Follow the trail's ups and downs as it works its way up the river valley, staying beneath sheltering trees and keeping an eye out for the flowers that thrive in the cool shade. At 2.5 miles reach Shelter Rock Camp, the namesake shelter now long gone, a popular rest stop before tackling the elevation ahead. With river access and plenty of room off the trail, this is also a good turnaround point for young hikers.

From Shelter Rock Camp, the trail begins a climbing traverse across the flanks of Buckhorn Mountain. While confined to the trees at first, the trail soon leads out through rocky avalanche fields increasingly blanketed with meadowy patches of green, spotted and dotted with the whites, yellows, blues, and reds of the abundant flowers here. Look upslope to the craggy points of Buckhorn Mountain and across the valley to the sharp points of Boulder Ridge. Pause often to enjoy the sweeping views, admire the colors brightly contrasting against the gray-brown talus, and in summer scoop up a handful of sun-ripened blueberries.

After 2 miles of climbing and a return to the trees, reach Camp Mystery at the 4.5-mile mark, a popular overnight spot and long a destination for the Boy Scouts who spend summers down at Camp Parsons. Not far beyond, the trees pull back to reveal a rocky headwall

OPPOSITE: *Wildflowers line the trail up to Marmot Pass.*

The trail cuts between the rocky shoulders of Buckhorn Mountain and expansive meadowlands.

and the trail switchbacking up it. Push onward, tackling the last big obstacle between you and Marmot Pass. Once you plateau, take a moment to look back down the valley, all the way down to Hood Canal with Glacier Peak in the far distance on the clearest of days. The pass is just a short climb from here.

At 5.2 miles from the trailhead, the trail intersects with the Upper Dungeness Trail #833.2 and the Tubal Cain Trail #840, both of which are part of the Pacific Northwest National Scenic Trail. From this well-trodden intersection, you have a commanding view. To the west find Mount Mystery, and as you swivel north, find Mount Fricaba, Mount Deception, the Needles, and Mount Clark, followed by Mount Walkinshaw and finally Gray Wolf Ridge.

There is plenty more trail from here, with trail #840 leading out to the Tubal Cain Mining District and a scramble to the summit of Buckhorn Mountain, and trail #833.2 switchbacking down to Boulder Shelter and eventually Camp Handy.

HISTORY

This hike traces its origins back to the late 1890s, when a road was rammed up the Big Quilcene River valley to access the Tubal Cain

mines on Buckhorn Mountain and Iron Mountain. The road was rough, required multiple river crossings, and was often plagued with lingering snow. Within a few years another road was built up the Little Quilcene River valley, and miners abandoned the first road. By 1903, Victor Tull consolidated most of the mining claims into the Tubal Cain Copper and Manganese Mining Company and built two large mining camps, Copper City and Tull City, remnants of which can still be found today. Even with the improved road, the company struggled with low yields until an avalanche in 1912 destroyed the heart of the operations and the mines were abandoned by 1920.

While the mining venture was a bust, the road attracted hikers and backpackers. The Mountaineers were leading hikes up past the Shelter Rock Ranger Station and pushing on to Camp Mystery and Marmot Pass at least as far back as 1924 and likely much earlier. It is at Marmot Pass that the trail meets the Pacific Northwest Trail, the brainchild of Ron Strickland, who proposed it in 1970 and spent years cobbling together the route and lobbying Congress for funds. It achieved federal recognition in 2000 as the Millennium Trail and became a National Scenic Trail in 2009.

5 LAKE OF THE ANGELS

DISTANCE: 7 miles
ELEVATION GAIN: 3400 feet
HIGH POINT: 4950 feet
DIFFICULTY: Hard
HIKING TIME: 7 to 10 hours
BEST SEASON: Summer
TRAIL TRAFFIC: Light foot traffic
MANAGING AGENCY: Olympic National Forest
PERMIT: None

MAPS: USGS Mount Washington, USGS Mount Skokomish; Green Trails Olympic Mountains East No. 168SX
TRAILHEAD GPS: 47.58342°N, 123.23360°W
NOTE: The last 4.3 miles of FR 25 are rough and unpaved; a high-clearance vehicle is recommended. Wilderness regulations apply in Mount Skokomish Wilderness; see Wilderness Guidelines in Hiking Best Practices.

Follow this challenging trail up through flower-filled subalpine meadows to a remote lake tucked between two craggy mountaintops. Explore this wild country on your way to the Valley of Heaven, where you'll find the Lake of the Angels and the gorgeous alpine landscape that inspired such divine names.

GETTING THERE: Take US Highway 101 along Hood Canal to Hamma Hamma Road (road signs also label it "Hamma Hamma Rec Area Rd"), 13.8 miles north of Hoodsport. Turn west, following the road, also known as Forest Road 25, for 7.6 miles to the end of the pavement at the Lena Lake Trailhead. Continue on gravel another 4.3 miles to the Putvin Trailhead, just beyond Boulder Creek.

Lake of the Angels nestled at the base of Mount Skokomish seen from the slopes of Mount Stone

FEATURED WILDFLOWER

MILK THISTLE
Silybum marianum

A prolific nonnative weed, milk thistle is found throughout most of the US and Canada. The plant grows in a single shaft and is easily identified by its spike-covered leaves and flower heads, which bloom from summer to early fall. The blooms are composed of red-tinged purple, threadlike petals that turn to white, dandelion-like tufts in the fall, when the wind picks up the seeds and distributes them. Milk thistle can grow quite tall, up to 6 feet.

In the past, the plant was often harvested for food, as the roots and leaves can be cooked and eaten. In recent years milk thistle has become a popular dietary supplement and a treatment for liver disease and various cancers, though the effectiveness of the supplement has yet to be scientifically verified.

Other Wildflowers on the Trail: American bistort, beargrass, broadleaf arnica, broadleaf lupine, bunchberry, cow parsnip, crevice alumroot, elephant's head, false hellebore, harebell, harsh paintbrush, Jeffrey's shooting star, leatherleaf saxifrage, oxeye daisy, pearly everlasting, pink mountain-heather, scarlet paintbrush, tiger lily, western columbine, western pasqueflower, western sweetvetch, yellow coralbells

From the trailhead, the Putvin Trail #813 enters a thick canopy of pine and hemlock, following Boulder Creek for 0.2 mile, past the short spur out to local settler Carl Putvin's grave. Climb past mossy boulders before switchbacking away from the rushing waters of Boulder Creek. Salal and huckleberry line the trail as you work your way up the mountainside, navigating a handful of creek basins and enjoying glimpses of Jefferson Peak and Mount Pershing peeking through the trees from the far side of the Hamma Hamma River valley. At 1.2 miles reach the now-closed Boulder Creek Road and an Olympic National Park registration station for those planning an overnight trip.

From the roadbed, begin the toughest section of the hike, made up almost entirely of steep grades and rough trail. Soon climb across the Mount Skokomish Wilderness boundary and enter the Whitehorse Creek valley. The trail stays high above the creek as you ascend, with occasional breaks in the trees offering views of Mount Skokomish towering over the rocky headwall you will need to clamber up to reach the Valley of Heaven. As you near the upper reaches of the valley, pause to catch your breath and watch Whitehorse Creek tumble down the headwall and into a broad alder-filled plateau before disappearing into the trees below. Continue to switchback and climb up rock ledges, a few steep enough to require handholds to get over them.

Crest the headwall and emerge into lovely subalpine meadows brimming with wildflowers. While Jefferson Peak dominates the skyline, on good days Mount Rainier makes an

OPPOSITE: *Glacial melt streams down rocky slopes near the shore of Lake of the Angels.*

appearance in the distance. Enjoy wandering across slow creeks and passing a large pond one might mistake for the Lake of the Angels at 2.7 miles. The temptation to think you've arrived is strong enough that the pond even has an apt name: the Pond of the False Prophet.

Press onward toward the lake, crossing into Olympic National Park and tackling a final series of steep, rocky switchbacks leading to the Valley of Heaven. Here, at 3.4 miles, Lake of the Angels rests in an alpine cirque. A bulky arm of Mount Skokomish rises above the lake, dominating the southern horizon and cradling the snowfields that feed the lake below. To the north, the commanding heights of Mount Stone stand guard at the opposite end of the lake basin. Wander along the lake, keeping an eye out for mountain goats and an ear open for whistling marmots, both of which often make

an appearance here. Settle in and enjoy a little slice of alpine heaven.

For those spending the night or just looking for a higher perch, trails from the lake lead out to Hagen Lake or Mount Stone and the Stone Ponds via a pass known as St. Peter's Gate.

HISTORY

Carl Putvin, the trail's namesake, was a pioneer and trapper who moved his young wife and toddler son to a trapping cabin near the Lake of the Angels around 1909. According to his great-granddaughter, in January of 1913 Putvin trekked down from the cabin to Eldon for supplies. On his return trip, a tree fell on him, and either the impact of the tree or the elements took the twenty-year-old far too early. After attempting to move his body, his wife decided to bury him where he died.

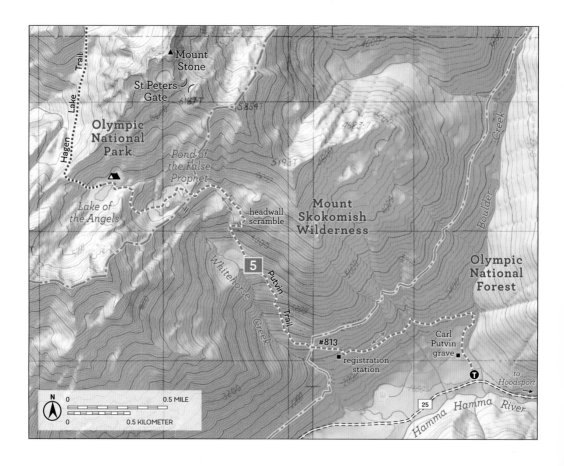

6 GOOSE ROCK

DISTANCE: 2.7 miles
ELEVATION GAIN: 400 feet
HIGH POINT: 480 feet
DIFFICULTY: Easy
HIKING TIME: 2 to 3 hours
BEST SEASON: Late spring to early summer
TRAIL TRAFFIC: Heavy foot traffic
MANAGING AGENCY: Washington State Parks

PERMIT: Discover Pass
MAPS: USGS Deception Pass; Green Trails
Deception Pass/Anacortes Community Forest
Lands No. 41S (out of print)
TRAILHEAD GPS: 48.40470°N, 122.64480°W
NOTE: The parking area for this very popular hike
is often full; arrive early to get a spot.

This short hike to the top of Goose Rock in Deception Pass State Park glides through several diverse ecosystems that support a wide variety of wildflowers and other flora while offering views of dynamic seascapes. Easily accessible and approachable for almost any hiker, this climb is the perfect introduction to Washington State's most popular state park.

GETTING THERE: Take I-5 exit 230 for Burlington/Anacortes and State Route 20. Turn left onto SR 20 west and continue 11.7 miles to a traffic circle. Stay on SR 20 west, avoiding the SR 20 spur leading to Anacortes. Continue another 6.1 miles to a small parking area on the right just after crossing the Deception Pass Bridge. The trail begins at a set of stairs at the north end of the parking lot. Privy available.

FEATURED WILDFLOWER

BROADLEAF STONECROP
Sedum spathulifolium
A low-growing succulent with rounded, waxy leaves and bright yellow, star-shaped blooms, broadleaf stonecrop thrives in a wide range of soil and environmental conditions and is often found in rocky areas where the soil is too thin for many other plants. Even when the plant is not in bloom, the small clusters of leaves may display eye-catching colors ranging from pale green to a deep pink blush. Its flowers bloom from spring to late summer and are popular with certain species of butterflies; as a result, it has become a popular ornamental ground cover in gardens.

Other Wildflowers on the Trail: Candy flower, chocolate lily, common camas, coralroot orchid, harsh paintbrush, Menzies' larkspur, mountain death camas, naked broomrape, nineleaf biscuitroot, Nootka rose, Pacific rhododendron, Puget Sound gumweed, sand verbena, scarlet paintbrush, sea blush, starflower, wild currant, woolly vetch, yarrow

Surveying the Strait of Juan de Fuca from the top of Goose Rock

Begin by taking a short set of stairs down to a path running under the bridge. Head right and pause a moment to take in this unique view of Deception Pass and the bridge's cantilevered construction. Just past the bridge is a junction with the Northwest Summit Trail, the trail you'll be returning on at the end of the loop. For now, veer left onto the Goose Rock Perimeter Trail as it weaves its way past the peeling trunks of the madrones prevalent here. Keep an eye trailside as all sorts of flowers, lichens, and succulents can be found, including the broadleaf stonecrop. At the same time, gaps in the trees offer glimpses of sparkling waters as well as forest-covered Strawberry and Ben Ure Islands.

At 1.1 miles reach the junction with the Southeast Summit Trail. Stick to the Perimeter Trail for now, as there are more seascapes and flowers to discover ahead. As you progress, pass tempting paths beckoning you toward the water, where you can get good views of the islands and Mount Baker in the distance. You'll pass

the junction with the Lower Forest Trail in 0.1 mile, reaching the Discovery Trail at the 1.3-mile mark. Take a sharp right on the Discovery Trail, gliding through a dense understory of salal and fern. Continue strolling through the forest, keeping an eye out for pink rhododendron blooms hidden in the surrounding greenery.

At 1.7 miles reach the junction with the Southwest Summit Trail and the beginning of the ascent. Turn right and climb another 0.1 mile, where the trail cuts across the Lower Forest Trail, and reach the Northwest Summit Trail at 1.9 miles. Veer right and follow it to the summit. As you climb, the trees soon thin, and the trail emerges onto an exposed outcropping at the top of Goose Rock. Technically known as an "herbaceous bald," it is carpeted with tiny plants and vegetation. Stick to the trails to avoid damaging this fragile area. At the 2.2-mile mark, find the views. This is the highest point on Whidbey Island, and on clear days Mount Rainier makes an appearance. Cranberry Lake

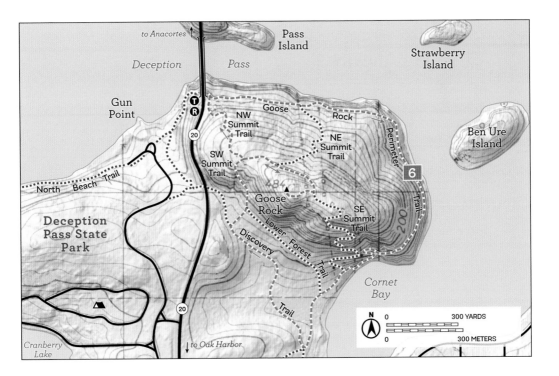

lies below, with the Strait of Juan de Fuca just beyond it. Some days the planes from Naval Air Station Whidbey Island practice maneuvers and put on a short (and loud) air show.

Take some time to settle in and enjoy the view before packing up and retracing your steps back to the junction with the Southwest Summit Trail. Keep to the right on the Northwest Summit Trail as it drops back down to connect with the Perimeter Trail. Turn left under the bridge to reach the steps and the parking area.

A tour of Goose Rock is a nice introduction to the many miles of trail found throughout the park, all with a lot of interesting plants and flowers to find. Explore beaches and islands, cabins and campsites, amphitheaters and diving sites in the sprawling state park.

HISTORY

Back in 1790, Spanish explorers were busily charting the area and naming everything they stumbled across. While some of those names are still with us—the Strait of Juan de Fuca, San Juan Islands, Fidalgo Island, for example—others did not last. Deception Pass was dubbed Boca de Flon by Manuel Quimper, a Spanish naval officer assigned to the area. In 1792, Captain George Vancouver named it Port Gardner, believing it was the entrance to a bay. After further exploration showed it to be a narrow strait between two islands, he renamed it Deception Passage, in a nod to its deceptive nature.

After Washington received its statehood in 1889, the federal government retained control of the area for military operations until 1922, when it was transferred to the state. At the time, Washington decided to make it a park but did not have the funds to build any infrastructure. Enter the Civilian Conservation Corps, who built most of the roads and buildings seen in the park today. Beginning in 1924, the small ferry *Deception Pass* provided access between the islands, captained by Berte Olson, Washington's first female ferry captain. The ferry ran between Yokeko Point and Hoypus Point until the modern cantilevered bridges were completed in 1935.

7 EBEY'S LANDING

DISTANCE: 3.7 miles
ELEVATION GAIN: 250 feet
HIGH POINT: 250 feet
DIFFICULTY: Easy
HIKING TIME: 2 hours
BEST SEASON: Early spring to midsummer
TRAIL TRAFFIC: Moderate foot traffic

MANAGING AGENCY: Washington State Parks, National Park Service
PERMIT: Discover Pass
MAPS: USGS Coupeville; Ebey's Landing website, www.nps.gov/ebla
TRAILHEAD GPS: 48.19230°N, 122.70830°W

Ebey's Landing State Park contains a great deal of varied landscape, and this short loop is a good way to get a taste of everything it has to offer. For those looking for a longer day, a trek out to the cemetery is well worth the time, as it includes several interesting historical monuments and buildings.

GETTING THERE: Take State Route 20 or State Route 525 to S. Ebey Road, located just west of Coupeville. Turn south onto S. Ebey Road. Follow Ebey Road 1.7 miles to Ebey's Landing State Park. If you're approaching from the south, you may find it easier to take the ferry from Mukilteo to Clinton on Whidbey Island. From Clinton, follow SR 525 north for about 22 miles to where it ends at SR 20. Then continue on SR 20 east for 6.2 miles. Turn left on S. Sherman Road, which in 0.3 mile, becomes Cook Road. When the road reaches a T junction, turn right onto Ebey's Landing Road and continue to the trailhead at a sharp turn in the road.

FEATURED WILDFLOWER

CHOCOLATE LILY
Fritillaria affinis

Also known as checker lily, chocolate lily has nodding, bell-shaped blooms with six tepals and can be a deep purple or chocolate color, but often the flowers bear a green or yellow mottling that gives rise to the "checker" description. Between early spring and early summer, flowers blossom from an unbranched stem that grows 8 to 24 inches tall with one or more whorls of lance-shaped leaves. Found in grassy areas or forest meadows in low to mid elevations, the lilies were a popular food source for coastal American Indians, who ate the bulbs or ground them into flour.

Other Wildflowers on the Trail: Bleeding heart, brittle prickly pear, broadleaf lupine, chickweed, coastal gumweed, common camas, field mustard, golden paintbrush, harsh paintbrush, harvest brodiaea, Hooker's onion, Nootka rose, orange honeysuckle, purple deadnettle, red campion, redstem storksbill, white campion, woolly vetch, yarrow

Field mustard (Brassica campestris) *is abundant at Ebey's Prairie.*

While hikers can start with a walk along the shore, we recommend climbing the stairs up to the bluff. Not only does this approach allow you to reach the hike's stunning views more quickly, but it also avoids a much steeper climb at the far end of the loop. From the stairs, the trail follows a dirt road sandwiched between the ocean and Ebey's Prairie, which includes active farmland that is also part of the sprawling Ebey's Landing National Historical Reserve. After a half mile of hiking, reach a junction with the Ebey's Prairie Trail, which connects the Bluff Trail with the Sunnyside Cemetery.

From the junction, the road becomes trail and begins a short climb to the top of the bluff, revealing the trail's most sweeping views. Perego's Lake (sometimes labeled Perego's Lagoon) is slowly revealed as you wind along the grassy bluff, passing a surprising variety of wildflowers along the way. Windswept trees make brief appearances as you progress, gently descending toward the beach. After you've walked the length of the lake, reach a junction at the 1.7-mile

mark. Here the trail switchbacks steeply down to the beach, and while others have cut through the switchbacks to reach the water a little more quickly, avoid the temptation to follow in their footsteps. The grasses that cover the sandy bluff hold it together; if they die, the slope will erode and collapse, destroying the trail. Take a few extra moments to follow the trail so that others can enjoy it in the future.

Once off the bluff, start heading south along what is often simply referred to as the "beach trail." In 2009 this stretch of beach was integrated into the Pacific Northwest National Scenic Trail, which stretches 1200 miles from Montana to the Pacific Ocean. And scenic it is; the rocky beach makes for a pleasant 1.7-mile walk back to the car, with mountains of driftwood to clamber around on, plenty of rocks and shells to check out, and a wide array of birds and wildlife to enjoy. All these features combine to make Ebey's Landing extremely popular. With gorgeous views, easy access, and appeal for hikers of all ages, this hike is perfect for a family outing on Whidbey Island.

HISTORY

As far back as the 1300s, Lower Skagit Indians lived in villages in the Coupeville area. In 1792 George Vancouver visited the area and named Whidbey Island in honor of one of his lieutenants, Joseph Whidbey. After that time, a few white settlers visited and explored Whidbey Island, but it wasn't until the Donation Land Claim Act of 1850 that settlement began in earnest. The act encouraged settlement by letting settlers claim 320 acres without charge, provided certain requirements were met. In 1851, Colonel Isaac Ebey was one of the first to file a claim; he quickly became a leader in the burgeoning community. His life was cut short in 1857 when he was targeted as a prominent white citizen and executed by an indigenous tribe seeking vengeance for an earlier attack that killed twenty-seven tribal members.

Eventually the Ebey homestead became part of a project seeking to preserve the pioneer legacy of Whidbey Island. In 1978, Congress authorized the formation of the reserve at Ebey's Landing, a national historical site that today encompasses 19,333 acres.

Wildflowers line the Bluff Trail above Peregos Lake and Puget Sound.

8 MIMA MOUNDS

DISTANCE: 3.3 miles
ELEVATION GAIN: Negligible
HIGH POINT: 240 feet
DIFFICULTY: Easy
HIKING TIME: 1 to 2 hours
BEST SEASON: Early spring to midsummer
TRAIL TRAFFIC: Moderate foot traffic
PERMIT: Discover Pass

MANAGING AGENCY: Washington State
Department of Natural Resources
MAPS: USGS Littlerock
TRAILHEAD GPS: 46.90530°N, 123.04760°W
NOTE: Dogs are prohibited in the preserve.
Check DNR website for hours of operation
(see Appendix).

Take a stroll through this unique landscape, following paths that wind among hundreds of grassy mounds gently rising from the wildflower-filled prairie. Short, easily accessible, and nearly flat, Mima Mounds is an excellent way to introduce youngsters to wildflowers.

Camas-covered mounds along the South Loop Trail

FEATURED WILDFLOWER

COMMON CAMAS
Camassia quamash
Found in wet meadows and prairies at low to mid elevations, common camas grows 1 to 3 feet tall with thick, grasslike leaves surrounding a central, multi-flowered stem. Six-petaled flowers bloom from early spring to early summer and vary in color from pale blue to deep purple as well as white. Camas was historically a very important food source for local tribes, who spent generations cultivating areas to encourage camas growth and harvest. Tribes would dig up the bulbs and then roast them in pits for days.

Other Wildflowers on the Trail: Broadleaf shooting star, chocolate lily, dune goldenrod, graceful cinquefoil, harebell, harvest brodiaea, hookedspur violet, kinnikinnick, meadow death camas, prairie lupine, Scotch broom, spring gold, western buttercup, woolly sunflower

GETTING THERE: Take I-5 to exit 95, then follow Maytown Road for 3.7 miles through the town of Littlerock to a T intersection. Take a right onto Waddell Creek Road SW and follow it for 0.8 mile to the signed Mima Mounds Natural Area on your left. Follow the paved road a short distance to the parking area. Privy available.

From the parking lot, the trail cuts through a short stretch of mixed forest before reaching the Mima Prairie. The namesake mounds are immediately visible as you work your way to a small interpretive center and observation deck. Take a few moments to read the interpretive signs on the history of the area before climbing the narrow steps to the roof. The view from the top lends some perspective on the sea of mounds stretching to the south, as well as a better view of the wildflowers that so often blanket the prairie with blues, whites, and yellows.

Once you've taken it all in and you're ready to explore, you have your choice of a short jaunt on the 0.5-mile, ADA-accessible loop, or the longer 2-mile trail that explores the southern end of the natural area. If you have the time, we recommend you do both to get the most out of your visit. The undulating mounds can be hypnotic, and each peak and trough holds the promise of something new hidden just beyond your line of sight. If you head south you'll find another observation platform where the pavement ends, offering another opportunity to appreciate this unique landscape and, if the weather cooperates, some decent views of Mount Rainier and Mount St. Helens.

While the route is short and flat, the wildflowers are the stars of this hike. The variety and number of wildflowers found at the Mima Mounds Natural Area Preserve is impressive and helps keep the prairie in bloom for most of the year. The wildflowers flourish here in part due to controlled burns that the Department of Natural Resources lights to help manage the natural area, as well as the diligent efforts of volunteers to stave off invasive species such as Scotch broom.

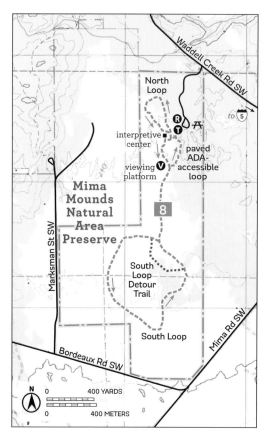

This little hike is a great option for bringing the kids out to explore an engaging landscape, and because it's accessible year-round, it's a destination for a good midwinter leg stretch. At the same time, it's worth noting that the rifle ranges at the nearby Evergreen Sportsman's Club are in frequent use and can sound a lot closer than they are. Despite the occasional noise, the mounds themselves are intriguing enough to merit a visit. Note that over the last few years, a group of nonprofits and government agencies has held an annual Prairie Appreciation Day in early May that includes guided wildflower walks, among a variety of other activities.

HISTORY

Formed approximately fifteen thousand years ago on a vast glacial outwash plain, Mima Prairie was part of a sprawling grassland system that once covered 180,000 acres. For generations, American Indian tribes lived around and managed the prairie, routinely setting fires to encourage the growth of camas and other useful bulbs. In 1841, the United States Exploring Expedition commanded by Charles Wilkes rolled through the area; he named it and theorized the mounds were American Indian burial sites. But after digging into a few, he found they were solid mounds of rock and dirt.

Since that time dozens of theories have been put forth for the origins of the mounds, and while some are more popular than others, there is no real consensus—earthquakes, glacial floods, winds, plant growth, and pocket gophers have all been suggested as possible explanations. The mystery only added to the allure of the unique landscape and helped prompt the designation of the area as a National Natural Landmark in 1966. Eight years later the 637-acre Mima Mounds Natural Area Preserve was established to further protect the area.

OPPOSITE: *Magic Mountain and Pelton Peak tower above the Stehekin River Valley near Cascade Pass (Hike 13).*

NORTH
CASCADES

9 SKYLINE DIVIDE

DISTANCE: 8.8 miles
ELEVATION GAIN: 2400 feet in; 200 feet out
HIGH POINT: 6500 feet
DIFFICULTY: Moderate
HIKING TIME: 5 to 6 hours
BEST SEASON: Summer; good fall color
TRAIL TRAFFIC: Heavy foot traffic; stock permitted between July and October
PERMIT: Northwest Forest Pass

MANAGING AGENCY: Mount Baker–Snoqualmie National Forest
MAPS: USGS Bearpaw Mountain, USGS Mount Baker; Green Trails Mount Baker No. 13
TRAILHEAD GPS: 48.88040°N, 121.86500°W
NOTE: Wilderness regulations apply in Mount Baker Wilderness; see Wilderness Guidelines in Hiking Best Practices.

Trek across wildflower-laden slopes to reach an exposed ridge with magnificent views of Mount Baker and the North Cascades. With big views and a moderate grade, it's no wonder that Skyline Divide has become one of the most popular hikes in the area.

GETTING THERE: Take I-5 exit 255 for Sunset Drive and Mount Baker, turning onto State Route 542 east, also known as the Mount Baker Highway. Continue 34.5 miles to Glacier Creek Road, about a mile past the town of Glacier. Turn right onto the road and then take a left almost immediately onto Forest Road 37. Follow FR 37 for 12.6 miles to the Skyline Divide Trailhead. Privy available.

Looking across Skyline Divide from a wildflower meadow with Mount Baker in the distance

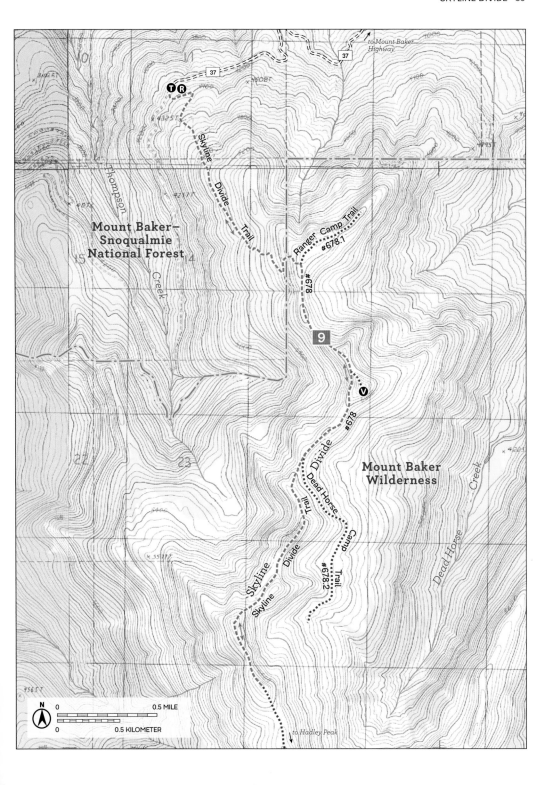

FEATURED WILDFLOWER

SPOTTED SAXIFRAGE
Saxifraga bronchialis
Relatively rare, spotted saxifrage grows in clusters of tight rosettes carpeting the ground. This perennial has short, leathery, fingerlike leaves that are often edged with hair. Its red stems grow to less than 1 foot high, branching to produce multiple blooms from late spring to midsummer. The flowers are white with bright pink, purple, and yellow spots; prominent, bulbous stamens; and a protruding center. Look for these lovely blooms in patches of gravel or amid rocks.

Other Wildflowers on the Trail: Alpine goldenrod, American bistort, broadleaf arnica, broadleaf lupine, cow parsnip, Davidson's penstemon, fireweed, fleabane, foamflower, glacier lily, harebell, harsh paintbrush, larkspur, Lewis's monkeyflower, oxeye daisy, partridgefoot, pink mountain-heather, pussytoes, scarlet paintbrush, silky phacelia, silverleaf phacelia, Sitka valerian, small-flowered penstemon, spreading phlox, spreading stonecrop, St. John's wort, subalpine aster, western columbine, white campion

Begin from the well-marked trailhead off FR 37, following the Skyline Divide Trail #678 as it works its way up the ridge under a thick canopy of fir and hemlock. Switchbacks and extensive log staircases help to smooth out what would otherwise be a rough climb on rock-and-root trail bed. The trail improvements wane as you near the ridgeline, crossing into the Mount Baker Wilderness at 1.7 miles. Find the first wildflower meadows here, with wide swaths of slope covered in blooms and bright color. Ahead the snowy summit of Mount Baker peeks over the treetops, drawing you out of the meadows to the ridgetop.

At 1.8 miles crest the ridge and arrive at a sprawling open vista with enormous views of Mount Baker and a ragged skyline full of peaks and crags. Find Mount Shuksan to the east of Baker and pick out Goat Mountain and Mount Larrabee from the mountaintop lineup. To the left, the Ranger Camp Trail #678.1 leads up a small rise, where the views are just as good and you can take a few steps away from the crowd that tends to gather here. When you're ready, push down the Skyline Divide Trail, skimming the rim of the grassy bowl below and following the ridge as it descends to a saddle, then immediately begins climbing straight up the next bump along the undulating ridgeline. Expect more of this drop-and-climb dance, as the trail has several more high points to navigate ahead.

Reach an unmarked junction 2.4 miles from the trailhead, with the main trail continuing to the right and a boot path snaking up a hefty prominence to the left. It's a steep climb and while the views from the sheltered top are excellent, they're somewhat spare, as trees obscure much of the view. There isn't a lot of

OPPOSITE: *Mount Baker peeks over the trees above a lupine-filled meadow.*

room up there, so bear in mind that it might be a little crowded when you arrive. However, a rough path leads down through open slope to reconnect with the main trail, so you will not have to retrace your steps.

Whether you opt for the side trip or not, press onward down the ridgeline, watching Mount Baker become ever larger and keeping an eye on the ground for the wildflowers found frequently along the trail. At 3.1 miles arrive at Dead Horse Camp Trail #678.2 snaking down the ridge to the left. Keep right for more ups and downs above open slopes, enjoying long 360-degree views of the surrounding landscape. Traverse below a particularly large ridgeline bump to reach a high point where the trail turns sharply south toward looming Mount Baker at 4.4 miles.

Here are good views of the peaks that surround Mount Baker—Hadley Peak, Colfax Peak, and Lincoln Peak. Find Twin Sisters Mountain just to the west of Baker and Shuksan to the east, and look north along the length of the Skyline Divide and beyond into the North Cascades and British Columbia, where dozens and dozens of peaks can be found. This is your turnaround point; the trail becomes more difficult as it heads out along Chowder Ridge toward Hadley Peak.

HISTORY

Like many glacier-covered peaks rising prominently on the horizon, Mount Baker has long attracted people. American Indian tribes knew it as Kulshan (among many other names and variations), and it played a starring role in mythology and legend. European explorers and settlers knew it as Baker, named by Captain George Vancouver in 1792. It wasn't long before mountaineers were scrambling up to the summit, an affair that required quite a bit of time and did not allow them to linger at the top.

In 1908, Charles Finley Easton decided that someone needed to spend more time on Baker's summit and organized an expedition to do just that. On what was grandly called the Easton-Sprague Research Expedition, Easton took along his brother Martin Easton; one R. B. Hess; and L. A. Sprague, a photographer, to document everything. They also wanted to try a new route, which involved following a long, unnamed ridge up the north side of the mountain. Easton dubbed it the Skyline Divide.

The expedition intended to spend a few days at the summit, which they ultimately did, but in fairly dire circumstances. Crevasses plagued their progress up the mountain, slowing them down and forcing them to spend the night on the mountainside. The next day a storm developed and they spent another night sheltered on a massive chunk of ice wedged into a crevasse. Despite these challenges, the group pressed on, reached the summit, and lived to tell the tale.

10 YELLOW ASTER BUTTE

DISTANCE: 7.6 miles
ELEVATION GAIN: 2500 feet
HIGH POINT: 6200 feet
DIFFICULTY: Hard
HIKING TIME: 4 to 6 hours
BEST SEASON: Late spring to midsummer; excellent fall color
TRAIL TRAFFIC: Heavy foot traffic
MANAGING AGENCY: Mount Baker–Snoqualmie National Forest

PERMIT: Northwest Forest Pass
MAPS: USGS Mount Larrabee; Green Trails Mount Shuksan No. 14
TRAILHEAD GPS: 48.94330°N, 121.66260°W
NOTE: The popular camps below Yellow Aster Butte fill up early. Set up camp in established sites or on snow or bare rock as alpine vegetation is sensitive and easily damaged. Wilderness regulations apply in Mount Baker Wilderness; see Wilderness Guidelines in Hiking Best Practices.

Hikers approach Yellow Aster Butte's flower-carpeted summit.

Popular with day hikers and backpackers alike, this flower-filled trek up into a rugged alpine landscape is full of sweeping vistas, glacier-carved lakes, and windy summits. Jagged peaks and tarn-dotted basins await at the top of Yellow Aster Butte, your reward at the end of a long climb, or a jumping-off point for further adventure.

GETTING THERE: Take I-5 exit 255 for Sunset Drive and Mount Baker, and turn onto State Route 542 east, also known as the Mount Baker Highway. Continue 46.2 miles to reach the WSDOT Shuksan Highway Maintenance Sheds and Twin Lakes Road (Forest Road 3065), 13 miles east of the town of Glacier. Turn left and follow the gravel road for 4.3 miles to the Yellow Aster Butte/Tomyhoi Lake Trailhead. Parking is very limited; be prepared to park along the forest road some distance from the trailhead.

From the trailhead, the climb begins by following the Tomyhoi Lake Trail #686 as it switchbacks up through an avalanche field thick with brush and vegetation before plunging into thick forest. Once under the canopy, cross into the Mount Baker Wilderness at 0.5 mile, climbing over a ridge and dropping into the Swamp Creek basin to emerge in a large meadow brimming with springtime blooms, the first of many flower-filled meadowlands to come. Return briefly to the trees as you work your way up the basin on a steady incline, trading forest for views and meadow-lined trail with every step. Pause where the trail briefly flattens on a grassy

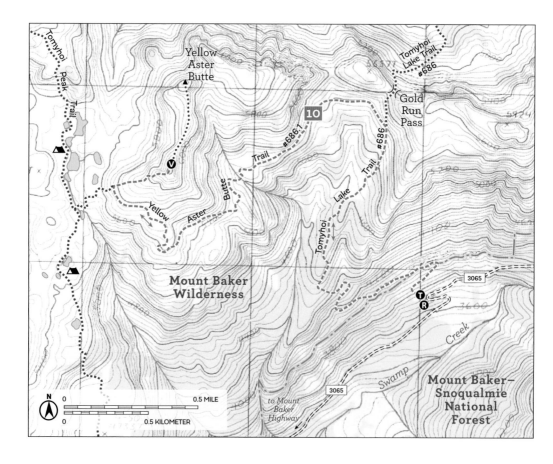

FEATURED WILDFLOWER

CUSICK'S SPEEDWELL
Veronica cusickii

Often growing in patches linked by an underground root system, Cusick's speedwell produces deep blue to purple flowers with exactly four petals (one larger than the others) and two stamens. A single stem stretches proudly upward between 2 and 8 inches. The stems are often covered in fine hairs with opposing pairs of oval leaves that grow smaller toward the top. Also known as mountain veronica, the plant is typically found in moist soils at high elevations and blooms from summer to early fall.

Other Wildflowers on the Trail: Alpine goldenrod, American bistort, bracted lousewort, Canada thistle, coast hedgenettle, Davidson's penstemon, Douglas spirea, fireweed, giant mountain aster, goatsbeard, harsh paintbrush, larkspur, leatherleaf saxifrage, Lewis's monkeyflower, mountain arnica, northwestern twayblade, pale paintbrush, pearly everlasting, pink mountain-heather, scarlet paintbrush, Sitka valerian, small-flowered penstemon, snow buttercup, spreading phlox, subalpine spirea, sweet coltsfoot, wandering fleabane, western columbine, western pasqueflower, yarrow

bench that overlooks the valley and showcases snowy Mount Baker.

After a few ups and downs, reach a well-signed junction with the Yellow Aster Butte Trail #686.1 at 1.8 miles. To the right, the Tomyhoi Lake Trail continues upward over Gold Run Pass before a long descent into the lake basin to the shore of Tomyhoi Lake, almost 2 miles distant. Veer left to continue your ascent of Yellow Aster Butte.

From the junction, traverse the shoulders of Yellow Aster Butte through meadowlands brimming with wildflowers and mountain blueberry. The increasingly rocky trail cuts through scree fields, crosses creeks, skips over bare rock, and passes through the occasional stand of trees as it winds its way around the mountain. Soon after climbing out of a large creek bowl, the trail flattens and curves into true alpine parklands, complete with big views

of Mount Baker and Mount Shuksan. Push onward, following the trail as it slowly reveals a spectacular glacial trough filled with more than a half dozen tarns, a perfect spot for an overnight stay. More than likely, the gray basin will already be dotted with brightly colored tents, as this popular backpacking destination fills up early in the day.

At the 3.5-mile mark, reach an unsigned junction. If you're planning on spending the night, follow the trail to the left as it zigzags down into the basin to find a campsite and drop your pack before continuing up to the summit. Otherwise, head right directly up the mountainside to the top of Yellow Aster Butte. This is the steepest and most difficult portion of the trail, where sections of loose rock and scree make the climb even more challenging. Climb 0.3 mile up, up, and up to reach a false summit and the end of the hike (the true summit lies

The trail cuts through one of the many wildflower meadows on the slopes of Yellow Aster Butte.

another 0.3 mile distant along the ridgeline and does not offer much more in views).

The views here are vast. Mount Baker, Mount Shuksan, Mount Larrabee, and Tomyhoi Peak all loom large. Cast your gaze north into British Columbia, with the Border Peaks rising above Tomyhoi Lake. Countless crags and peaks line the horizon in every direction from this perch. Find a good spot to settle down, break out a map, and see how many you can identify.

HISTORY

There is a long history of mining and prospecting in this area, going back as far as 1858, when gold nuggets were found in the Nooksack River by idle gold rushers passing time while waiting to access the Fraser River valley. Over the coming decades, claims pushed farther east, with miners and prospectors building roads and blazing trails along the way. By 1894, the road-trails reached what would become the Mount Baker Mining District, soon followed by the discovery of gold in 1897 on the slopes of

Bear Mountain above Silesia Creek, known as the Lone Jack vein.

A gold rush soon followed, with mining tent cities mushrooming up along the mining road: Gold Hill, Trail City, Wilson's Townsite, and Gold City. In 1901 William Boyd and W. L. Martin filed the Gold Run claim on the slopes of Mount Larrabee (then known as Red Mountain), accessing it either from Twin Lakes up to High Pass or via Gold Run Pass. They were joined by brothers LeRoy and Clyde Gargett in 1910, soon combining forces to form the Gold Run Mining and Milling Company in 1911. For decades they hauled up equipment, built a mill, and tunneled thousands of feet into the mountain, building what became known as the Gargett Mine. In 1938, five tons of ore were shipped down the mountainside to Tacoma for smelting. It yielded very little valuable material and the mine was abandoned with the onset of World War II. Today, we follow the same trails first pounded out by prospectors more than one hundred years ago.

11 CHAIN LAKES LOOP

DISTANCE: 6 miles
ELEVATION GAIN: 1700 feet
HIGH POINT: 5400 feet
DIFFICULTY: Moderate
HIKING TIME: 4 to 5 hours
BEST SEASON: Summer; good fall color
TRAIL TRAFFIC: Heavy foot traffic
PERMIT: Northwest Forest Pass

MANAGING AGENCY: Mount Baker–Snoqualmie National Forest
MAPS: USGS Shuksan Arm; Green Trails Mount Shuksan No. 14
TRAILHEAD GPS: 48.84660°N, 121.69340°W
NOTE: Wilderness regulations apply in Mount Baker Wilderness; see Wilderness Guidelines in Hiking Best Practices.

This loop romps through lake basins, zips across rocky slopes, showcases massive glacier-covered volcanoes, and leads up to lofty viewpoints. Ever popular with backpackers and climbers, this area has plenty of lakeside campsites, solitary viewpoints, and wildflower-dotted greenery to explore.

GETTING THERE: Take I-5 exit 255 for Sunset Drive and Mount Baker, turning onto State Route 542 east, also known as the Mount Baker Highway. Continue on SR 542 for 57.1 miles to the end of the road at Artist Point. Privy available.

FEATURED WILDFLOWER

ELEPHANT'S HEAD
Pedicularis groenlandica
Spikes of tightly clustered blossoms top the hairless stalks of elephant's head from early to midsummer. Saw-toothed, fernlike leaves can be found at the base of each stalk, which is reddish in younger plants and matures to a deeper green. Growing up to 2.5 feet high, this wildflower prefers the well-hydrated soil along lakes and riverbeds at moderate to high elevations but may also be found in lower wetlands. The plant is named for the shape of its blooms, each one bearing an uncanny resemblance to the ears and trunk of an elephant. Blooms are generally magenta, but can be white or almost purple.

Other Wildflowers on the Trail: American bistort, bog orchid, broadleaf lupine, common butterwort, common monkeyflower, fan-leaf cinquefoil, fireweed, glacier lily, leatherleaf saxifrage, Lewis's monkeyflower, marsh marigold, mountain arnica, mountain aster, orange agoseris, paintbrush, pale paintbrush, partridgefoot, pink mountain-heather, pussytoes, rusty saxifrage, Sitka valerian, small-flowered penstemon, spreading phlox, subalpine spirea, tufted saxifrage, western pasqueflower

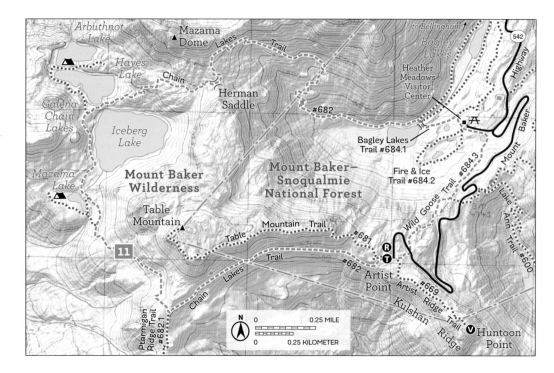

From the Artist Point parking area, head toward white-capped Mount Baker along Chain Lakes Trail #682. (Make sure to avoid the Table Mountain Trail #681, which also begins in the area.) Traverse the treeless slopes beneath Table Mountain, cutting through talus fields and intermittent meadows and taking in views of Mount Shuksan. Below, the Swift Creek valley spreads out, with Baker Lake shimmering in the distance. After 0.6 mile, cross into the Mount Baker Wilderness. Push onward to the end of Table Mountain at the 1-mile mark and arrive at the junction with the Ptarmigan Ridge Trail #682.1—the lumpy prominence ahead is the beginning of the trail's namesake ridge. Veer right, continuing along the Chain Lakes Trail.

From the junction, begin working your way around the back end of Table Mountain, dropping downward toward the lake basin as the trail alternates through boulder fields and increasing meadows. The scattered wildflowers begin to concentrate here, multiplying as you reach the lip of the basin and see little Mazama Lake below, the first of

the Galena Chain Lakes. Drop steeply down into the basin, soon passing the trail out to Mazama's campsites and backcountry toilet at 1.8 miles. The meadows and marshes around Mazama are full of wildflowers, so consider doing a little exploring here before pressing up a small rise 0.2 mile to reach the shores of Iceberg Lake. The lake rests at the bottom of Table Mountain's rubble-covered slopes, with Mazama Dome rising almost directly across the water.

Glide along the trail as it hugs the lakeshore, soon arriving at a spur trail to the left leading out to Hayes and Arbuthnot Lakes at 2.2 miles. More campsites and another backcountry toilet can be found there. Keep right, cutting across a narrow bridge of land between Hayes and Iceberg Lakes before beginning your climb to Herman Saddle. Switchback your way across exposed rock above Iceberg Lake to reach the saddle at 3 miles and a sweeping vista almost entirely dominated by Mount Shuksan, though Ruth Mountain and Panorama Dome make an appearance. Look for one of the Bagley Lakes

Mount Shuksan looms large from the shoulders of Table Mountain.

tucked into the valley below, the next stop on your journey.

From the pass, drop steeply toward the Bagley Lakes, switchbacking down through more boulders and more scattered greenery. The trail flattens near the lake and follows the shore to the junction with the Bagley Lakes Trail #684.1 near the lake's outlet creek at the 4.8-mile mark. Turn right, crossing the creek on a sturdy concrete bridge, then gently climb toward Heather Meadows Visitor Center. Reach the visitor center after 0.3 mile, then follow the road to find the Wild Goose Trail #684.3 at 5.2 miles. Turn right, climbing your way back toward Artist Point alongside the highway, with staircases helping navigate the steepest sections. Cross the highway and arrive back at the parking area, closing the loop at 6 miles.

HISTORY

Back in the 1890s, prospectors and miners were roving the lake basins and creek valleys around Mount Baker looking for signs of gold or other valuable minerals. When they found some promising formations in a large four-lake basin, they named them Galena Lakes in the hopes that the area would soon yield gold and silver. A few prospects were dug in the area and a zinc mine was blasted out of the slopes of Barometer Mountain above Arbuthnot Lake.

Around the same time, the Portland Mazamas were frequenting the area, and, in the summer of 1906, they spent some time at the lakes, called a committee, and decided to name the lakes. Collectively, they were called the Chain Lakes, as they appear to be chained together. They named the first lake in the chain Mazama, for the club;

the next and largest was dubbed Iceberg, as ice often lingers in the lake through the summer. After Iceberg, the next lake was the Mazamas' primary swimming hole, which they named Natatorium Lake. Later it was renamed in honor of Frances S. Hayes, an avid outdoor enthusiast who famously took an icy skinny-dip in the lake and later went on to join the faculty of the Bellingham State Normal School (now known as Western Washington University). They named the last lake Arbuthnot, after James Arbuthnot, who, along with his partner, had blasted a tunnel between Arbuthnot Lake and Hayes Lake to gain better access to a vein of ore.

The two different names for the lakes caused some confusion, if only for the mapmakers, so the name Galena Chain Lakes was the compromise. That same confusion probably led to the o in Arbuthnot being changed to an e on most maps.

12 SOURDOUGH MOUNTAIN

DISTANCE: 9 miles
ELEVATION GAIN: 5000 feet
HIGH POINT: 5985 feet
DIFFICULTY: Hard
HIKING TIME: 7 to 8 hours
BEST SEASON: Late spring to early summer
TRAIL TRAFFIC: Light to moderate foot traffic
PERMIT: None for dayhike

MANAGING AGENCY: North Cascades National Park
MAPS: USGS Diablo Dam, USGS Ross Dam; Green Trails North Cascades Ross Lake No. 16SX
TRAILHEAD GPS: 48.71760°N, 121.14520°W
NOTE: A permit, which can be difficult to get in this popular area, is required for overnight stays. Trekking poles are useful on the way back down.

The vast panoramic views from Sourdough Mountain's uppermost slopes are as breathtaking as the grueling ascent required to reach them. Along the way, switchback through dense forest and traverse flower-filled meadows to reach a sprawling summit and a fire lookout cabin.

GETTING THERE: Take State Route 20 to Diablo Street, located on the north end of Gorge Lake Bridge, 5.3 miles east of Newhalem. Turn onto the road, following signs pointing toward Diablo. Drive 0.9 mile through town to a riverside parking area across from the community pool. Park and cross the street, following signs pointing to the trailhead hidden in the trees. Privy available.

From the trailhead, the Sourdough Mountain Trail begins to climb immediately, following a boot-pounded trail scratched into the side of the mountain. Quickly leave the maples and alders behind as you work your way into firs and hemlocks. After crossing a sturdy bridge, the trail rockets uphill, steeply ping-ponging up a long series of switchbacks. Not far beyond the switchbacks, cross into the North Cascades National Park and continue to push your way ever upward on slightly less daunting grades.

The trees begin to thin as you approach Sourdough Camp at the 4-mile mark, just before crossing Sourdough Creek. Find tent sites tucked into the mountainside along with some of the first views of the hike. Catch part of Diablo Lake sparkling below a horizon filled with snowcapped peaks. Colonial Peak and Pinnacle Peak loom largest, while Ruby Mountain and Mount Logan are also easy to pick out.

Cross Sourdough Creek and begin a long, climbing traverse through open mountain

OPPOSITE: *Pink mountain-heather offers splashes of trailside color with Mount Baker looming on the horizon.*

FEATURED WILDFLOWER

FIREWEED

Chamaenerion angustifolium

Fireweed's bright colored purple-pink blossoms line the top of a leafy, reddish stem that grows up to 8 feet high. Narrow, willow-like leaves are arranged in a spiral up the stem to a raceme flower cluster that blooms from late spring to early fall. In the fall, pollinated seed capsules split open and silky-haired seeds are distributed by the wind. Each plant produces approximately eighty thousand seeds while also propagating by rhizomes. As a result, one individual plant is capable of creating an entire patch, allowing fireweed to effectively colonize a disturbed area extremely quickly.

Plentiful across the Northern Hemisphere, this flower is named for its ability to propagate in burnt soil left in the wake of a wildfire. It also grows in areas disturbed by logging, construction, and soil erosion, and somewhat famously in bomb craters during World War II. Small and large mammals, including rabbits, deer, and cattle, eat the young shoots of this plant. Historically, humans found it useful for a wide variety of agricultural, medicinal, and nutritional purposes.

Other Wildflowers on the Trail: Broadleaf lupine, calypso orchid, Indian pipe, Indian thistle, Lewis's monkeyflower, mountain aster, pearly everlasting, scarlet paintbrush, small-flowered penstemon, subalpine spirea, tiger lily, western columbine

meadows carpeted with wildflowers set against a dramatic backdrop of jagged summits and glacier-draped mountainsides. Huckleberries also flourish here, providing yet another reason to pause and take in the scenery. Continue to skirt through occasional stands of trees on your way to the last set of switchbacks leading up to the exposed summit ridge. Push your way up to the top, leaving the trees and meadows behind for barren rock and vast sweeping views.

Take a moment to catch your breath and reorient yourself to the refreshingly flat terrain of this expansive summit. When you're ready, begin a wonder-filled wander toward the lookout cabin, letting the views wash over you as you progress. Find a space near the cabin to drop your pack and take it all in.

To the north the snowy peak of Mount Redoubt rises in the distance above Sourdough Lake. The lake rests on the flanks of Peak 6607, and the jagged top of Hozomeen Mountain juts up from the horizon just to the east. Continue turning east to find Jack Mountain dominating the ridgeline above Ross Lake, with Crater Mountain rising behind. Next slide your gaze over a jumble of peaks before your eyes rest on Ruby Mountain's now-familiar prominence to the south. Continuing to sweep south, now even more mountaintops can be seen—Buckner, Boston, Primus—before reaching the somehow more impressive glacier-cloaked Colonial Peak. To the west, Davis Peak is close at hand, and you can easily pick out Mount Degenhardt, Elephant Butte, Luna Peak, and the high points of Stetattle Ridge before rounding back to your

ABOVE: *Diablo Lake from the summit of Sourdough Mountain*
BELOW: *The Sourdough Mountain Fire Lookout has a commanding view of the North Cascades.*

starting point. There are dozens and dozens more mountains to be seen, so break out your map and see how many you can find. Take your time at the top—you've earned it. And if nature calls, there's even a backcountry toilet near the lookout cabin.

Linger long before gearing up for your return trip. For most, that means retracing your steps, but backpackers can make a long loop by following the trail as it continues from the cabin and drops down off the north slopes of the mountain to the shores of Ross Lake, then following the water back to the parking area. Either way, descent will be relentlessly steep and hard on the knees, so break out the trekking poles for your return trip.

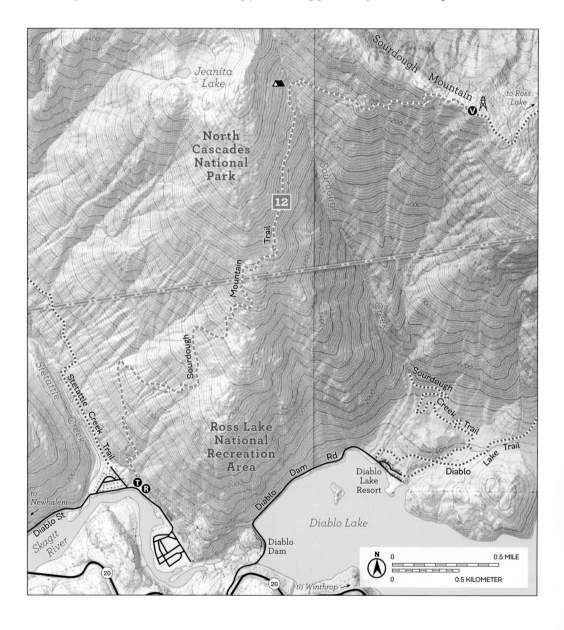

HISTORY

Throughout the mountain ranges up and down the West Coast, there are more than a few lakes, creeks, mountains, and other geographical features bearing the name "sourdough." In most cases their names' origins trace back to the miners and prospectors who brought sourdough starters from San Francisco up to the Yukon and subsisted primarily on sourdough bread and pancakes. As a result they were often referred to simply as "sourdoughs," and the areas they prospected or spent time in became known as sourdough country. Sourdough Mountain and Sourdough Creek get their names from those miners, while Sourdough Lake was named for its resemblance to the ubiquitous frying pan used to bake the bread over the campfire.

After the mining era waned, the US Forest Service decided that Sourdough Mountain's unobstructed views and broad, open summit would be an ideal site for a fire lookout, a program they began around 1915 to combat forest fires. The original cabin was built in 1917 and lasted until 1933, when the Civilian Conservation Corps built the current lookout cabin. It was the first of the 1930s-era lookout cabins to be built in the North Cascades. The roof was replaced in 1980, and four years later, the lookout was added to the National Register of Historic Places. Despite its new recognition as an important part of history, the elements continued to wear away at the cabin, and more extensive restoration work was done in 1998 and 1999 to bring it up to its current condition.

13 CASCADE PASS AND SAHALE ARM

DISTANCE: 11.2 miles
ELEVATION GAIN: 4000 feet
HIGH POINT: 7600 feet
DIFFICULTY: Hard
HIKING TIME: 7 to 9 hours
BEST SEASON: Mid to late summer
TRAIL TRAFFIC: Heavy foot traffic to Cascade Pass; moderate to Sahale Camp
PERMIT: None for dayhike

MANAGING AGENCY: North Cascades National Park
MAPS: USGS Cascade Pass; Green Trails North Cascades Ross Lake No. 16SX
TRAILHEAD GPS: 48.47550°N, 121.07490°W
NOTE: Dogs are prohibited on this trail and within North Cascades National Park except designated areas. A permit, which can be difficult to get for this popular area, is required for overnight stays.

Tackle dozens of switchbacks as you climb up to a historic mountain pass before pressing on through vast wildflower meadows to an alpine climber's camp. Along the way, drink in spectacular vistas, explore lake basins, and enjoy a colorful floral show.

GETTING THERE: Take State Route 20 to Marblemount. Where the highway makes a sharp bend in town, turn onto Cascade River Road, immediately crossing a bridge over the Skagit River. Follow the road for 10 miles to the end of the pavement, and then continue another 13 miles to the end of the road and the Cascade Pass Trailhead. Privy available.

The Cascade Pass Trail is the most popular hike in North Cascades National Park, and the reason is readily apparent the moment you arrive at the trailhead. Tucked at the head of the North Fork Cascade River, the parking area is a viewpoint in and of itself, with glacier-coated Johannesburg Mountain looming mightily above. The mountain's pointed subpeaks—Cascade Peak and the Triplets—add further bulk to the imposing cliffs above. It's difficult to find a setting this impressive without ever lacing up your boots.

The Cascade Pass Trail begins from the parking area, wasting little time ducking into the trees and starting an impressively steep ascent. Crisscross up the mountainside, ricocheting off more than thirty switchbacks, with breaks in the canopy providing pocket views of Johannesburg as you climb. Eventually, after 2.5 miles of climbing, reach the last switchback and begin a long traverse to Cascade Pass.

As you progress, wildflower slopes begin to crowd out the trees. The open, blooming meadows are a welcome change from the forested climb. Enjoy the views, the flowers, and the occasional

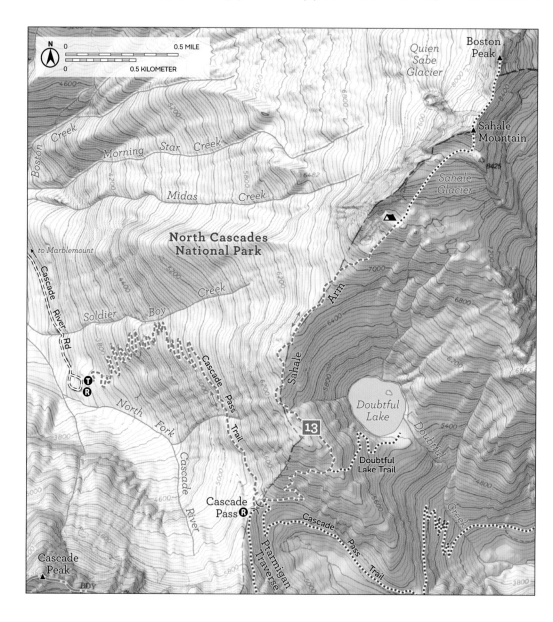

FEATURED WILDFLOWER

AMERICAN BISTORT
Bistorta bistortoides

Perched atop a single reddish stem 1 to 2 feet tall, American bistort's oblong-shaped cluster of white or pale pink blooms appears soft and feathery due to its long stamens. Long, leathery, lancelike leaves typically grow near the base of the plant, a member of the buckwheat family. The plant's roots, leaves, seeds, and bulbs were an important food source for the indigenous peoples of the American West. This flower prefers moist soil at moderate to high elevations and blooms from late spring to midsummer.

Other Wildflowers on the Trail: Common butterwort, common monkeyflower, glacier lily, Indian thistle, mountain arnica, oxeye daisy, partridgefoot, pearly everlasting, pink mountain-heather, rusty saxifrage, scarlet paintbrush, Sitka valerian, small-flowered penstemon, snow cinquefoil, spreading phlox, subalpine spirea, western columbine

sound of ice breaking off Johannesburg's glaciers as you progress, then cross a wide, barren talus field before arriving at the stone platform marking Cascade Pass at 3.4 miles.

The views from this mountain crossroads are stunning. To the north, the trail leads up Sahale Arm, with Mount Torment, Eldorado Peak, and the Triad filling out the horizon as you swing west. To the south look for Mix-Up Peak, then Magic Mountain and Pelton Peak as you swing east. This is the turnaround point for many—the views are gorgeous, there's a pit toilet, and there's plenty of space to break out lunch. For others, more adventure awaits. The Cascade Pass Trail continues from here, tracing an ancient trade route down toward Stehekin more than 20 miles distant. To the right, boot paths lead toward scramble routes to the top of Mix-Up Peak, best left to those with mountaineering and routefinding experience. For now, head left, following signposts for Sahale Arm.

From the pass, the trail becomes a little rougher as it climbs upslope. Switchback through wide meadows of wildflowers and huckleberry, brimming with the colors of the season. After a strenuous climb, reach the ridgeline at 4.2 miles and peek over the edge into a deep basin, where Doubtful Lake and its tiny island lie at the base of snowcapped Sahale Mountain. A web of trails leads down to the lake should you want to explore the basin. To stick to the featured route, keep left, following the ridge on a gentler grade toward Sahale Camp. Along the way, traverse flower fields above Doubtful Lake with ever-increasing views of Sahale Mountain and Buckner Mountain. As meadows yield to boulder fields and exposed rock, look to the moonscape-like Boston Basin on Sahale's western slopes. Push up the last stretch of trail composed entirely of rock and rubble, reaching the wide mountainside bench that is Sahale Camp at 5.6 miles. Tent sites here are marked by low rock walls built to shield against the wind.

Drop your gear and marvel at the ocean of peaks and craggy summits spread out before you. Mountains you looked up to earlier are below you now. Glacier Peak rises in the distance above Mix-Up and Magic while Mount Baker makes an appearance to the west. Settle in and enjoy this expansive, hard-won view.

HISTORY

Cascade Pass has long served as a gateway between the Skagit River valley and Lake Chelan. As far back as 7500 BC, indigenous peoples built fires and set up temporary camps at the pass. More recently, fur trader Alexander Ross explored the route in 1811, finding it more difficult than passes farther south. The area's mining boom brought prospectors over the pass, where the earliest claims around Doubtful Lake and Horseshoe Basin date back to 1875. Some of the most successful mines were located in Horseshoe Basin, such as the Black Warrior mine that continued to see activity until the 1950s.

All that activity had miners clamoring for a "mine-to-market" road over Cascade Pass. Several routes were considered in 1895, and work on the road began the following year. The primitive road was cut, but floods and avalanches in 1897 destroyed much of the work. Undeterred, boosters organized "pilgrimages" to Cascade Pass to build support for the road. Washington State earmarked money for the Cascade Wagon Road project, but construction challenges and delays led to the abandonment of the route in 1940. Ultimately the route over Rainy Pass won out, and over the next several decades, various iterations of the road that would become Highway 20 were slowly completed. The road officially opened in 1972. Around the same time, in 1967, the first iteration of today's hiking trail to Cascade Pass was built, and the year after that, the area became a part of the newly created North Cascades National Park.

Sahale Mountain, rising to the north above Cascade Pass, was named by the Mazamas, a climbing club based in Portland, Oregon. The name comes from Chinook Jargon and means "top, highest, or upper" or, more romantically, "away up high."

Wildflowers brighten the trail near Cascade Pass with the Triplets in the distance.

14 MAPLE PASS LOOP

DISTANCE: 6.6 miles
ELEVATION GAIN: 2100 feet
HIGH POINT: 6950 feet
DIFFICULTY: Moderate
HIKING TIME: 4 to 6 hours
BEST SEASON: Mid to late summer; golden larches enhance excellent fall color
TRAIL TRAFFIC: Heavy foot traffic
PERMIT: Northwest Forest Pass

MANAGING AGENCY: Okanogan-Wenatchee National Forest
MAPS: USGS Washington Pass, USGS Mount Arriva, USGS McGregor Mountain; Green Trails North Cascades Ross Lake No. 16SX
TRAILHEAD GPS: 48.51520°N, 120.73580°W
NOTE: Camping is prohibited within 0.25 mile of Rainy Lake or Lake Ann.

Explore a spectacular loop trail that climbs through high-alpine landscapes bursting with bright hues from late-spring floral shows and vibrant fall colors to reach sweeping views of lake basins and mountaintops from Maple Pass.

GETTING THERE: Take State Route 20 to the Rainy Pass Picnic Area, located 37 miles east of Newhalem and 35.2 miles west of Winthrop. The trailhead is located near the south end of the lot. Privy available.

FEATURED WILDFLOWER

SUBALPINE SULPHUR-FLOWER
Eriogonum umbellatum var. *majus*
This wild buckwheat can be difficult to identify, as the species varies a great deal. The base of the plant is a mat of dark green leaves, with 6-to-9-inch stems extending upward and crowned with a cluster of small flowers akin to an umbrella (*umbellatum* means "umbrella-like"). This particular variant has blooms that eschew the yellows normally associated with a flower with the word *sulphur* in its name. Instead, the buds begin pinkish and fade to white as the flower opens from summer to early fall.

Other Wildflowers on the Trail: Alpine leafybract aster, broadleaf lupine, columbine, cow parsnip, Cusick's speedwell, false hellebore, fireweed, foamflower, gentian, glacier lily, harebell, Indian thistle, Lewis's monkeyflower, magenta paintbrush, marsh marigold, Menzies' larkspur, mountain arnica, partridgefoot, pearly everlasting, pink mountain-heather, scarlet paintbrush, shrubby cinquefoil, Sitka valerian, spreading phlox, spreading stonecrop, spring beauty, subalpine spirea, threadleaf sandwort, twinflower, western bluebells, western Labrador tea, woolly pussytoes, yarrow

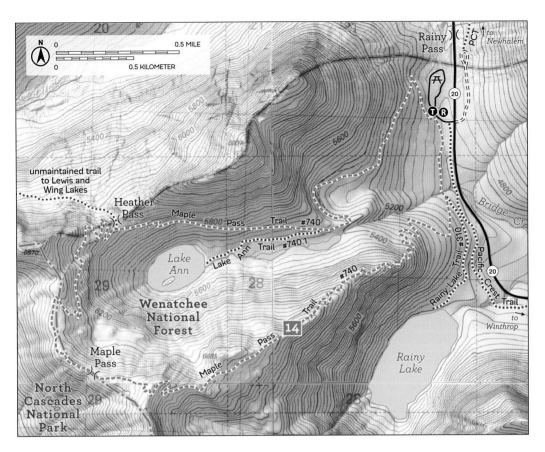

The Maple Pass Trail #740 begins from the parking area, where you will need to decide which way to go on the loop. The more popular approach outlined here has hikers heading right (counterclockwise), where gentler grades ease the climb up to Maple Pass. The trail to the left is much steeper but gets all the hard work out of the way early and allows for a more leisurely descent. Choose the route that works best for you.

Heading right, begin the hike along boot-hardened trail, climbing through a quiet, mature forest of fir and hemlock, where trunks rise from the huckleberry-carpeted forest floor. After a few switchbacks, work your way along the shoulders of a hefty ridge known as Crooked Bum and cross into a wide avalanche meadow brimming with wildflowers. Take a moment to enjoy the myriad colors from the wide variety of blooms before returning to the trees. Drop a short distance into the basin of Lake Ann, reaching the Lake Ann Trail #740.1 at 1.2 miles, which branches off to the left and leads down to the lakeshore.

Keep on the Maple Pass Trail, soon leaving the forest for a long climbing traverse above Lake Ann across boulder fields interspersed with a few scattered trees. Climb higher into alpine country, switchbacking through meadows to reach aptly named Heather Pass at 2.2 miles. The boot path here leads down toward Lewis Lake in the distance and Wing Lake beyond. Push onward, staying on the Maple Pass Trail, for better perches that offer views of Porcupine Peak and Mount Hardy to the north,

OPPOSITE: *Ascending the wildflower-lined trail to Heather Pass*

The expansive view to the east from Maple Pass

Black Peak above Lewis Lake to the west, and Whistler Mountain to the east.

From the pass, the trail steepens, climbing up into true alpine territory. Pick your way across talus fields and meadows, ascending the ridge that runs between Corteo Peak and Frisco Mountain. Wildflowers proliferate in the meadows as the views across these open sections of trail get bigger and bigger. Skirt along the edges of the North Cascades National Park boundary before reaching Maple Pass at 3.8 miles, where commanding views of the surrounding landscape await. To the south, peer down Maple Creek valley to find Glacier Peak in the far distance. Frisco Mountain rises on the left side of the valley to the southeast, while Corteo Peak and Black Peak are the craggy mountains to the west. To the east, Winchester Mountain stands opposite the glacial trough cupping Lake Ann. In addition to the views, the meadowy slopes near Maple Pass are bursting with flowers in the summer, set against this panoramic backdrop of snowy mountaintops. Take some time to linger and explore.

When you're ready, begin the long, steep descent down the open ridge dividing Lake Ann and Rainy Lake. More flower-filled fields await as you zigzag downward, savoring views and getting your first glimpses of Rainy Lake. Glance over to Lake Ann's steep-sloped cirque, where rushing cascades often tumble into the lake below. Eventually the trail leaves the alpine highlands and returns to the huckleberry and the trees, continuing the steep drop off the rocky ridge.

After a long downhill trek, the trail begins to flatten as you near Rainy Lake Trail #310. At 6.3 miles, turn left onto the flat, paved trail to breeze your way back to the parking area and complete the 6.6-mile loop.

HISTORY

The grand views from Maple Pass include a look down Maple Creek valley, where its namesake creek tumbles down toward Bridge Creek. Back in the 1880s, the Stehekin Mining District encompassed the valley, and by 1897, prospectors were working more than a dozen claims along the creek. As mining activity waned, sheepherders took advantage of ferries to Stehekin to reach remote allotments in the creek valleys above the Stehekin River. In the summer of 1917, around seventy-five thousand sheep were ferried up Lake Chelan and driven along the Stehekin River. Some made their way to Maple Creek valley to graze until fall.

While miners cut tracks and trails south of Maple Pass in the 1880s, the first permanent trail up to Rainy Pass wasn't blazed until 1906. Ranger Tommy Thompson undertook the challenge, likely building on paths cut by surveyors mapping out possible routes for the proposed Cascade Wagon Road in 1895 (see Hike 13). The first attempt at a road through the area was over Cascade Pass in 1896, but washouts and avalanches destroyed it. In subsequent years further attempts were made, but by 1940 the Cascade Pass route was abandoned. Nearly two decades later, construction began on a road that would run from Diablo Dam to Early Winters Creek via Rainy Pass, which was known as the North Cross-State Highway. The gravel road was completed in 1968, then was paved and officially opened in 1972, when it became better known as the North Cascades Highway.

15 WINDY PASS

DISTANCE: 7.8 miles
ELEVATION GAIN: Negligible on the way in; 700 feet out
HIGH POINT: 7000 feet
DIFFICULTY: Easy
HIKING TIME: 4 to 5 hours
BEST SEASON: Summer
TRAIL TRAFFIC: Light to moderate foot and equestrian traffic
PERMIT: Northwest Forest Pass

MANAGING AGENCY: Mount Baker–Snoqualmie National Forest
MAPS: USGS Slate Peak, USGS Pasayten Peak; Green Trails North Cascades Ross Lake No. 16SX
TRAILHEAD GPS: 48.73210°N, 120.67500°W
NOTE: Sections of the road to Harts Pass are quite narrow with very steep drop-offs; use caution. Wilderness regulations apply in Pasayten Wilderness; see Wilderness Guidelines in Hiking Best Practices.

Stroll down some of the most picturesque sections of the Pacific Crest Trail, complete with big mountainside meadows overflowing with wildflowers, on a flat, well-graded trail. Add on a short side trip up to a fire lookout tower and a trek above a mining ghost town, and you'll be hard pressed to find a hike that has more to offer.

GETTING THERE: Take State Route 20 to Lost River Road, located 13.2 miles west of Winthrop and about 22 miles east of Rainy Pass, easily found by following road signs directing you toward Mazama. Turn onto Lost River Road, proceed for 0.4 mile, and then take a left to continue on the road through Mazama. Just after you cross the Lost River, the pavement ends and Forest Road 5400 begins. Continue 12 miles to Harts Pass on this narrow dirt-and-gravel forest road with potholes and steep drop-offs. Turn right onto FR 5400-600 (Slate Peak Road), proceeding for 1.3 miles to the parking area at the first switchback.

From the trailhead, follow the gravel Pacific Crest Trail #2000 (PCT) out toward the rim of Slate Creek valley. The wildflower-lined, flat trail wanders past a scattering of trees to open country and wide views of the valley below and a jagged horizon of peaks and crags. Soon enough spy the Slate Peak Lookout perched on the peak's flat-top summit. Watch for squirrels and pika flitting between the rocks as you traverse Slate Peak's boulder-strewn flanks.

Work your way across several avalanche chutes, some brightened with more blooms than others. Enjoy the sweeping vistas that are momentarily interrupted by a stand of trees just before the trail spills into Benson Creek basin and sprawling meadowlands. A multitude of flowers greet you here and hug the trail as you progress through open country. Cross Benson Creek at 2.1 miles. Not far beyond, the trail crests the ridgeline to briefly reveal the sprawling Pasayten Wilderness, with forested valleys and rocky summits. Push onward, skimming the wilderness border through more delightful open country to Buffalo Pass at the 2.9-mile mark and another chance to take in what the Pasayten River valley has to offer.

From here, it's another mile to Windy Pass, traversing the slopes above Bonita Creek. The boomtown of Barron was situated in this creek valley, and it's easy to pick out the jeep tracks and surface-mining works scratched into the mountainsides. There are still buildings and crumbling foundations to be found, most easily seen with a pair of binoculars, though it should be easy enough to spy the ski yurt known as Barron Hut from the trail near Windy Pass.

At 3.9 miles, arrive at Windy Pass. Follow boot paths into the trees (or continue a short distance up the PCT) to find long panoramic views of rugged peaks and snowy mountaintops rising above tree-filled river valleys. Take a moment to survey it all: Ahead to the west are the heights of Tamarack Peak. Behind you Azurite Peak and Mount Ballard rise to the south. Swing your gaze northeast, back

Lupine flourishes in the meadows on the approach to Windy Pass.

FEATURED WILDFLOWER

BLUE STICKSEED
Hackelia micrantha

This delicate wildflower blooms from early to mid-summer atop a smooth stem 1 to 3 feet tall. Growing from a base of wide lancelike leaves, the stem, which may sport a few narrower leaves, generally branches to hold several clumps of small, bright blue flowers, each with five petals and a yellow or white center. Blue stickseed prefers moister soils and is often found near streams, though it is also common in meadows or on open slopes. After germination, the plant produces a small prickled seed, which explains how it got its name.

Other Wildflowers on the Trail: Alpine buckwheat, alpine leafybract aster, annual agoseris, bog orchid, broadleaf lupine, Cusick's speedwell, Drummond's cinquefoil, elephant's head, larkspur, lobeleaf groundsel, moss champion, mountain arnica, orange agoseris, partridgefoot, pink mountain-heather, scarlet paintbrush, small-flowered penstemon, spotted saxifrage, spring gold, spreading phlox, wandering fleabane, western columbine, western pasqueflower, yarrow

to the Pasayten Wilderness topped by Pasayten Peak. Look down the Bonita Creek drainage and imagine what it was like when it was thronged by thousands of people all trying to strike it rich.

If you're wanting more trail time, the PCT continues north through stunning landscapes. Wander until you get your fill. For hikers with extra energy and who are experienced with off-trail travel, a boot path heading west from here leads to a scramble route up Tamarack Peak. When you're ready, turn around and retrace your steps to the trailhead.

HISTORY

Back in 1892 a prospector named Alex Barron found gold along Bonita Creek below Tamarack Peak, not far from present-day Harts Pass. This discovery sparked a small gold rush, and the boomtown of Barron sprang up around the claim. The town quickly expanded to include three hotels, a general store, saloon, power plant, sawmill, and even a post office. Almost overnight, roughly 2500 people were living in Barron, either digging for gold or providing services to the miners.

Gaining access to the new town to get equipment in and gold out was suddenly urgent, so in 1892, Colonel Thomas Hart built a road to Barron, expanding on mining tracks to a mountain pass later named for him. As with most booms, there was a bust, which happened for Barron between 1899 and 1900, when gold was discovered in Alaska. As quickly as it sprang into existence, Barron was abandoned, with store shelves still stocked and mail sitting at the post office. Interest in the mines returned in the 1930s, and the road to Harts Pass was widened enough for modern vehicles to use it. With that upgrade, Harts Pass became the

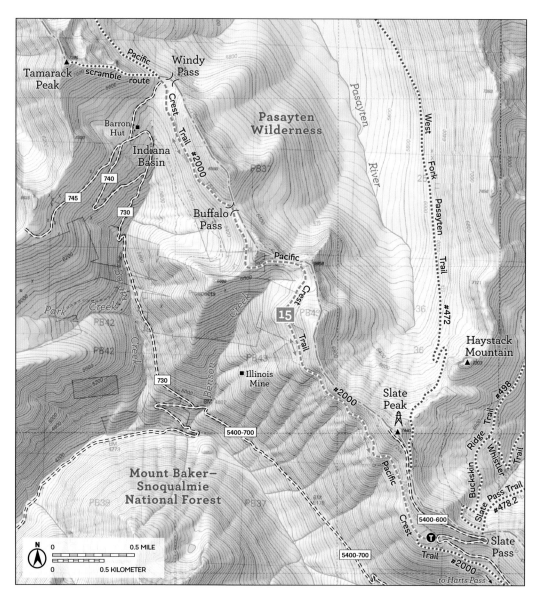

highest drivable point in Washington State and retains that status to this day.

Slate Peak has been home to a lookout since 1924, when a cabin was built there. In 1956, the Department of Defense wanted to put a radar station on Slate Peak, so they removed the cabin and blew 40 feet off the top of the mountain to level and enlarge the summit, but the station was never built. When the peak was turned back over to the Forest Service in the 1960s, they renewed plans for a fire lookout and quickly discovered that, to be effective, a lookout cabin needed the 40 feet of missing mountaintop. The current lookout tower was the solution.

OPPOSITE: *Slate Peak Lookout from the Pacific Crest Trail*

16 LEWIS BUTTE

DISTANCE: 5.4 miles
ELEVATION GAIN: 1100 feet
HIGH POINT: 3340 feet
DIFFICULTY: Moderate
HIKING TIME: 3 to 4 hours
BEST SEASON: Spring to early summer
TRAIL TRAFFIC: Light foot and mountain bike traffic
MANAGING AGENCY: Washington Department of
Fish and Wildlife

PERMIT: Discover Pass
MAPS: USGS Lewis Butte
TRAILHEAD GPS: 48.50630°N, 120.22040°W
NOTE: The newly built route outlined here cuts
across old jeep tracks and unofficial social trails
that are now decommissioned. Stay off these
trails and allow the wildflowers to reclaim them.
Rattlesnakes are common in this area; pay close
attention to your environment as you hike.

This short climb up a wildflower-covered butte follows new trail bed to reach 360-degree views of the
Methow Valley and a horizon full of North Cascade mountaintops. It's a great option for families or
groups with younger hikers or for a quick day trip out of Winthrop.

GETTING THERE: Take State Route 20 to Winthrop. On the west edge of town, head north on West
Chewuch Road, following road signs directing you to the ranger station. Continue on West Chewuch
Road for 0.9 mile and veer left on Rendezvous Road. Continue another 1.1 miles to Gunn Ranch Road and
veer left. Drive 0.8 mile to the nondescript trailhead and parking area on the left. Privy available.

FEATURED WILDFLOWER

ARROWLEAF BALSAMROOT
Balsamorhiza sagittata
A drought-tolerant plant, arrowleaf balsamroot is
commonly found on dry eastern slopes of the Cascades in large, slope-covering colonies, blooming from
late spring to late summer. As the name suggests, the
large silvery-gray leaves are arrow shaped, larger at
the base and becoming smaller and more oval higher
on the stem. The floral stem generally supports one
bright yellow, sunflower-like bloom, consisting of a
dark yellow disc surrounded by yellow petals 2 to 4
inches wide. The taproot is large and can extend down
several feet into the soil. Indigenous peoples cooked
and ate the root and used it as medicine; they also
used the seeds for oil and medicinal purposes.

Other Wildflowers on the Trail: Ballhead waterleaf,
fernleaf biscuitroot, harsh paintbrush, nineleaf biscuitroot, Nuttall's larkspur, prairie lupine, small bluebells,
spring gold, yarrow

Approaching the summit of Lewis Butte

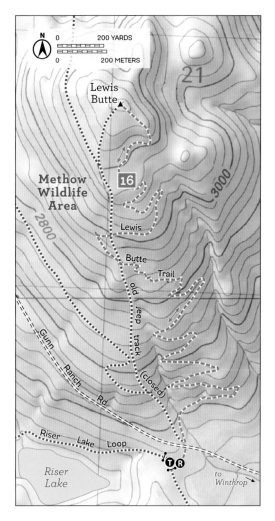

take a few years for plantings and restoration efforts to make these former trails less noticeable. When in doubt, continue on the more gently graded trail, following any signs directing you to stay on the trail. Around the half-mile mark, the trail splits into a loop. While either trail will get you there, the quickest path to the summit is to the right. Push onward and upward, switchbacking up the butte and crossing the old jeep track at 1.7 and 1.9 miles. After a final, steep push, reach the top of the butte at 2.7 miles.

Once you arrive, drink up the long views from the bald summit. The Methow Valley spreads out before you, with Gardner Mountain rising above the western end. To the south, Oval and Hoodoo Peaks stand tallest, likely dappled with snow. Swing eastward to find Winthrop, with Lookout Mountain and McClure Mountain rising above. Further east is Pearrygin Lake at the base of lumpy Blue Buck Mountain. Finally, look north, where you'll find the tips of more than a dozen North Cascade peaks.

When you're ready, retrace your steps back down the switchbacks, quickly zigzagging back down to the parking area. For hikers wanting a little more, the well-signed loop trail continues, dropping off the summit, heading north, then doubling back to close the loop via a long traverse across the lower reaches of the butte. With all the switchbacks, it's about the same mileage whether you take the loop or not. Back at the parking area, it's a short jaunt down to Riser Lake, adding 0.5 mile to the day. A longer option is the full Riser Lake Loop, 3.8 miles around the low hills opposite the butte.

HISTORY

Lewis Butte is likely named for Harmon Lewis, a stockman who owned a large portion of the butte in the early part of the last century. Beginning in 1991, the Washington Department of Fish and Wildlife (WDFW) began buying up parcels in the area to create a winter range for mule deer and to protect migratory corridors. The process was completed in 2007, and Lewis Butte became part of the Rendezvous Wildlife

Beginning from the parking area, walk across Gunn Ranch Road and follow the Lewis Butte Trail toward Lewis Butte. Wander through sagebrush on rocky tread to the first of many wide, open switchbacks that slowly work their way up the slope. In spring and early summer, these slopes explode with vibrant yellow and purple blooms as the balsamroot and lupine create a thick carpet of brilliant color that contrasts sharply with the dry browns found in the sagelands below.

Occasionally the trail intersects with decommissioned jeep track or an old trail that is now closed to prevent further erosion. It will

Fields of balsamroot cover the butte's slopes in bright shades of yellow.

Unit within the larger 34,600-acre Methow Wildlife Area.

The trails on and around Lewis Butte are popular with hikers, bikers, snowshoers, and skiers. Historically, hikers made their way to the top of Lewis Butte either via a jeep track that shot straight up the side of the butte or an informal trail that was just as steep. The high level of use and poor design led to trail deterioration and damage. In 2018, in collaboration with the Methow Valley Trails Collaborative and the Evergreen Mountain Bike Alliance, the WDFW announced trail improvements that, among other things, would decommission the jeep track and build a more sustainable trail. The improvements were completed in 2019 after hundreds of hours of volunteer work.

17 TIFFANY MOUNTAIN

DISTANCE: 4.2 miles
ELEVATION GAIN: 1700 feet
HIGH POINT: 8245 feet
DIFFICULTY: Moderate
HIKING TIME: 4 to 5 hours
PERMIT: None
BEST SEASON: Summer; golden larches glow in the fall

TRAIL TRAFFIC: Moderate foot and equestrian traffic
MANAGING AGENCY: Okanogan-Wenatchee National Forest
MAPS: USGS Tiffany Mountain; Green Trails Tiffany Mountain No. 53
TRAILHEAD GPS: 48.66330°N, 119.96640°W

Climb through a recovering burn area brimming with wildflowers and traverse meadowy ridgelines offering mountain-filled vistas as you make your way to an 8200-foot summit that was once home to a fire lookout. Best of all, while the dirt road to the trailhead is rough, the high starting elevation makes Tiffany Mountain's rugged slopes and lofty mountaintop fairly approachable for most hikers.

GETTING THERE: Take State Route 20 to Winthrop. At the four-way stop, take Bridge Street a few blocks to Bluff Street. Turn right and continue for 6.2 miles (Bluff Street becomes East Chewuch Road) to Forest Road 37, which is not well signed. If you cross the Chewuch River, you've gone too far. Follow FR 37 as it first

FEATURED WILDFLOWER

SMALL-FLOWERED PENSTEMON
Penstemon procerus
The perennial small-flowered penstemon (aka littleflower penstemon) grows up to 24 inches tall, with floral stems rising from a base of loosely clustered, lance-shaped leaves. It grows on subalpine rocky slopes and in meadows, though it can be found at higher elevations. The lipped flowers, typically bluish purple with a white tube floor, form dense whorled clusters near the top of the stalk. The plant blooms from late spring to midummer and is ideal for hummingbirds, as they can easily reach the nectar deep inside the tubular blossoms. Small bees are also able to crawl up into the blossoms to reach the pollen.

Other Wildflowers on the Trail: Alpine buckwheat, alpine leafybract aster, alpine yellow fleabane, American bistort, broadleaf lupine, fireweed, harsh paintbrush, lanceleaf stonecrop, lobeleaf groundsel, lousewort, milkvetch, mountain arnica, prairie smoke, pussytoes, rusty saxifrage, shooting star, stonecrop, threadleaf sandwort, western columbine, yarrow

OPPOSITE: The meadows on Tiffany Mountain are brimming with wildflowers.

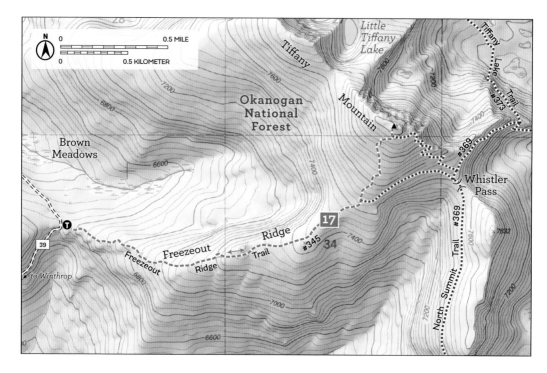

crosses, then follows Boulder Creek for 12.8 miles to FR 39. Turn left and continue on rough road for another 3.2 miles to the trailhead, marked by a cattle guard where the road widens slightly for limited parking.

From the roadside trailhead, the Freezeout Ridge Trail #345 begins by slipping past a barbed-wire fence and entering a stand of derelict pine trees, bleached and charred from the 2006 Tripod Fire. Below them, the forest is hard at work rebuilding itself, and the wildflowers are abundant. Blooms line the trail, leading the way and adding appealing color to the burn zone, which is dominated by ashen tones. The well-trodden trail dodges boulders as it begins to climb up and over Freezeout Ridge's exposed bedrock. Here, with no canopy to block your view, look upslope toward the rocky summit of Tiffany Mountain awaiting your arrival.

Work your way up the ridgeline, reaching the edge of the burn after 0.75 mile, finding a few green trees that quickly yield to desert meadows. Leave the trees entirely for open country, taking in views of Brown Meadows off the north side of Freezeout Ridge, with dozens of North Cascade peaks lining the horizon. To the south,

pick out neighboring Clark Peak and Old Baldy. Press onward, passing through seemingly endless wildflower fields, home to flowers big and small. Keep an eye out for smaller blooms tucked close to the ground or nestled against rock, seeking shelter from the wind.

At 1.6 miles reach a junction with a trail branching off to the right, leading out to Whistler Pass and the North Summit Trail #369. Keep left here, following the trail as it begins to climb more steeply toward Tiffany's summit. Switchback through even more flower-filled grasslands. The boulder-studded slopes here are a testament to Tiffany Mountain's glaciated past, the rocks having been strewn about the mountainside by retreating ice. That same ice scooped out the cirques holding the soon-to-be-seen Tiffany Lakes.

Reach the rock-jumbled summit at 2.1 miles and clamber your way across the exposed rock to the former lookout site. The lookout is long gone, though a firesight mounting pipe serves as a reminder of what once was. The views are tremendous. There are innumerable peaks and valleys—a vast expanse that encompasses wildernesses, a national park, and the Columbia Basin. Below peek down into the larch-filled cirque holding Little Tiffany Lake, which can put on quite a color show in the fall. Beyond find Tiffany Lake, surrounded by a blackened matchstick forest. Find the perfect rock and settle in to soak up the views.

HISTORY

Back in the early 1890s, a group of wealthy New York socialites, including three brothers, set up camp around a mountain lake at the base of a rugged mountain. One of those brothers was William Tiffany. The group spent two years on the lakeshore before returning to the East Coast. William Tiffany joined Theodore Roosevelt's volunteer army to fight in the Spanish-American War, a group better known as the "Rough Riders." He fought in Troop K and survived the 1898 Battle of San Juan Hill but succumbed to yellow fever soon afterward. Tiffany Lake and Mountain were named in his honor.

In 1900 a US Geological Survey crew scaled Tiffany Mountain to install a triangulation station (the current marker dates from 1924). While Tiffany and his compatriots undoubtedly scrambled to the top, the first recorded ascent was by the survey crew. In 1931 the Forest Service installed a lookout cabin at the summit atop an 8-foot tower, which lasted until 1953, when it was removed. Aside from some rusted metal and some anchor points, the most obvious legacy of the old lookout is the metal pipe at the summit that was used to mount the fire finder.

In 2006 the lightning-sparked Tripod Fire ravaged Tiffany Mountain's slopes from June to October, eventually merging with other wildfires and consuming more than 175,000 acres. It remains one of the largest wildfires in Washington State history.

Tiffany Mountain has abundant wildflower-covered slopes.

18 SUMMER BLOSSOM TRAIL

DISTANCE: 4 miles
ELEVATION GAIN: 1500 feet
HIGH POINT: 7850 feet
DIFFICULTY: Moderate
HIKING TIME: 3 to 4 hours
BEST SEASON: Early to midsummer
TRAIL TRAFFIC: Light foot traffic
MANAGING AGENCY: Okanogan-Wenatchee
National Forest

PERMIT: None
MAPS: USGS South Navarre Peak, USGS Marin
Peak; Green Trails Prince Creek No. 115
TRAILHEAD GPS: 48.11990°N, 120.30300°W
NOTE: It is not uncommon to hear motorbikes
in the distance on the sole hiker-only trail in the
Sawtooth Backcountry. Wilderness regulations
apply in Lake Chelan–Sawtooth Wilderness; see
Wilderness Guidelines in Hiking Best Practices.

If you can bear the bumpy ride to reach the trailhead, the Summer Blossom Trail offers gorgeous views, fields of flowers, and less traveled trail. The dozens of miles of forest road to the trailhead aside, the panoramic views from North Navarre Peak are approachable for most hikers.

GETTING THERE: From US Highway 97, just south of Pateros, turn onto State Route 153 signed for Twisp and Winthrop. Follow SR 153 for 16.8 miles to Gold Creek Loop Road. Turn left, and in 0.8 mile turn left

FEATURED WILDFLOWER

WESTERN LABRADOR TEA
Rhododendron columbianum
This short, woody native shrub grows between 1 and 4 feet high, with smooth, dark brown bark that occasionally peels. Western Labrador tea is a member of the rhododendron family, so the leaves will likely be familiar: dark green, oblong, alternating, and often slightly drooping. The tops of the leaves are smooth, while the undersides are lighter in color and dusted with shiny hairs. When the plant flowers, from early summer to midsummer, branches end in clusters of bright white flowers, each with five rounded petals and long, protruding stamens. This water-loving plant is usually found at lower elevations near bogs and marshes, in partly shady areas.

The leaves, which give off a distinctive spicy aroma, have long been used in making herbal medicinal tea to address various ailments. Over time the name of the plant and the name of the beverage have become synonymous: Labrador tea. However, the plant contains toxins that can be released if the leaves are steeped too long.

Other Wildflowers on the Trail: Alpine buckwheat, bracted lousewort, broadleaf lupine, Davidson's penstemon, harsh paintbrush, lanceleaf stonecrop, lobeleaf groundsel, mountain arnica, rock clematis, scarlet paintbrush, small-flowered penstemon, spring gold, tall groundsel, wandering fleabane

The Summer Blossom Trail lives up to its name.

onto Gold Creek Road, with a sign pointing you toward South Fork Gold Creek, Foggy Dew Group Site, and Crater Creek Camp. In 1 mile turn left onto South Fork Gold Creek Road (FR 4330). Continue for 13.4 miles to the junction of Grade Creek Road (FR 8200) and Cooper Mountain Road (FR 8020). Turn right onto Grade Creek Road and continue 8.3 miles to the Summer Blossom Trailhead.

From the roadside parking area, cross Grade Creek Road to the trailhead. As you cross, note the green slopes of Summer Blossom basin on the flanks of Bryan Butte just to the north. From here, you can see only a small portion of the meadowlands, but after some climbing, you will find pocket views that showcase the whole basin.

The Summer Blossom Trail #1258 begins by entering open pine forest, pressing down narrow trail at a gentle grade. After about 0.25 mile of hiking, the trail steepens as it starts to work its way up one of the ribs of Sawtooth Ridge. Wide switchbacks lead out toward the edge of Summer

Blossom basin, offering a bird's-eye view of the meadows and Falls Creek drainage. Sometimes narrow and rocky, the trail climbs through thinning forest interspersed with wildflower-filled meadows brightening the trailside.

At 1.1 miles break out of the trees into a large wildflower meadow, often filled with the deep blues and reds of lupine and paintbrush. Push upward on increasingly rocky trail to begin a climbing traverse up one of the shoulders of North Navarre Peak. The talus slopes are largely open here, offering views of Lake Chelan shimmering in the distance. Find flowers and darting

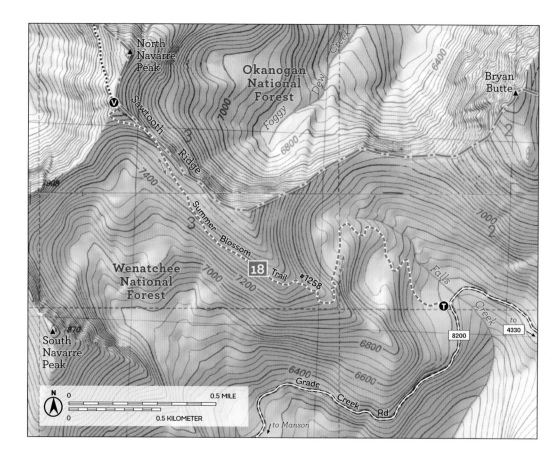

South Navarre Peak from the Summer Blossom Trail

squirrels eking out an existence between the rocks as you progress, dodging dwarf-sized trees stunted by the elevation and tough terrain as you go. Eventually attain the ridgeline of Sawtooth Ridge and get your first taste of the hike's sweeping views before pressing up the last few hundred feet to a high shoulder of North Navarre Peak at 2 miles.

This remote, rubble-strewn point offers tremendous views. To the south, the Columbia Plateau spreads out in the distance beyond Lake Chelan, while closer, the exposed crags of South Navarre Peak rise from the Falls Creek valley. To the west, white-capped Glacier Peak and Bonanza Peak stand above a crowded horizon of peaks and summits. Gaze below into the Safety Harbor Creek valley to find vast swaths of burn, a legacy of multiple wildfires, most recently the Uno Peak Fire in 2017. To the east, view Bryan Butte and the Foggy Dew Creek drainage. To the north, find a short boot path leading up to the top of North Navarre Peak, where you can find excellent views of the Lake Chelan–Sawtooth Wilderness and more Sawtooth Ridge peaks.

HISTORY

The Summer Blossom Trail traces its roots back to the sheep allotment system established between the 1880s and 1905. Grazing allotments were an attempt to control the number of sheep and livestock grazing on public lands. Every year, sheepherders would drive sheep up to higher elevation grazing lands, such as those on Sawtooth Ridge. Many of the roads, trails, and large camps in the Sawtooth Backcountry are a legacy of those sheepherders. Summer Blossom was likely named by those sheepherders, who would have stopped at the quasi-wetland basin. Presumably the basin was named for the ample flowers, or simply the relative lushness of the area compared to its more arid surroundings. The allotments were largely phased out by the 1950s.

North and South Navarre Peaks were named for Judge Ignatius Navarre, a mineral surveyor for the federal government and local judge, who was among the first white settlers along Lake Chelan, arriving in 1886. Wenatchee National Forest supervisor Albert Hale "Hal" Sylvester climbed South Navarre Peak in 1899, though he was likely not the first to make it to the top. He was, however, a prolific namer of peaks, rivers, and ridges in the area, and was, therefore, probably responsible for getting the name Navarre on the map.

OPPOSITE: *The Stuart Range from Tronsen Ridge (Hike 29)*

CENTRAL CASCADES

19 OLD SAUK TRAIL

DISTANCE: 6 miles
ELEVATION GAIN: 100 feet
HIGH POINT: 800 feet
DIFFICULTY: Easy
HIKING TIME: 2 to 3 hours
BEST SEASON: Late spring to early summer
TRAIL TRAFFIC: Moderate foot traffic
MANAGING AGENCY: Mount Baker–Snoqualmie National Forest

PERMIT: Northwest Forest Pass
MAPS: USGS Helena Ridge; Green Trails Silverton No. 110
TRAILHEAD GPS: 48.21518°N, 121.55960°W
NOTE: Three trailheads access the Old Sauk Trail. The middle trailhead, 1.5 miles down the Mountain Loop Highway, provides access to a mile-long ADA-accessible loop with a river viewpoint.

Explore a quiet riparian forest steeped in history and wander beneath the shadows of towering old-growth sentinels on this easily accessible river walk. When alpine meadows and heather-topped summits are out of reach, enjoy the flowers and other flora (and fauna!) that thrive along this section of the Sauk River.

GETTING THERE: Take I-5 exit 208 for Arlington/Darrington and State Route 530. Turn east on SR 530 and drive to Darrington. Follow the signs to the Mountain Loop Highway, heading south out of town. After 4 miles, find the signed Old Sauk River Trailhead on your left. Privy available 1.5 miles farther down the road at the ADA-accessible trailhead.

The Sauk River is designated a Wild and Scenic River.

FEATURED WILDFLOWER

INDIAN PIPE
Monotropa uniflora

These pale white or light pink plants rise 4 to 8 inches up from the forest floor, with a single bloom nodding down toward the ground on a stem of the same color. Small scaled leaves grow along the length of the stem. Indian pipe blooms from early summer to early fall and can appear as a single plant or in clusters. As the flower matures, it rises to become perpendicular to the stem before releasing its seeds. After that, the plant begins to gradually darken. The edges turn gray and then become black before the plant eventually collapses into decay.

These plants may seem to appear suddenly, emerging to their full height within just a few days. They do not employ photosynthesis but instead take their nutrients through a parasitic attachment to underground fungi. Nicknamed "ghost pipe" or "ghost plant," this wildflower prefers dense or shaded areas of forest.

Other Wildflowers on the Trail: Bleeding heart, bunchberry, foamflower, pink wintergreen, starflower, trillium, twinflower, wood violet

From the gravel parking area, follow the wide, forested Old Sauk Trail #728 toward the Sauk River. The river is part of the Skagit Wild and Scenic River System, a designation it received in 1978 to ensure that the river remains free-flowing and unobstructed. Wander through a mixed forest of evergreens and maples intermingling with looming old-growth firs that survived the last round of logging in the 1930s. Spy moss-covered boulders nestled in the ferns, and wildflowers finding shelter near stumps and nurse logs.

If the water level allows, take a path down to the rolling river to spend some time watching the water tumble over the rocky riverbed and scan the area for wildlife. Raptors are common here, as are deer and other wildlife attracted to the river. Push onward, paralleling the river, to the viewpoint, enjoying a trailside thick with moss, berry bushes, and views of the river. Here you can explore the mile-long ADA-accessible loop, which offers the opportunity to spend some time a little deeper under the canopy.

From the viewpoint, press onward along the river. Take your time on this nearly flat trail, as there is always something to pause and take a closer look at—whether it's blooming flowers, a handful of huckleberries, or a bald eagle. Reach the end of the trail at Murphy Creek and the highway at the 3-mile mark. Turn around and enjoy this river ramble in reverse.

Ideal for hikers of all ages and abilities, the Old Sauk Trail is a chance to slow down and take a closer look at the landscape. With almost no elevation gain to speak of and year-round access, this trail is a great little escape during the winter or as a spur-of-the-moment walk with the family during the summer months.

The Washington Trails Association has put a lot of work into the Old Sauk Trail, updating the main trailhead and repairing trail damage from recent floods. The ADA-accessible trailhead was added in 2011, and the increased access means that the Old Sauk Trail should see more use in the future.

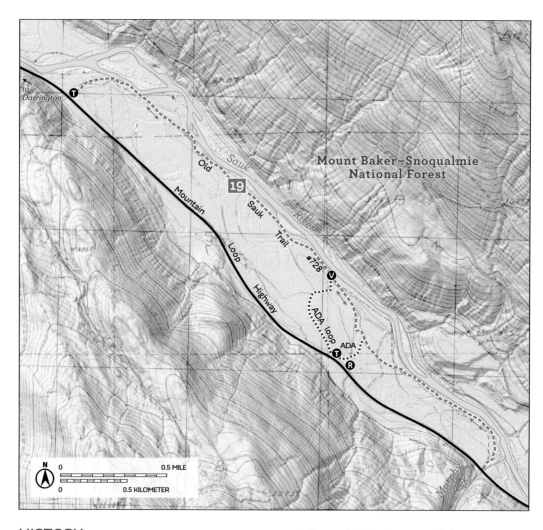

HISTORY

For generations, the Sauk-Suiattle Tribe plied the Sauk, Suiattle, Cascade, Stillaguamish, and Skagit Rivers before signing a treaty with the United States government in 1855. The town of Darrington was founded not long after, in 1867, and the 1889 discovery of gold at Monte Cristo caused a development boom that rapidly expanded the settlement. A wagon road was quickly built to lead equipment and miners into the Monte Cristo area and haul minerals and ore out. Predictably, as more space was needed to fuel Darrington's expansion, the Sauk-Suiattle were slowly but surely pushed out.

When tribal leaders signed the 1855 treaty, it is estimated that the tribe had around four thousand members; by 1924 their numbers had dwindled to eighteen. Facing extinction, the tribe spent the next fifty years attempting to get federal recognition. In 1973 the tribe achieved their goal, which helped establish a reservation just outside of Darrington, and today, the tribe has rebounded to more than three hundred members.

Boots still pound parts of that old Monte Cristo wagon road: hikers on the Old Sauk Trail follow the same route taken by prospectors more than a century ago.

The Old Sauk Trail cuts through sheltering forest.

20 GREEN MOUNTAIN LOOKOUT

DISTANCE: 7.6 miles
ELEVATION GAIN: 3000 feet
HIGH POINT: 6500 feet
DIFFICULTY: Hard
HIKING TIME: 5 to 6 hours
BEST SEASON: Late spring to summer; excellent fall color
TRAIL TRAFFIC: Moderate foot traffic
PERMIT: None

MANAGING AGENCY: Mount Baker–Snoqualmie National Forest
MAPS: USGS Huckleberry Mountain, USGS Downey Mountain; Green Trails Cascade Pass No. 80
TRAILHEAD GPS: 48.26820°N, 121.23690°W
NOTE: Wilderness regulations apply in Glacier Peak Wilderness; see Wilderness Guidelines in Hiking Best Practices.

Switchback up through green, open slopes and wildflower-bursting meadows to reach a rocky perch that first hosted a fire lookout more than a century ago. Because the route is rarely under the forest canopy, the long trek up to the summit offers big views that widen with each passing step and culminates in spectacular vistas from the catwalks of Green Mountain Lookout.

GETTING THERE: Take State Route 530 to Suiattle River Road (Forest Road 26), located 7.1 miles east of Darrington and 11.1 miles west of Rockport. Take Suiattle River Road for 10 miles to the end of the pavement and then continue another 8.7 miles to Green Mountain Road (FR 2680). Turn left and follow the road 5.5 miles to the Green Mountain Trailhead. Parking is limited.

The striking view from Green Mountain Lookout

From the parking area, the Green Mountain Trail #782 slips into the trees and quickly climbs past the trailhead registration station. Follow a dusty, steep trail through mature forest under the only sheltering canopy found along this hike. Quickly reach a large meadow that foreshadows the rest of the hike: trailside wildflowers dot the greenery with color for a few

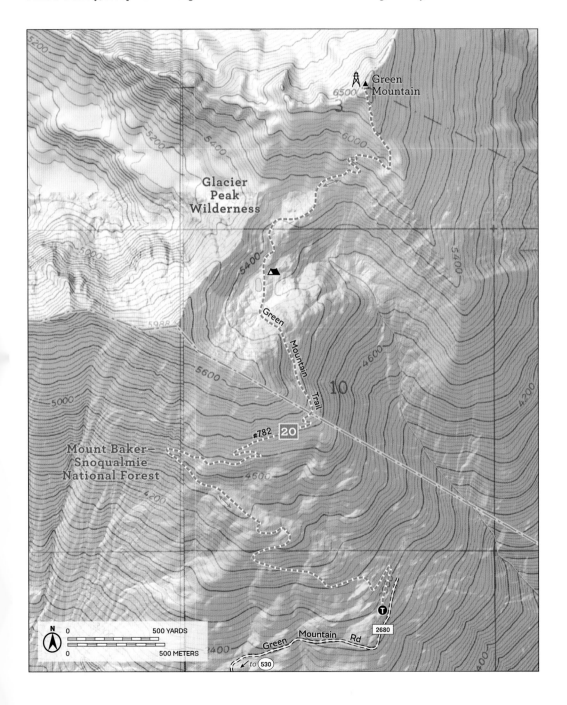

FEATURED WILDFLOWER

WESTERN PASQUEFLOWER
Anemone occidentalis

Before the snow fully melts in spring, the finely divided, light green, fernlike leaves of western pasqueflower emerge in moist subalpine meadows and on open mountainsides heavy with snowmelt. Each stem, growing up to 12 inches high, holds a single large cuplike flower. Blooming from late spring to midsummer, the flower boasts creamy-white petals surrounding hundreds of yellow stamens, while the undersides of the petals are often lightly tinged with blue. The flowers quickly fade after pollination and are soon replaced with silky hairs in a tufted top. During this process the stem lengthens, allowing the wind to spread the flower's seeds when the tufts dry out.

The word *pasque* alludes to Easter or Passover, around when the flowers bloom, as well as to the pure white color of the flowers. Indigenous peoples used the stems and seeds of pasqueflower for medicinal purposes.

Other Wildflowers on the Trail: American bistort, Cascade penstemon, cow parsnip, Douglas spirea, fireweed, glacier lily, harebell, harsh paintbrush, Lewis's monkeyflower, Nootka rose, pearly everlasting, pink mountain-heather, pioneer violet, Sierra pea, Sitka valerian, spring beauty, tall bluebells, tiger lily, western columbine

moments before you briefly return to the firs. Soon the trees give way to encroaching meadowlands, flower-filled slopes, and a first peek at horizons soon to be filled with snowcapped volcanoes and jutting mountaintops.

Push ever upward, switchbacking upslope to reach the Glacier Peak Wilderness at 1.7 miles. From here, it is a stiff climb up the back of a ridge to the edge of a shallow basin, passing a few stands of trees and views of Glacier Peak and the Suiattle River valley along the way. Drop into the basin, reaching a few small tarns and scattered camps at 2.7 miles. High up ahead you might be able to spot the lookout cabin, clinging to one end of Green Mountain's rocky crown. Work your way through the sometimes-marshy basin, where surrounding slopes are often teeming with glacier lilies. Pause to take in the rolling meadows broken up by swaths of huckleberries that glow with reds and oranges in the fall.

The trail steepens again on the climb out of the basin, switchbacking up through endless flower fields to the ridgeline, then rocketing straight up the open ridge to the lookout cabin at the 3.8-mile mark. Whereas the views below were largely dominated by Glacier Peak, the summit's 360-degree vistas offer a commanding perspective over an enormous amount of stunning landscape. Look north to find Mounts Baker and Shuksan rising behind Mount Chaval and Snowking Mountain. To the west, White Chuck Mountain, Whitehorse Mountain, and Three Fingers fill the skyline. Swing south past

OPPOSITE: *Hiking through Green Mountain's namesake meadows*

Mount Pugh and Sloan Peak for more big views of Glacier Peak and the Suiattle River valley. Finally, the eastern horizon is largely filled with Dome Peak set above the Downey Creek valley as well as flat-topped Bonanza Peak just to the southeast. There is room to explore the summit area, so take some time to wander and enjoy this breathtaking panorama.

HISTORY

Green Mountain has been used to spot fires since 1919, when lookouts manned the mountaintop by day and camped in tents below the summit by night. That changed in 1933, when the Civilian Conservation Corps loaded up a string of pack mules with lumber and led them more than 20 miles up to the top of Green Mountain, where they built a lookout cabin. From that cabin, the lookouts scanned the horizon for smoke and, for a few years during World War II, watched the skies for signs of enemy aircraft. Over the decades, the cabin was pounded by heavy snows and harsh conditions, requiring extensive repairs.

By the early 1980s, advances in fire detection made the cabin obsolete, and though it was no longer staffed by the Forest Service, it remained popular with hikers, and in 1987, it was added to the National Register of Historic Places. Despite efforts by volunteers to care for the cabin, by 2002 the required repairs were so extensive that the cabin was disassembled, with each piece carefully numbered and then helicoptered out and stored for future reassembly. Lack of funding and poor weather resulted in a seven-year delay before restoration of the lookout began.

That effort in 2009 involved at least sixty-seven helicopter trips and other machinery that is not normally allowed in the wilderness. The project caught the attention of Wilderness Watch, a wilderness advocacy group that filed a lawsuit seeking to remove the lookout cabin because the use of machinery violated the Wilderness Act. They eventually prevailed in 2012, when a federal judge sided with Wilderness Watch and ordered the removal of the cabin. Local leaders and lookout volunteers decried the ruling, and in 2014, in the wake of the Oso Landslide that devastated the small town of Oso, Washington, on March 22, killing forty-three people, Congress passed the Green Mountain Lookout Heritage Protection Act. The legislation protected the cabin and ensured that the Forest Service could continue to maintain the structure into the future.

21 WALT BAILEY TRAIL

DISTANCE: 9 miles
ELEVATION GAIN: 2100 feet
HIGH POINT: 4800 feet
DIFFICULTY: Hard
HIKING TIME: 6 to 8 hours
BEST SEASON: Spring to summer
TRAIL TRAFFIC: Light foot traffic

MANAGING AGENCY: Mount Baker–Snoqualmie National Forest
PERMIT: None
MAPS: USGS Mallardy Ridge, USGS Wallace Lake; Green Trails Silverton No. 110, Green Trails Index No. 142
TRAILHEAD GPS: 48.02387°N, 121.64360°W

Follow this route down the nearly legendary Walt Bailey Trail, the result of a volunteer effort to rebuild a long-lost trail that once led out to a set of pristine alpine lakes and big views of Spada Lake.

GETTING THERE: Take the Mountain Loop Highway to Mallardy Road (Forest Road 4030), located 17.6 miles east of Granite Falls and 35.5 miles southwest of Darrington. Turn south and follow the road 1.3 miles to FR 4032. Veer right onto FR 4032 and continue 5.7 miles to the end of the road and the trailhead.

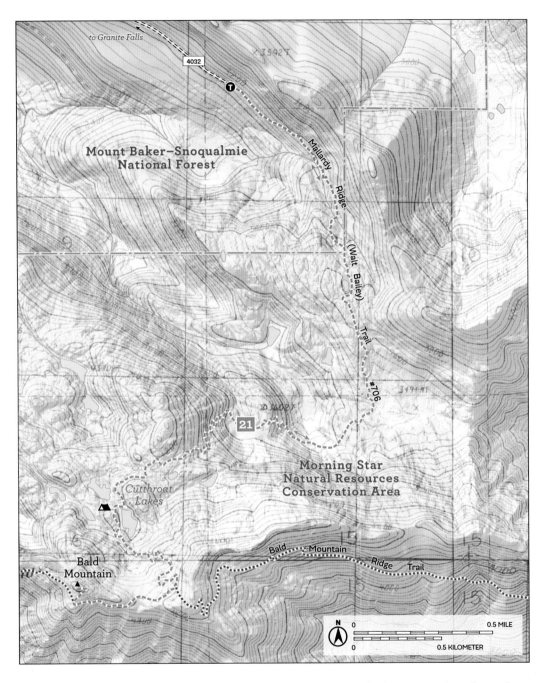

Officially known as the Mallardy Ridge Trail #706, this hike begins from the end of the forest road and enters a mixed forest of alder, cedar, and hemlock. The narrow Walt Bailey Trail wanders through the trees to broad meadows dotted with marshy ponds. At 1 mile, it enters the Morning Star Natural Resources Conservation Area (NRCA), which protects more than

FEATURED WILDFLOWER

TIGER LILY
Lilium columbianum

Able to exceed 4 feet in height, the stems of tiger lily branch outward to produce a column of numerous blooms. The yellow-orange flowers face the ground, with a tight cluster of thick, orange-tipped stamens in the center of petals that curve gracefully back toward the stem. Dark red freckles dot each petal closer to its center. Examine the lower half of this plant to notice the pattern of the lance-shaped leaves, arranged in whorls around the stem. This wildflower blooms from late spring to midsummer and can be found at a wide range of elevations, from sea level to subalpine.

Many indigenous peoples harvested this lily for its bulbs, which could be cooked to impart a bitter or peppery flavor to soups or other dishes. The name *columbianum* refers to the Columbia River, where samples of this plant were first collected. Tiger lily is also known as Columbia lily.

Other Wildflowers on the Trail: Alpine speedwell, bog orchid, copperbrush, coralroot orchid, golden arnica, Jeffrey's shooting star, leatherleaf saxifrage, lobeleaf groundsel, marsh marigold, partridgefoot, pink mountain-heather, queen's cup, subalpine lupine, subalpine spirea, wandering fleabane, western columbine, white mountain-heather

37,000 acres of land around Spada Lake. Back in 2007 the Mount Pilchuck and Greider Ridge NRCAs were merged into today's Morning Star NRCA—though references to the defunct Mount Pilchuck NRCA linger.

Push upward, following trail that may not always meet Forest Service trail standards, but that never poses much difficulty to follow or navigate. During the summer, find plenty of trailside huckleberries to snack on as you work your way along Mallardy Ridge. At 1.5 miles reach large grassy meadows that are home to many of the wildflowers found along the route. Beyond the largest of the alpine meadows, the trail steepens and begins to switchback up through talus fields toward Cutthroat Lakes. At 2.9 miles, arrive at the ridgeline and a small

tarn with a fairy-tale view of the lakes spread out below like a hidden kingdom. This is the realm of fisherfolk and backcountry adventurers, one not often frequented by day hikers. You're unlikely to meet too many folks on your trek across the lake basin.

From here, follow the winding path as it descends to the lakes. Along the way, you'll pass footpaths snaking off from the main trail to secluded lakeshores, tranquil campsites, and quiet lunch spots. Stay on the widest path as it curves around the lakes and begins to climb up out of the lake basin toward Bald Mountain. Switchback up the mountainside to the ridgeline and the junction with Bald Mountain Ridge Trail at 3.9 miles. Veer right, following the spine of the mountain to the summit. Navigating this

TOP: *Looking out over Cutthroat Lakes and beyond from the summit of Bald Mountain*
BOTTOM: *Hiking past one of the Cutthroat Lakes*

sometimes-brushy section can be a little diffi-cult, but the path is clear and the views worthy of the extra effort.

Arrive at the summit 4.5 miles from the trail-head. The views from here are enormous. To the south, Mount Rainier rises above Spada Lake and the Sultan Basin. Turn to the east to find Del Campo and Vesper Peaks, Big Four Mountain, and Mount Pugh. To the north pick out Three Fingers and Whitehorse Mountain. Mount Pilchuck can be seen to the west. Settle in, break out your lunch, and enjoy this tranquil view.

HISTORY

During the Stillaguamish River's mining hey-day around the turn of the last century, miners worked claims all along the river. One enter-prising miner began working at the mouth of a creek along the Stillaguamish but never bothered to officially file the claim. Perhaps for that reason, folks started referring to the creek by the name of the miner: Mallardy. Over the years, Mallardy Creek and Mallardy Ridge have played host to innumerable travelers making their way up the ridge to Cutthroat Lakes and beyond.

Back in the 1930s, the Mallardy Ridge Trail ran from the Stillaguamish River up the mountainside to the Blackjack Ridge fire look-out before circling back down to the river. The pole-tower lookout was built in 1935 and a cabin was added in 1942. In 1950, the deci-sion was made to remove the lookout, and the trail fell into disuse. At the same time, logging operations destroyed some sections of the trail. What was left of the trail was abandoned, and it wasn't until 1991 that Walt Bailey, a veteran of the Civilian Conservation Corps, began work on an alternative route for the Mallardy Ridge Trail. Built entirely by volun-teers, including the then seventy-three-year-old Bailey, today's Walt Bailey Trail provides access to Cutthroat Lakes and connects to the Bald Mountain Ridge Trail.

22 GLACIER BASIN

DISTANCE: 13 miles
ELEVATION GAIN: 2200 feet
HIGH POINT: 4400 feet
DIFFICULTY: Hard
HIKING TIME: 7 to 8 hours
BEST SEASON: Summer
TRAIL TRAFFIC: Heavy foot and mountain bike traffic to Monte Cristo townsite; light foot traffic to Glacier Basin
PERMIT: Northwest Forest Pass

MANAGING AGENCY: Mount Baker–Snoqualmie National Forest
MAPS: USGS Blanca Lake; Green Trails Mountain Loop Highway No. 111SX
TRAILHEAD GPS: 48.02569°N, 121.44380°W
NOTE: The route crosses South Fork Sauk River, either by fording (typically easy in summer) or walking across a large log. Wilderness regulations apply in Henry M. Jackson Wilderness; see Wilderness Guidelines in Hiking Best Practices.

It's a rough climb to reach this often-overlooked alpine cirque, but what you'll find is well worth the effort. The secluded basin feels like a hidden wonderland, complete with waterfalls, wildflowers, and relics of Monte Cristo's mining past.

GETTING THERE: Take the Mountain Loop Highway to Barlow Pass, located 30 miles east of Granite Falls and 23 miles south of Darrington. Park and find the gated Monte Cristo Road on the south side of the road opposite the Barlow Pass Trailhead parking lot. Privy available.

FEATURED WILDFLOWER

LEWIS'S MONKEYFLOWER
Erythranthe lewisii
Lewis's monkeyflower, a perennial, can grow more than 3 feet tall, with tiered pairs of deeply veined, spade-shaped leaves climbing the stalks. The bright pink or reddish-purple tubular flowers bloom in summer and consist of five petals flaring outward into what resembles a set of laughing lips, perhaps of a grinning monkey. The plant was also once classified in the *Mimulus* genus—*mimus* is Latin for a comedic actor. Reputed to be among the many flowers first documented by Lewis and Clark's westward expedition, the plant is said to have been named in Lewis's honor. Look for it alongside streams and in wet soil at moderate to high elevations.

This flower's reproductive success depends on bees, which transfer pollen from one flower to another as they collect nectar. Look closely to find two hairy ridges that emerge from the center of this flower, sometimes highlighted in yellow.

Other Wildflowers on the Trail: Broadleaf lupine, common monkeyflower, false hellebore, false Solomon's seal, fireweed, foamflower, goatsbeard, pearly everlasting, pink mountain-heather, rusty saxifrage, subalpine spirea, wandering fleabane, western columbine

From the parking area, cross the highway to the gated Monte Cristo Road, built on the Everett and Monte Cristo railroad grade. Wide and flat, the trail breezes down the old railbed alongside the South Fork Sauk River. Openings in the mixed forest canopy offer glimpses of craggy summits above, including Sheep Mountain, Foggy Peak, and the shoulders of Del Campo Peak. At 1.1 miles reach the junction with the Weden Creek Trail #724, which leads up to Gothic Basin, but that is an adventure for another day. Press onward for another 0.1 mile to reach the river ford and site of the washout that destroyed the bridge in 1980. Decide whether to ford the river or brave the log bridge—fording is easy in high summer when the water is low. Use caution if you opt for the log, as it is often slippery.

Beyond the ford, on the 3-mile stroll to the townsite, note the imposing, often-snowcapped peaks ahead—Wilmans, Monte Cristo, and Cadet Peaks. Glacier Basin and your destination sit below. At 4.2 miles, pass the Monte Cristo Campground, which makes for a good base camp for climbers and scramblers to explore this area. Reach the townsite and the grass-covered former rail yard at the 4.5-mile mark. A few outbuildings and cabins, the old railroad turnaround, and a powerhouse are lingering reminders that this ghost town was once home to around two thousand people.

From the townsite, cross Seventysix Creek and follow Dumas Street for 0.2 mile to an intersection. To the right the former road wanders deeper into the townsite, past a few crumbling buildings. To the left, you can get a closer look at the concentrator, where ore from the Glacier Basin Mines was collected and processed. The basin lies straight ahead, and the work begins.

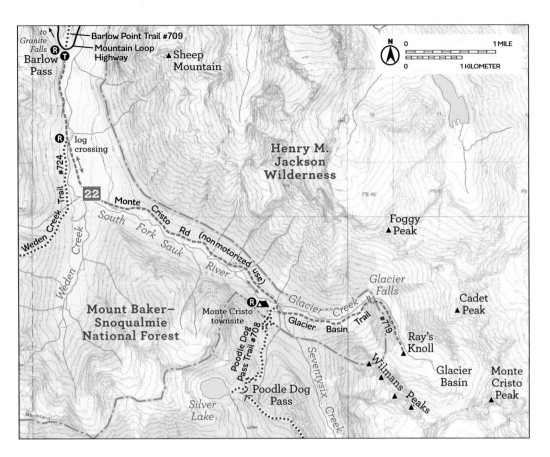

Follow Glacier Basin Trail #719 as it rapidly transitions from road to trail to half-scramble alongside Glacier Creek. Find wayside cascades, some hidden in boulders and talus, that make for good stopping points as you navigate your way up the steep mountainside. At its worst, there is a short section of rock so steep that a rope is (usually) on hand to help you make it over the hump. Push onward, entering the Henry M. Jackson Wilderness at the 5.7-mile mark near Glacier Falls, a tumbling cascade easily seen from the trail.

Continue to follow the rushing creek, and eventually the grade will ease. Spy rusting bits of pipe and cable in the surrounding rock and increasing wildflowers as you round Mystery Hill and enter the basin 6.5 miles from the trailhead. Here the surrounding peaks loom above—

Cadet to the north, Monte Cristo to the east, and Wilmans Peaks to the south. Meadows of wildflowers line Glacier Creek and lead toward a hill known as Ray's Knoll. Work your way across the basin bottom, marveling at the talus-strewn slopes, towering mountaintops, and bright, contrasting colors of the wildflowers. Find a campsite on Ray's Knoll as well as plenty of space to quietly enjoy the solace of this alpine wonderland.

HISTORY

Tucked at the foot of Monte Cristo Peak, Glacier Basin was named for the glaciers that scooped out the cirque as they retreated north thousands of years ago. Though the glaciers are long gone, you're still likely to run into patches of lingering snow.

OPPOSITE: *Monkeyflowers brighten Glacier Basin.*

Glacier Basin and Rays Knoll

Gold was discovered near Monte Cristo in 1889 in what soon became known as Seventysix Gulch. Hoping to strike it rich, brothers Fred and Mac Wilmans, along with Frank Peabody, hiked into Glacier Basin looking for their own pot of gold. What they found would become known as the Mystery and Justice Mines, encompassing thirty-three claims—the epicenter of Monte Cristo mining operations and the source of the vast majority of the district's output.

A number of adits were driven into the rock—Mystery, Justice, Pride of the Woods, Pride of the Mountains, New Discovery, and Golden Cord—and they were all soon connected by underground tunnels and stopes. In 1892, construction began on the Rockefeller-funded Everett and Monte Cristo Railway, and an aerial tram was built to transport ore down to the concentrator near Monte Cristo. The trams traversed an 1100-foot span of cable above Glacier Basin to the ridge known as Mystery Hill, then continued along a series of towers that guided the tram to a downslope terminal. Another tramway was built in 1896.

Operations were in full swing in 1897, but washouts on the railway that year were expensive and time-consuming to repair. Investors pulled out, and mining activity began to wane. The railroad washouts continued, and increasing levels of arsenic were found in the lower levels of the mine. After 1915, the mines were abandoned, but their mark on the land continues. Mining equipment and crumbling buildings are easily found among Glacier Basin's talus fields, including what remains of the tram tower on Mystery Hill. The arsenic, too, lingered until 2013, when the US Forest Service and the Washington State Department of Ecology secured funds from a settlement against ASARCO to clean up the toxic tailings. ASARCO is particularly notorious in Washington State for its longtime copper smelter in Tacoma that operated until 1985. The cleanup in Glacier Basin was completed in 2016.

23 SCORPION MOUNTAIN

DISTANCE: 8 miles
ELEVATION GAIN: 2300 feet in; 300 feet out
HIGH POINT: 5540 feet
DIFFICULTY: Hard
HIKING TIME: 4 to 5 hours
BEST SEASON: Late spring to early summer;
excellent fall color
TRAIL TRAFFIC: Light foot traffic
PERMIT: None

MANAGING AGENCY: Mount Baker–Snoqualmie
National Forest
MAPS: USGS Captain Point; Green Trails
Benchmark Mountain No. 144
TRAILHEAD GPS: 47.79648°N, 121.26240°W
NOTE: Wilderness regulations apply in Wild Sky
Wilderness; see Wilderness Guidelines in Hiking
Best Practices.

Follow a fading and sometimes-rough trail along Johnson Ridge on a lonesome trek out to dazzling wildflower meadows set against ever-more-enormous views of countless peaks and mountaintops. While it's a rough-and-tumble journey, these impressive views are well worth the effort, and because this often-overlooked hike doesn't get a lot of trafficyou'll likely have the summit all to yourself.

FEATURED WILDFLOWER

GLACIER LILY
Erythronium grandiflorum
Blooming until midsummer, glacier lilies are particularly impressive in the early spring, when they often burst through receding snow, bringing a bright splash of yellow to trailside snowfields and signaling the coming of spring. Thin, bright green stems ascend straight up 2 to 3 inches, before turning sharply downward, holding the bell-like flowers facing the ground with bright yellow petals curving upward. Underground, the stem grows down to a depth of up to 7 inches, widening into a bulblike structure called a *corm*, which plants use to survive harsh environmental conditions. The corm is a favorite food of squirrels, rodents, and bears.

The stamens are long and furry and may be white or tipped with yellow, red, or brown. Each flower is accompanied by two thick, broad leaves, similar to tulip leaves. Find glacier lilies on open slopes and areas where snowmelt keeps the soil moist.

Other Wildflowers on the Trail: Bracted lousewort, broadleaf lupine, false hellebore, fireweed, harebell, lobeleaf groundsel, mountain arnica, pearly everlasting, scarlet paintbrush, Sitka valerian, small-flowered penstemon, subalpine aster, tiger lily, trillium, wandering fleabane, white mountain-heather, western columbine

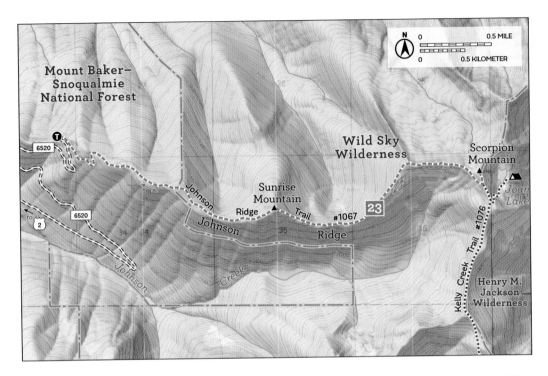

GETTING THERE: Take US Highway 2 to Beckler Road (Forest Road 65), located 0.8 mile east of Sky-komish and 15.2 miles west of Stevens Pass. Turn north, following signs for Beckler River Campground, and proceed 7 miles to a junction, taking a sharp right up FR 6520 and following it for 2.7 miles to an unsigned junction. Keep left here, continuing on FR 6520 for another 4.1 miles to the end of the road and the Johnson Ridge Trailhead.

From the parking area at the end of the road, the Johnson Ridge Trail #1067 begins steeply, following a decommissioned road through a recovering clear-cut for 0.3 mile before veering sharply uphill to the ridgeline on a short but steep trail. This area was last logged in the late 1980s, leaving openings in the canopy that reveal a taste of the panoramas to come. Press upward along the ridge, watching as the forest begins to deepen, and cross into the Wild Sky Wilderness at 1.3 miles.

From here, work your way up the flanks of Sunrise Mountain, climbing through stands of old-growth subalpine fir and hemlock as you near the summit. At 2 miles, break out of the trees into semi-exposed summit meadows. Pause to take in some decent views before pressing onward; look for Mount Fernow and

Mount Daniel to the south, as well as your final destination: the grassy top of Scorpion Mountain directly to the east.

The trail drops from the top of Sunrise back into the trees and down to a ridgeline saddle at the foot of Scorpion Mountain. There's nowhere to go from here but straight up. Climb steeply to the edge of the wildflower meadows at 3.5 miles. Leave the trees and travel through an abundant floral display. Huckleberries flourish here as well, turning the mountainside red in the fall. Continue your climb along the open ridge as a wider and wider sea of surrounding mountaintops is revealed with each step. As you near the summit, the trail returns to sheltering trees before reaching the meadows crowning Scorpion Mountain, often blanketed with glacier lilies just after the snow recedes. At 3.8 miles

Approaching the summit of Scorpion Mountain

Glacier lilies blanket the slopes of Scorpion Mountain.

reach an unmarked junction with a trail veering off to the left and leading up to the hike's end. Take those final steps to the top to reveal a staggering 360-degree view. Just below the summit to the east is little Joan Lake (easily reached 0.4 mile farther down the trail from the unmarked junction, along with the Kelly Creek Trail #1076). To the north, snowy Glacier Peak catches your eye; to the south Mount Fernow dominates the horizon. Between Glacier and Fernow are dozens and dozens of peaks. Catch your breath, drop your pack, then pull out a map and see how many you can identify.

HISTORY

Back before the area was extensively logged in the late 1970s and early 1980s, a sizeable trail system connected the Beckler River to a number of lakes and peaks in the area, many reached by way of the Johnson Ridge Trail. While today's trail officially ends at Joan Lake, it once continued on to Captain Point via the Kelly Creek Trail. Other trails and connectors led to Alpine Baldy, the Mount Fernow Potholes, and Beckler Peak.

The logging destroyed large portions of these trails, and they were largely abandoned—though a few intrepid hikers try to follow what remains before bushwhacking to their destination. In 2008, much of this area was protected from future logging by being designated a wilderness, now known as the Wild Sky Wilderness. Part of that protection included the requirement to build more trails in the new wilderness. Today there is an ongoing effort by forest managers and trail volunteers to do exactly that, and there are proposals to revive some of these old routes.

24 ALPINE LOOKOUT

DISTANCE: 9.6 miles
ELEVATION GAIN: 2400 feet in; 200 feet out
HIGH POINT: 6235 feet
DIFFICULTY: Moderate
HIKING TIME: 5 to 6 hours
BEST SEASON: Summer; good fall color
PERMIT: Northwest Forest Pass

TRAIL TRAFFIC: Moderate foot and equestrian traffic
MANAGING AGENCY: Okanogan-Wenatchee National Forest
MAPS: USGS Lake Wenatchee; Green Trails Wenatchee Lake No. 145
TRAILHEAD GPS: 47.79230°N, 120.79440°W

Wander along a rolling ridgeline through scattered wildflower meadows set against a marvelous backdrop of rugged terrain, glimmering lakes, and vast forested valleys. End your journey at a lookout cabin with panoramic views. With most of the hike's climbing work frontloaded on your trek up to the crest of Nason Ridge, you won't need to focus on the trail, allowing you to enjoy every view and flower along the way.

GETTING THERE: Take US Highway 2 to Butcher Creek Road (Forest Road 6910), an unsigned road located 0.1 mile east of the Nason Creek rest stop, 17.4 miles east of Stevens Pass, and 17 miles west of Leavenworth. Turn north onto FR 6910 for 4.5 miles to FR 6910-170. Turn right and continue 0.1 mile to the Round Mountain Trailhead.

FEATURED WILDFLOWER

BITTERROOT
Lewisia rediviva
The fleshy, fingerlike leaves of bitterroot, which grows up to 3 inches high, often wither before bloom time. The flowers bloom from mid-spring to midsummer and are quite large compared to the rest of the plant, approaching 3 inches in diameter, with twelve to eighteen petals that overlap or layer around colorful stamens. The petals vary from white to gradients of pink and purple. Find bitterroot in rocky soils at low to mid elevations.

These showy wildflowers are among those named for Meriwether Lewis, who collected specimens while on expedition with William Clark. The plant, whose taproot can easily rot from excessive moisture, is extremely resistant to drought and known for regenerating after long periods in dry soil, thus the species name *rediviva*. The carrotlike taproot was prized among indigenous peoples, who boiled and ate it.

Other Wildflowers on the Trail: Alpine goldenrod, bush penstemon, Davidson's penstemon, fireweed, Pacific lupine, scarlet paintbrush, showy Jacob's-ladder, small-flowered penstemon, spreading phlox, threadleaf sandwort, tiger lily, Tweedy's lewisia

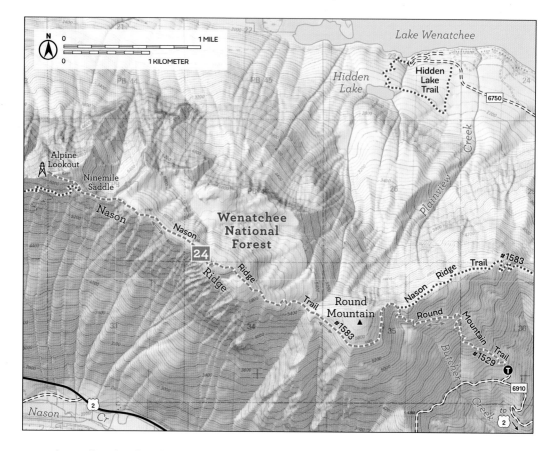

From the trailhead at the edge of a young forest still in recovery from being logged, the climb begins immediately, following the Round Mountain Trail #1529 as it ascends the shoulders of Nason Ridge. Here the trees are older, a mix of fir and pine that litter the dusty trail with needles and cones. The route is confined to the trees for the first half mile or so, but soon enough the forest abruptly ends as you reach a decades-old burn. Skeleton trees rise high above a brush-heavy infant forest, their bone-white trunks long ago stripped of blackened burn by the elements. Where there is a recovering burn, there are wildflowers, and there are plenty here—with paintbrush and lupine most commonly found along the trailside.

Climb through the burn and return to living forest, soon reaching the junction with the Nason Ridge Trail #1583 at 1.5 miles. Take a moment to catch your breath, knowing that the trail is fairly gentle from here and most of the stiff climbing is behind you. When you're ready, head left, working your way around the sides of Round Mountain, one of the larger prominences along Nason Ridge. The sparsely forested traverse offers some of your first views of the Nason Creek valley below and the Enchantment and Chiwaukum Peaks in the distance.

Beyond Round Mountain, the ridgeline walk begins, soon revealing views of Lake Wenatchee and Glacier Peak as your route alternates through stands of trees and wildflower meadows.

OPPOSITE: *Alpine Lookout clings to the mountaintop.*

Lake Wenatchee from Alpine Lookout

Navigate your way across 3 miles of ups and downs along the ridge, stopping often to admire a view or take a closer look at some wildflowers. Eventually you will spy Alpine Lookout in the distance, looking much farther away than it is. As you near the lookout, the trail drops down to Ninemile Saddle, a narrow stretch of ridgeline near the trail's 9-mile mark (the trail's numbering is calculated from the trailhead on the south shores of Lake Wenatchee). The talus-filled avalanche chutes on either side of the saddle offer some unique views of Lake Wenatchee and the Nason Creek valley below.

Push onward to the marked junction with the Alpine Lookout spur trail at 4.5 miles. Continuing on the Nason Ridge Trail would take you down toward Merrit Lake and the Merrit Lake Trail, which some use as an alternative (and more strenuous) approach to the lookout. Instead, turn up the rocky spur trail and climb the 0.3 mile to the lookout cabin. The true summit is a bit beyond the cabin, marked by a tall pipe. Find it by heading uphill past the helipad and then a weather station before reaching the top. Mountain goats frequent this area, so be prepared to give them a wide berth if you encounter them.

Whether from the cabin or the true summit, drop your gear and take a look around at these truly massive views. Look north to Dirtyface Peak just above Lake Wenatchee; the peak was also once home to a fire lookout. Gaze up the White River valley to find Glacier Peak jutting into the horizon, then turn to the sprawling Little Wenatchee River valley to find the tip of Sloan Peak. Keep turning west, looking down Nason Ridge toward hulking Mount Howard flanked by Mount Mastiff and Rock Mountain. As you swing to the south, you can make out Mount Rainier and Mount Daniel in the far distance, followed by the Chiwaukums. Admire Mount Stuart and the other Enchantment Peaks to the southeast. With views like these, it's not hard to guess how Alpine Lookout got its name. Find a spot to settle down and savor this sprawling panorama.

HISTORY

Around the turn of the last century, long after settlers, explorers, and adventurers had begun climbing up Nason Ridge to survey their surroundings, Albert Hale "Hal" Sylvester, then supervisor of Wenatchee National Forest, gave the ridge a name. He named the ridge after the creek, which was named in 1890 for a local American Indian rancher who lived along the creek and went by Charlie Nason. One of Sylvester's ongoing challenges was to combat wildfires—often ironically sparked by the cinders shooting out of logging locomotives—and one way he did that was by giving geographic features names to help direct crews to the locations of fires. Another tactic was developing lookout sites, and Nason Ridge made for an excellent site.

The first lookout station on Nason Ridge consisted of a sighting device known as an alidade, a phone that was connected to other nearby lookouts, and a tent that lookouts often just called a "rag house." By 1927, there were 430 miles of telephone wire connecting lookout stations in the region. In 1936 the old rag house was upgraded to a cabin, which stood until the mid-1970s, when the aging cabin needed to be replaced. The plan in the summer of 1975 was to helicopter the Dirtyface Peak lookout cabin to the Alpine Lookout site. Presumably this is at least part of the reason for the helipad found next to the cabin. Unfortunately, they were unable to lift the cabin from Dirtyface (they ended up burning it to the ground) and were instead forced to build a new cabin at Alpine Lookout the following year.

In 1995, the lookout was added to the National Historic Lookout Register, and in 2006 the cabin was again replaced. Today, after more than a hundred years, lookouts still report to Alpine Lookout during the summer months to scan the horizons for smoke.

25 ICICLE RIDGE

DISTANCE: 4.6 miles
ELEVATION GAIN: 1800 feet
HIGH POINT: 3000 feet
DIFFICULTY: Moderate
HIKING TIME: 2 to 3 hours
BEST SEASON: Spring to early summer
PERMIT: None

TRAIL TRAFFIC: Heavy foot, equestrian, and mountain bike traffic
MANAGING AGENCY: Okanogan-Wenatchee National Forest
MAPS: USGS Leavenworth; Green Trails Leavenworth No. 178
TRAILHEAD GPS: 47.56860°N, 120.68090°W

Icicle Ridge is part of the sprawling mountainous terrain that makes up the northern wall of the Icicle Creek valley. Just minutes from bustling downtown Leavenworth and easily accessible, the first section of the Icicle Ridge Trail #1570 is a very popular day hike in spring and summer, as hikers come to enjoy the wildflower-lined trail and the spectacular views from the top.

GETTING THERE: Take US Highway 2 to Icicle Road (Forest Road 76), located just west of Leavenworth. Turn south on the road, continuing 1.4 miles to the sign for the Icicle Ridge Trailhead on the right side of the road. Turn right and then take a left almost immediately into the trailhead parking area.

Icicle Ridge Trail #1570 begins from a small parking lot just off Icicle Road. With little ceremony, the route opens with a long series of switchbacks that relentlessly climb up the shoulders of the ridge, offering no reprieve until you reach the ridgeline. Early sections of the trail pass behind a few houses before zigzagging through thin forest and patches of wildflowers. Here, too, you will pass the only water to be found on the hike before pressing upward toward the dusty reaches of the trail. As you climb, clusters of trees offer welcome shade, while breaks in the tree cover provide a window into Icicle Creek valley in the distance.

Find the purple hues of the woolly vetch along the first mile of trail. As you climb, you may pass glacier lilies or paintbrush before graduating to the lupine and balsamroot that dominate the ridgeline. If you're hiking between the early spring and late summer, the sheer variety of wildflowers and flowering shrubs found along this trail all but guarantees you'll encounter some blooms on your trek to the top.

Eventually the trail crests in a welcoming clearing, complete with several logs to rest on, at 2.1 miles. Peer down the other side of the ridge for your first peek at the Wenatchee River.

If it's early enough in the season, you may be able to see the waters of Drury Falls tumbling down the exposed cliffs to the north. While this clearing is a tempting place to stop, veer to the right and continue down the trail for a few hundred more feet to find the biggest views. Leavenworth is spread out below, with the Wenatchee River sparkling and shimmering in the sun. Note the charred remains of the trees that once covered this viewpoint, a reminder of the fires that made this panorama possible.

With abundant wildflowers and a spectacular view, the Icicle Ridge Trail has a lot to offer. At the same time, climbing 1800 feet in 2.3 miles makes this short trail a little challenging, especially on a hot day, so remember to pack sufficient water for the climb. This trail is also crowded on summer weekends, so be prepared to share the trail. As always, yield to the hikers who are climbing up.

Looking out over Leavenworth from wildflower-covered Icicle Ridge

FEATURED WILDFLOWER

WOOLLY VETCH
Vicia villosa

Woolly vetch is a common wildflower found at lower to mid elevations. The vinelike plant sprawls across hillsides or climbs nearly anything available. Its compound leaves have anywhere from twelve to eighteen narrow oblong leaflets. The flowers bloom from late spring to early summer, grow in elongated clusters known as racemes, and vary in color from pinkish purple to deep violet. A legume, the plant sports long seedpods in the fall.

Other Wildflowers on the Trail: Alpine groundsel, arrowleaf balsamroot, barestem biscuitroot, broadleaf lupine, bush penstemon, coralroot orchid, fireweed, glacier lily, harsh paintbrush, Hooker's fairybell, kinnikinnick, little pipsissewa, Lyall's mariposa lily, nineleaf biscuitroot, phlox, queen's cup, sedge, snowbrush, spreading dogbane, white campion, yarrow, yellow salsify

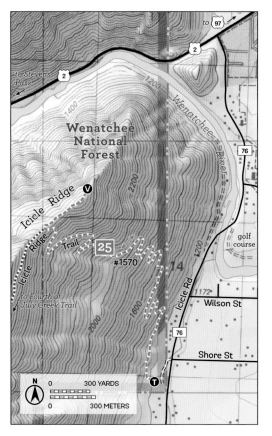

For those looking for more trail to explore, the Icicle Ridge Trail continues up the ridge from the clearing, passing Fourth of July Creek Trail at the 9-mile mark before pressing into the Alpine Lakes Wilderness, eventually reaching Frosty Pass at the end of the 29.6-mile trail.

HISTORY

From the overlook, you'll see hundreds of charred silver snags silently standing watch over Leavenworth. They burned in 1994 in a lightning-sparked wildfire now known as the Hatchery Creek Complex, and they serve not only as a reminder of the devastating fire season that year, but also just how close the flames came to the town. The fire consumed more than 43,000 acres and burned for weeks, one of four simultaneous major fires in the area, hemming Leavenworth in on two sides while collectively destroying 180,000 acres of forest. The blazing mountainsides could be plainly seen from the town's homes and businesses as nearly three thousand firefighters and one thousand US Marines tirelessly worked fire lines to contain the encroaching flames. They fought the fires for thirty-three days, and while thirty-five cabins burned down, the flames never made it to Leavenworth.

26 MOUNT DEFIANCE

DISTANCE: 10.4 miles
ELEVATION GAIN: 3400 feet
HIGH POINT: 5584 feet
DIFFICULTY: Hard
HIKING TIME: 6 to 7 hours
BEST SEASON: Late spring to early summer
TRAIL TRAFFIC: Heavy foot traffic to Mason Lake; moderate to Mount Defiance
MANAGING AGENCY: Mount Baker–Snoqualmie National Forest

PERMIT: Northwest Forest Pass
MAPS: USGS Bandera; Green Trails Snoqualmie Pass Gateway No. 207S
TRAILHEAD GPS: 47.42463°N, 121.5833°W
NOTE: Parking can be challenging in summer; arrive early or be prepared to park up to 0.25 mile away on Forest Road 9031. Wilderness regulations apply in Alpine Lakes Wilderness; see Wilderness Guidelines in Hiking Best Practices.

Push past the popular shores of Mason Lake to reach the expansive wildflower meadows carpeting the summit of Mount Defiance, as well as the vast views of the Alpine Lakes Wilderness interior and Snoqualmie Valley below.

GETTING THERE: From I-90 between North Bend and Snoqualmie Pass, take exit 45. Eastbound, turn left to go under the freeway and join the westbound exit, following Forest Road 9030 as it veers left and continues 0.9 mile to a fork. Veer left onto FR 9031 and follow it for 2.9 miles until the road terminates at the Ira Spring Trailhead. Privy available.

Mount Rainier fills the southern horizon from the wildflower-lined trail near the summit of Mount Defiance.

FEATURED WILDFLOWER

BEARGRASS
Xerophyllum tenax

Commonly found on open mountainsides through-out the region, beargrass sprouts a dense clump of grasslike leaves surrounding a central flower stalk that can grow up to 5 feet tall. The thick green stalk is punctuated by green fibers protruding toward a dense raceme of hundreds of small white blossoms. The pleasantly fragrant plume of flowers blooms from late spring to late summer; each clump blooms only once and then dies. Beargrass was an important resource for indigenous peoples of the region, who used the leaves to construct baskets and ornamen-tal braids and roasted the root for food.

Other Wildflowers on the Trail: Avalanche lily, bleed-ing heart, broadleaf lupine, coralroot orchid, David-son's penstemon, fireweed, fleabane, foamflower, glacier lily, hookedspur violet, Indian thistle, marsh marigold, mountain arnica, pink mountain-heather, pioneer violet, scarlet paintbrush, serviceberry, Sitka valerian, small-flowered penstemon, spread-ing phlox, subalpine spirea, tiger lily, wandering fleabane, western columbine, white campion, yarrow

From the trailhead, the Ira Spring (Mason Lake) Trail #1038 begins on the bones of a repur-posed fire road that was built to combat a per-sistent wildfire on Bandera Mountain back in 1958. Both the grade and still-wide road are well suited for conveying heavy machinery and fire-fighters up a mountainside. Skip across a few streams, including Mason Creek, and through sections of young mixed forest before entering the Alpine Lakes Wilderness at 1.2 miles.

Once in the wilderness, it's not long before the trail leaves the old roadbed at 1.5 miles. Arrive at a signed junction directing you steeply up the mountainside. Clamber up rock steps on increasingly dusty trail. The trees thin, and the beargrass proliferates as the yielding canopy reveals ever-increasing glimpses of the Sno-qualmie Valley below. Eventually, after a steady climb, shed the last of the trees to reach enor-mous views of surrounding mountaintops from beargrass-covered slopes.

Push upward to the 2.9-mile mark, reach-ing the junction with the Bandera Mountain Trail to the right. Veer left to continue up to the west through subalpine meadows and talus fields, passing the Ira Spring Memorial plaque just before the short descent to Mason Lake. At 3.4 miles reach the lakeshore, which is rid-dled with little nooks and crannies that offer an abundance of campsites and the possibility of a refreshing dip. There is plenty of room, so keep going until you find the perfect spot to break out your lunch and enjoy a gorgeous picnic or some time splashing in these alpine waters on a sunny summer afternoon.

While it's tempting to linger on the shim-mering shores of Mason Lake, it's another 1.5 miles up to the summit of Mount Defiance. To reach it, continue following the trail around Mason Lake to the junction with the Mount Defiance Trail #1009 at 3.6 miles. Veer left, climbing through the trees along rough and rocky trail. Sections are steep and somewhat difficult to navigate, but exposed roots will help you work through some of the rougher sections. Eventually break out of the trees to reach the meadows of Mount Defiance, bursting with wildflowers in the high season and set against a backdrop of jagged peaks and views that stretch to Bellevue's glimmering skyscrapers.

Find a small rock cairn at 5 miles marking the spur trail to the right leading to the summit. From here it's a short 0.2-mile flower-filled romp up to the top, with sections chipped straight out of the summit block. On the best of days, you can see five volcanic peaks: Adams, Baker, Glacier, Rainier, and St. Helens. Below find the sea of green broken up by a half-dozen lakes tucked into the bowl between Bandera and Defiance—Lake Kulla Kulla is the largest, with Blazer Lake and Rainbow Lake just to the east. Little Mason Lake is nestled below familiar Mason Lake. To the northeast you can make out a portion of Pratt Lake resting at the base of Pratt Mountain. Cast an eye across I-90 to

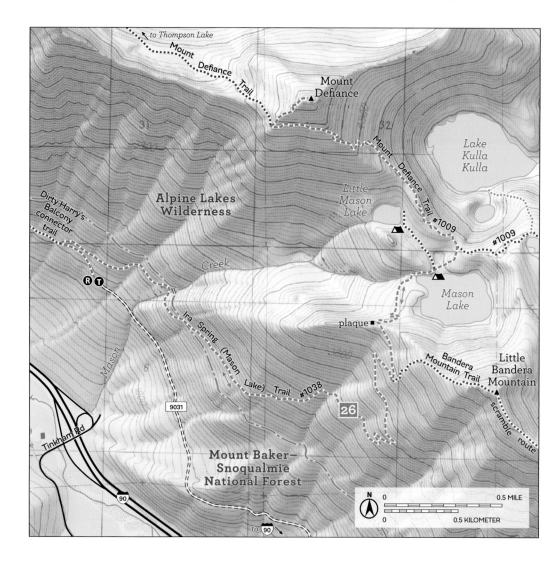

look down on craggy McClellan Butte. To the west a treeless ridge known as West Defiance (aka Putrid Pete's Peak) extends out from the summit, rising above Spider Lake below.

HISTORY

Since it was first blazed in 1958 to fight a wildfire on the slopes of Bandera Mountain, the predecessor to the Ira Spring (Mason Lake) Trail was infamously tough, steep, and dusty. Despite the roughness of the trail, the allure of Mason Lake's cool waters and Bandera Mountain's sweeping views brought tens of thousands of boots up the old fire track. Over the years, all that foot traffic badly eroded the trail, and hikers soon found themselves tackling rocks and boulders rather than earthen trail.

Eventually the beloved trail became nearly too difficult to navigate. At the urging of wilderness advocate Ira Spring, a new route was proposed to address the steep grade and give some relief to the mountainside that had dutifully borne so much trail traffic for so many years. In 2003 and 2004, volunteers in coordination with the Forest Service made the new trail a reality. With Spring's passing in 2003, the trail was dedicated the Ira Spring Memorial Trail.

Beargrass thrives along the trail on the approach to Mount Defiance.

27 LODGE LAKE

DISTANCE: 4 miles
ELEVATION GAIN: 450 feet in; 350 feet out
HIGH POINT: 3500 feet
DIFFICULTY: Easy
HIKING TIME: 2 to 4 hours
BEST SEASON: Summer
PERMIT: Northwest Forest Pass

TRAIL TRAFFIC: Light to moderate foot and equestrian traffic
MANAGING AGENCY: Mount Baker–Snoqualmie National Forest
MAPS: USGS Snoqualmie Pass; Green Trails Snoqualmie Pass Gateway No. 207S
TRAILHEAD GPS: 47.42734°N, 121.42140°W

On this hike out to a solitary alpine lake, follow the Pacific Crest Trail up snow-free ski slopes through wildflower meadows to an open ridgeline with big views of the surrounding peaks. A perfect choice for hikers of all ages, this short trek has a little of everything—from flowers to forest, landscapes to lakes—along a trail you can follow to your heart's content, even if that means hiking all the way to the Mexico border.

GETTING THERE: Take I-90 to the Summit at Snoqualmie ski area. From the west, take exit 52 for West Summit, keeping right and veering onto State Route 906 under the "Snoq Summit" sign. Almost immediately turn left into the gravel parking area.

FEATURED WILDFLOWER

SUBALPINE SPIREA
Spiraea splendens
This 1-to-2-foot-tall shrub has soft, serrated oval leaves that spiral up the length of its woody red stem. Subalpine spirea blooms from late spring to late summer. Its young blossoms resemble berries, but in bloom the protruding stamens create a pom-pom effect, topping the plant with bright pink flower clusters, which persist late in the season. Pleasantly fragrant when in bloom, the shrub is also showy in the fall as its leaves turn bright yellow to orange before falling to the ground.

Other Wildflowers on the Trail: Alpine goldenrod, bunchberry, dwarf bramble, false hellebore, fireweed, foamflower, foxglove, harsh paintbrush, Indian thistle, magenta paintbrush, marsh marigold, orange hawkweed, oxeye daisy, pearly everlasting, queen's cup, rosy twistedstalk, rusty saxifrage, scarlet paintbrush, shooting star, Sitka valerian, tiger lily, yellow pond lily

OPPOSITE: *A chairlift hangs silently above ski slopes that burst with color when not covered by snow.*

From the east, take exit 53 for East Summit, turning left onto the unsigned Yellowstone Trail Road. Pass under I-90 and turn right onto SR 906 toward Alpental and Summit West. Continue 0.5 mile to the parking area on the left.

Once you are on gravel, drive 0.3 mile to the back end of the largest lot to find the trailhead.

From the trailhead, follow the Pacific Crest Trail #2000 (PCT) as it enters a stretch of forest, a short 0.2-mile jaunt to the open slopes of the Summit ski area. Wander up the green slopes beneath now-silent ski lifts and over small streams bringing the last of the spring

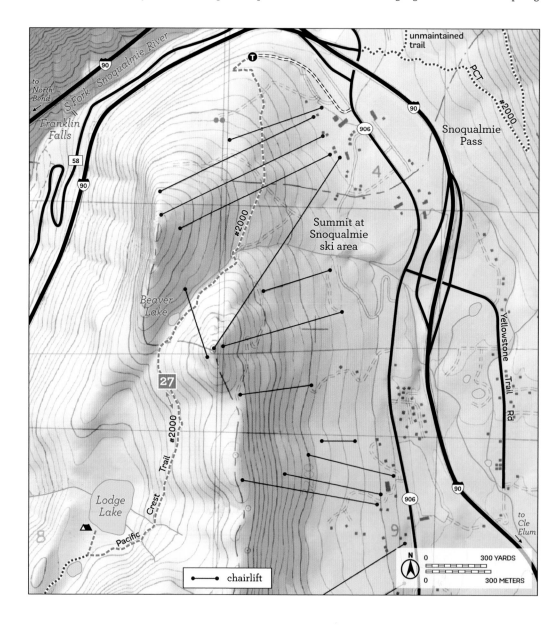

unmaintained trail

S Fork Snoqualmie River

90

to North Bend

Franklin Falls

58

90

#2000

PCT

#2000

90

906

Snoqualmie Pass

4

Summit at Snoqualmie ski area

Beaver Lake

Yellowstone Trail Rd

27

Pacific Crest Trail #2000

Lodge Lake

8

9

906

90

to Cle Elum

chairlift

N

0   300 YARDS

0   300 METERS

melt down the mountainside, and watch the floral show unfold along the way.

As you work your way up, the views get more impressive. At the ridgeline, the northern horizon is filled with familiar summits, starting with Denny Mountain to the northwest, followed by hulking Snoqualmie Mountain directly to the north behind Guye Peak. Turning east, find distinctive Red Mountain, then Kendall Peak, and finally Mount Margaret.

The mountain views are made all the better by the vibrant colors of the wildflowers blanketing the slopes, from bright-red paintbrush and brilliant-white daisies to light-purple fireweed. After 1 mile, return to the shade of hemlock and cedar and arrive at Beaver Lake. No need to linger here, as there are fairer lakeshores ahead. Continue skirting the water and begin a gradual descent to Lodge Lake. As the trail levels out, you will be able to catch glimpses of the water shimmering through the trees. Push onward to the far end of the lake to find a spur trail at 1.8 miles with a sign pointing the way to Lodge Lake. Take this trail 0.2 mile down to the forested lakeside, following boot paths to private lunch spots tucked into the shore. Take some time to enjoy the quiet and solitude, somewhat unexpected so close to the freeway.

HISTORY

In 1914, The Mountaineers leased land around Snoqualmie Pass from the Forest Service and built their Snoqualmie Lodge near the Chicago, Milwaukee, and St. Paul Railroad station in Rockdale. It's this lodge that Lodge Lake was named for, as it was only a quarter mile from the front door. Built by volunteers, largely from the trees and materials found on-site, the lodge was open year-round, could house seventy, and was staffed with a cook and a caretaker.

At first the lodge was primarily used as a base for hiking and climbing the surrounding peaks, with club members taking the train from Seattle to Rockdale, then hiking 1.5 miles up to the lodge for weekends of snowy outdoor excursions, snowshoeing the nearby peaks, and late-night dances to the windup Victrola.

But the rising popularity of skiing meant that by the 1920s, the lodge was becoming something of a ski camp, and many of the first skiers at Snoqualmie Pass were members of The Mountaineers.

The hike to Lodge Lake follows a section of the PCT, a 2650-mile trail from Canada to Mexico that was finally completed in the 1990s, after decades of effort to connect Washington's Cascade Crest Trail to other regional networks in Oregon and California. This portion of the PCT was built on top of trail first blazed by The Mountaineers in 1919 to access the lodge in the summer months.

The Snoqualmie Lodge burned down in 1944 after a spark from the fireplace lit up the shingled roof. Volunteers rebuilt the structure in 1948 on a different 77-acre parcel closer to the Summit at Snoqualmie ski area, where it stood until another fire burned it to the ground in 2006. After the fire, The Mountaineers used the property as an area for picnicking and winter recreation for club members. By 2015 they decided to sell it to the surrounding ski area but added an easement for the PCT to be rerouted across the land in accordance with Forest Service recommendations, leaving a lasting legacy for future mountaineers.

Paintbrush and spirea are prolific on the slopes.

28 ESMERALDA BASIN

DISTANCE: 6.8 miles
ELEVATION GAIN: 1700 feet
HIGH POINT: 6000 feet
DIFFICULTY: Moderate
HIKING TIME: 3 to 4 hours
BEST SEASON: Summer
PERMIT: Northwest Forest Pass

TRAIL TRAFFIC: Moderate foot, mountain bike, and equestrian traffic
MANAGING AGENCY: Okanogan-Wenatchee National Forest
MAPS: USGS Mount Stuart; Green Trails Alpine Lakes East No. 208SX
TRAILHEAD GPS: 47.43680°N, 120.93690°W

Follow a crumbling mining road as it climbs through open pine forest and trailside flower fields on the way up to Fortune Creek Pass and big views. While the trailhead is usually busy, nearly everyone heads up toward Lake Ingalls, leaving Esmeralda Basin for you to enjoy.

GETTING THERE: Take I-90 to exit 85, following signs to State Route 970; merge onto SR 970 and continue 6.5 miles to Teanaway Road. Turn left and continue 13.1 miles, trading pavement for gravel, to reach a fork just past 29 Pines Campground. Veer right onto Forest Road 9737 (North Fork Teanaway Road), following it 9.6 miles to the road's end and the Esmeralda Basin Trailhead. Note that there are additional forks that branch off of FR 9737 that could cause confusion. Once you're on FR 9737, always veer left when in doubt. Privy available.

FEATURED WILDFLOWER

JEFFREY'S SHOOTING STAR
Dodecatheon jeffreyi
Named in honor of botanist John Jeffrey, Jeffrey's shooting star is found in wet soils near streams and marshes. A dark green stem grows up to 20 inches tall and is surrounded by slightly wrinkled lancelike leaves near the base. Nodding purple-pink flowers bloom from early to midsummer and have four or five reflexed petals that are white near the base. The petals and stamens of this aptly named perennial grow in opposite directions, giving the impression of a flower that has turned inside out as it attempts to launch itself into orbit. This flower does not produce nectar, but its pollen is a rich source of nutrition. It is a favorite of bumblebees in particular, which cling upside down to the stamens and vibrate their bodies to shake the pollen out.

Other Wildflowers on the Trail: Alpine pennycress, blue stickseed, bog orchid, bracted lousewort, broadleaf arnica, broadleaf lupine, butterwort, cotton-grass, elephant's head, nineleaf biscuitroot, phlox, pioneer violet, small-flowered penstemon, snow dwarf primrose, spring beauty, Tweedy's lewisia

A meadow filled with Jeffrey's shooting star below Esmeralda Peaks

A mule deer in Esmeralda Basin

Esmeralda Basin Trail #1394 begins on a wide track that still bears some passing resemblance to its former life as a mining road. Meander alongside the North Fork Teanaway River and its boulder-and-log-clogged riverbed. The sound of rushing water tumbling past this rubble will be with you for a good portion of the hike. That same water feeds the many wildflowers you'll pass as you work your way up the valley, with small patches of flowers beginning almost immediately.

Progress through thin forest that never obscures the surrounding cliffsides, pausing to enjoy a riverside flower or two. At 0.3 mile reach the junction with the Lake Ingalls Trail #1390 and veer left, leaving the crowds and Lake Ingalls for another day. Push onward to the 1-mile mark and a large meadow that shelters a wide variety of flowers and interesting plants, including the insectivorous butterwort. Linger here awhile before continuing up through the basin on fairly gentle grade and skipping over a few flower-lined creeks along the way.

Trek through open country for the next mile, passing more flower fields before the trees begin to crowd the trail. Not far beyond, the trail begins a series of long switchbacks up the talus flanks of the ridgeline toward the pass. After the last switchback, leave the trees behind and begin an exposed, rocky traverse, passing the junction with the County Line Trail #1226.2 at 3.2 miles, which leads out to Lake Ann. Stay on the Esmeralda Basin Trail and climb up more barren, rocky slope to Fortune Creek Pass.

Arrive at the windswept pass 3.4 miles from the trailhead. Drop your gear and drink in the view. Look west to find Hawkins Mountain looming over Fortune Creek valley, with snow-capped Mount Daniel in the distance. Fortune Peak and Ingalls Peak are to the north, and as you swing east, find Longs Peak and a lovely long view of the basin you've just climbed out of. As you turn south, you can't miss the distinctive fingers of Esmeralda Peaks looking down on the valley below.

From here, a scramble route leads out along the ridgeline toward the Esmeralda Peaks. Those looking for a quiet viewpoint can follow the dusty boot path 0.1 mile up to the top of a small bump on the ridge for more sweeping views. Ambitious day hikers can continue on the Esmeralda Basin Trail from here, switchbacking down to Fortune Creek and the Fortune Creek Jeep Trail #4W301 and many more miles of trail to explore.

HISTORY

The Teanaway River drainage has a long history of mining activity. Miners and prospectors roamed creek valleys and lake basins in search of mineral wealth around the 1870s, and there was plenty to find. The Cle Elum Mining District was formed in 1883 to help organize the hundreds of claims that were popping up.

One of those claims was the Tip Top prospect, located at the head of the North Fork Teanaway River valley. Tip Top was owned by the Ballard Gold Mining and Milling Company, and workings eventually included several adits and a mine shaft. While it was never prolific, the site yielded enough gold that a primitive mill was built on-site and a road was built down through Esmeralda Basin to help bring equipment up and send the processed ore down to Cle Elum to be sold. Today, sections of the Esmeralda Basin Trail follow what remains of that old road.

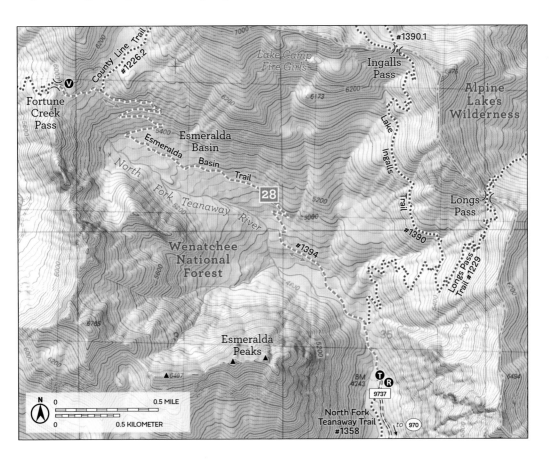

29 TRONSEN RIDGE

DISTANCE: 4.6 miles
ELEVATION GAIN: 800 feet in; 300 feet out
HIGH POINT: 4850 feet
DIFFICULTY: Easy
HIKING TIME: 3 to 4 hours
BEST SEASON: Late spring to early summer; golden larches in fall
TRAIL TRAFFIC: Moderate foot, equestrian, mountain bike, and ORV traffic
PERMIT: Northwest Forest Pass

MANAGING AGENCY: Okanogan-Wenatchee National Forest
MAPS: USGS Tiptop, USGS Blewett Pass; Green Trails Liberty No. 210
TRAILHEAD GPS: 47.39230°N, 120.57570°W
NOTE: The forest road to the trailhead can be difficult to navigate; high-clearance vehicles are recommended. The trail is open to motorcycles and ORVs between June 15 and October 15.

Balsamroot adds vibrant color along the trail up to Tronsen Ridge.

FEATURED WILDFLOWER

TWEEDY'S LEWISIA
Lewisiopsis tweedyi

Somewhat difficult to find, Tweedy's lewisia tops many flower hunters' lists. The plant consists of numerous thick, dark green leaves reminiscent of a succulent. Leathery stems extend a few inches above the leaves, each supporting a single bloom that is creamy yellow with a blush of pink or delicate orange, with pointed petals that may curl inward. Look for this plant in the shade at lower elevations and in more exposed, dry soil and gravel at higher elevations. Flowers bloom from mid-spring to early summer.

While the plant currently occupies its own genus, *Lewisiopsis*, this alluring and mysterious bloom has been reclassified several times since its earliest documentation in 1882 by Frank Tweedy, a topographic engineer who worked for forty-three years with the United States Geological Survey. Working on railway development, Tweedy was among the first nonindigenous persons to summit Mount Stuart, which is in the very limited geographical range of this flower.

Other Wildflowers on the Trail: Arrowleaf balsamroot, ballhead waterleaf, bitterroot, bracted lousewort, broadleaf lupine, bush penstemon, glacier lily, longleaf phlox, Lyall's mariposa lily, mountain arnica, nineleaf biscuitroot, scarlet gilia, scarlet paintbrush, serviceberry, small-flowered paintbrush, snow dwarf primrose, tall groundsel, Thompson's paintbrush, upland larkspur, yarrow

Explore a ridgeline of desert meadows with big views and a mountain-filled skyline on this wildflower romp. Other than a challenging drive down a rough forest road to reach the trailhead, most hikers will find this hike with its views and flowers easily accessible. And for those craving additional trail miles, Tronsen Ridge has more to explore.

GETTING THERE: Take US Highway 97 to Five Mile Road (Forest Road 7224), located 4.8 miles north of Blewett Pass. Turn east, following the rough gravel road 3.1 miles to the signed trailhead with a small parking area and campsite.

From the trailhead, begin following the Tronsen Ridge Trail #1204 almost directly along the ridgeline. Stands of pine and larch are not particularly dense, and you'll find yourself moving through mostly open terrain. Desert meadowlands are frequent and vary in size, but the wildflowers don't seem to mind. Balsamroot is particularly prodigious and crowds the trail for much of the hike. Look closer to spot the wide variety of flowers found along the ridge as you gain enough elevation to get some longer views.

At 1.9 miles reach a vista with some of the best views of the hike. From here you can pick out the cones of three surrounding volcanoes: Mount Rainier, Glacier Peak, and Mount Adams. Mount Stuart and its neighboring

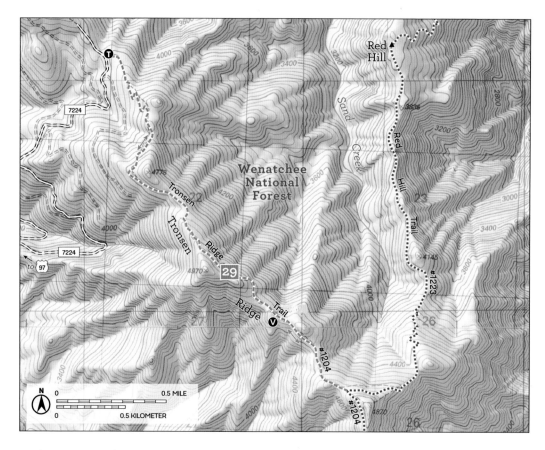

Enchantment Peaks are easy to spot. Further down Tronsen Ridge, find Mission Peak and Mount Lillian. Keep pushing onward past ponderosa pines and more wildflower-covered slopes, keeping an eye out for Tweedy's lewisia tucked in among the balsamroot.

Reach the junction with the Red Hill Trail #1223 and a decent turnaround point for a leisurely ridgeline stroll 2.3 miles from the trailhead. To extend your trip, take the Red Hill Trail, drop down off Tronsen Ridge, and head out to Red Hill, or keep pushing onward another few miles to the southern end of the Tronsen Ridge Trail. There are plenty more wildflowers to find along the way, though most of the best views are on this end of the trail.

When you've had your fill, retrace your steps back to the car, enjoying the views and trailside blooms in reverse.

HISTORY

Tronsen Ridge has a long history of human activity. Some field surveys indicate that it was used as a trade route and as a means to access higher elevation food sources during prehistoric times. More recently, since the mining boom times that gave rise to the mining communities of Blewett and Liberty, areas around Tronsen Ridge saw prospectors roving the ridge in search of riches. When the miners left, the sheepherders sought allotments to graze their sheep, likely following some of the same trails still in place today.

OPPOSITE: *Admiring the Stuart Range to the northwest from Tronsen Ridge*

MOUNT RAINIER & SOUTH CASCADES

30 SPRAY PARK AND SPRAY FALLS

DISTANCE: 8.2 miles
ELEVATION GAIN: 1600 feet
HIGH POINT: 6400 feet
DIFFICULTY: Moderate
HIKING TIME: 5 to 7 hours
BEST SEASON: Late spring to late summer
TRAIL TRAFFIC: Moderate to heavy foot traffic
PERMIT: National Park Pass

MANAGING AGENCY: Mount Rainier National Park
MAPS: USGS Mowich Lake; Green Trails Mount
Rainier Wonderland No. 269SX
TRAILHEAD GPS: 46.93264°N, 121.86300°W
NOTE: Dogs are prohibited on this trail and
elsewhere in Mount Rainier National Park
except designated areas. A permit is required
to backpack and stay overnight.

Mount Rainier's parklands are famous for their wildflower displays, and Spray Park certainly lives up to the reputation. Spray Park's flowers transform the grassy meadows into a sea of color while Spray Falls puts on a watery show of its own. For those willing to go the extra distance, there's a spectacular view of Mount Rainier.

GETTING THERE: From Buckley, take State Route 165 south for 1.6 miles to a junction. Turn left to continue on SR 165 toward Wilkeson. In 8.6 miles keep right at the Carbon River Road/Mowich Lake Road junction, veering toward Mowich Lake. Follow the Mowich Lake Road for 16.7 miles to the end of the road and the trailhead. Privy available at trailhead.

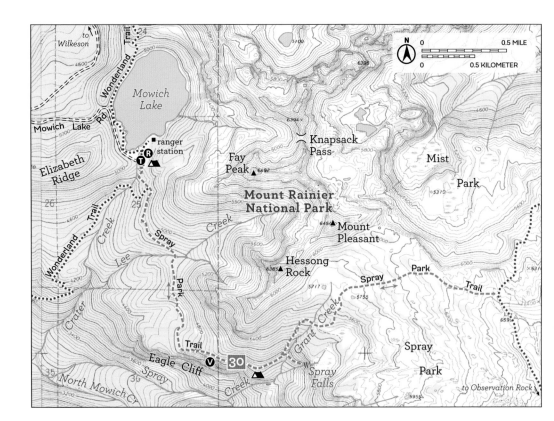

Spray Park's meadows are blanketed by wildflowers in season.

The trail glides past a tarn reflecting Mount Rainier.

From the Mowich Lake camping area, the well-signed Spray Park Trail begins by descending into a forest of cedar and fir rising out of a blanket of greenery. After a few switchbacks and 0.2 mile of hiking, find yourself at a junction with the Wonderland Trail. Veer left, following the sign that points toward Spray Park and Eagle's Roost Camp. Legions of boot steps keep this trail clear and easy to navigate as it crosses over creeks and traverses forested ridges. After another 1.4 miles, arrive at the Eagle Cliff viewpoint, a small area where trees have been cleared to offer a lovely pocket view of Mount Rainier. This is a good place to drop your pack for a short rest before continuing onward.

From Eagle Cliff, continue down the trail, passing Eagle's Roost Camp in 0.4 mile and reaching the spur trail leading out to Spray Falls at the 1.9-mile mark. This short side trip is not to be missed, as a visit to the falls adds less than 0.5 mile of hiking. Descend to Spray Creek and crane your neck to try to catch a glimpse of the upper reaches of the tumbling falls. Slightly better views are possible if you can find an easy way to cross the creek. After you've taken in the namesake falls, head back up to the main trail and get ready for a climb. The trail begins a series of tight switchbacks straight up the mountainside.

After 0.7 mile of climbing, cross Grant Creek to the edge of Spray Park at 2.8 miles. Wander through a meadow and follow the trail as it continues to open up, getting that much better with every step. While it is hard to find a stopping point that isn't stunning, if you continue to climb, the crowds quickly disappear. Press on to the high point of the trail that divides Spray Park and Seattle Park, 4.1 miles from the trailhead. Here you'll find big views of both parks and a side trail that leads out to Observation Rock. No need to follow that trail too far—a short scramble will get you face-to-face with Mount Rainier.

Whether you're visiting Spray Park for the day or just passing through on your way to your next campsite, the experience is sure to linger. This hike should be approachable for most hikers, though the elevation gain may put it out of reach for very young or inexperienced hikers.

While backpackers will continue onward from Spray Park down to the Carbon River and the Wonderland Trail, that is far too much mileage for most day hikers. Instead, to add more hiking mileage to your day, head back to the Spray Park Trailhead at Mowich Lake and follow the signs around the lake toward Tolmie Lookout. It adds about 5.5 miles to your day, but the views are spectacular, and there are more than a few wildflowers along the way.

FEATURED WILDFLOWER

SMALL-FLOWERED PAINTBRUSH
Castilleja parviflora
Sometimes called Indian paintbrush or prairie fire, these common wildflowers are easy to identify, though determining the specific species of paintbrush can be a little tricky, as quite a wide variety can be found in Washington State. Small-flowered paintbrush blooms from late spring to late summer and is typically found in drier areas in meadows and forest openings at mid to high elevations.

Multiple unbranched stems grow in a cluster from the base, up to about 10 inches tall, with tiered sets of lance-shaped leaves divided into three to five narrow lobes. The plant's actual flowers are hidden among the brightly colored bracts associated with all paintbrush species; the bracts are often bright red but also come in shades of magenta, pink, and purple.

Other Wildflowers on the Trail: Avalanche lily, beargrass, bog orchid, bunchberry, common monkeyflower, cow parsnip, Davidson's penstemon, fireweed, glacier lily, harebell, leatherleaf saxifrage, magenta paintbrush, marsh marigold, mountain arnica, mountain bistort, pink mountain-heather, pioneer violet, pipsissewa, queen's cup, scarlet paintbrush, small-flowered penstemon, subalpine lupine, tall bluebells, trillium, white mountain-heather, woolly pussytoes

Spray Falls

HISTORY

More than one hundred thousand years ago, vents opened on the northern side of Mount Rainier, spewing out a thick layer of lava that hardened to become the foundation of Spray and Mist Parks. These vents are clearly visible today and are now known as Echo Rock and Observation Rock. Around 1881, the Northern Pacific Railroad became interested in the northwest portion of Mount Rainier and sent geologist Bailey Willis to search for coal and to see if the area would be suitable for tourism. Part of Willis's expedition involved cutting a trail from Wilkeson to Mowich Lake that became known as the Grindstone Trail. From Mowich Lake, Willis explored the region, and by 1883 he had built a route to Spray Park, known simply as the Bailey Willis Trail, and was leading visitors up into the alpine wonderland. The legacy of Professor Willis's explorations can be found elsewhere on the mountain as well: the famous Willis Wall is named for him, as was Willis Glacier, now known as the North Mowich Glacier.

It was likely during the construction of the Bailey Willis Trail that Spray Falls was first popularized. At the falls, Spray Creek tumbles hundreds of feet down steep cliffs to break into a misty spray of water. The creek, falls, and park are all named for this display. Over time, the Bailey Willis Trail to Spray Park was replaced by the Spray Park Trail used today, though a few sections still follow the old route.

31 GRAND PARK

DISTANCE: 8.5 miles
ELEVATION GAIN: 1100 feet
HIGH POINT: 5600 feet
DIFFICULTY: Moderate
HIKING TIME: 4 to 5 hours
BEST SEASON: Spring to late summer
TRAIL TRAFFIC: Moderate foot traffic
MANAGING AGENCY: Mount Rainier National Park

PERMIT: None for dayhike
MAPS: USGS Sunrise; Green Trails Mount Rainier Wonderland No. 269SX
TRAILHEAD GPS: 46.99626°N, 121.64150°W
NOTE: Dogs are prohibited on this trail and elsewhere in Mount Rainier National Park except designated areas. A permit is required for overnight stays.

The traditional approach to Grand Park is a scenic 12.6-mile trek that begins at the Sunrise Visitor Center. In recent years, this "backdoor" approach, which shaves more than 4 miles off the hike, has become a popular alternative. Whichever route you choose, Grand Park boasts dramatic and stunning views of Mount Rainier from a wildflower wonderland, making this hike a must for any flower lover.

GETTING THERE: From Enumclaw, take State Route 410 east for 25 miles to Huckleberry Creek Road (Forest Road 73). Turn right onto FR 73 and follow it for 6 miles to cross the Huckleberry Creek bridge. Continue on FR 73 as it climbs for another 4 miles to the bridge crossing Eleanor Creek, which is signed. There is no official trailhead, but there is room near the creek for several cars to park.

To reach this enchanting parkland, follow an easy-to-find boot path along the edge of Eleanor Creek, directly off FR 73. The hike quickly enters a mixed forest and soon begins a moderate climb toward Lake Eleanor. Almost immediately, the trail crosses into Mount Rainier National Park and in 1.5 miles arrives at the lakeside. There are a few backcountry campsites around Lake Eleanor that provide nice views of the lake and pleasant places to break for a snack, though most hikers will be eager to push on to the meadowlands ahead.

FEATURED WILDFLOWER

AVALANCHE LILY
Erythronium montanum
Often found in alpine meadows, avalanche lily is closely related to glacier lily, and sometimes the names are used interchangeably. The primary distinction is the color: where glacier lily is yellow, avalanche lily is snow white with a yellow center. Blooming from late spring to midsummer, the avalanche lily grows up to about a foot off the ground, and a single six-petaled flower sprouts from the end of a lone leafless stem emerging from the base. Two oblong leathery leaves radiate from the base of the center stem.

Other Wildflowers on the Trail: American bistort, beargrass, broadleaf lupine, coralroot orchid, elephant's head, glacier lily, hookedspur violet, Jeffrey's shooting star, magenta paintbrush, marsh marigold, Mount Rainier paintbrush, nineleaf biscuitroot, spreading phlox, tiger lily, wandering fleabane, western pasqueflower, woolly pussytoes

From the lake, the trail officially becomes the Lake Eleanor Trail as it steepens and climbs through larger stands of hemlock and fir. The moderate climb is broken up by short wanderings through progressively larger meadows that offer little gardens of glacier and avalanche lilies and a taste of what is to come. Push onward and upward to the wide expanses of Grand Park. Bursting with wildflowers during the spring and summer months, the miles-long grassland can seem to be awash in color from the moment you arrive. Resist the temptation to linger at the edges, and press onward to the meadow's high point at 4 miles for outstanding views of Mount Rainier. Find a comfortable spot to settle in and soak up the panorama.

Shorter and approachable for almost all hikers, the Lake Eleanor route is understandably popular. As an added bonus, this approach is usually accessible long after the road to Sunrise is closed for the season. While the trek from FR 73 to Lake Eleanor isn't exactly official yet, its popularity has brought thousands of boots to soften it up, and today the path is almost as well maintained as the official trail. One word of caution: the area around Grand Park is the perfect breeding ground for mosquitoes and other bugs. Be sure to come prepared during the spring and summer months.

Those looking for more trail miles can continue along the Lake Eleanor Trail another 0.3 mile through Grand Park's meadows to connect with the Northern Loop Trail. From here you can work your way down to Berkeley Park or Sunrise Meadows, both of which are excellent for wildflowers (see Hike 32).

HISTORY

Half a million years ago, a cycle of volcanic activity built the mountain we now know as Mount Rainier by piling layer upon layer of whatever bubbled up to the surface. Different materials

OPPOSITE: *Mount Rainier rises above the sprawling meadowlands of Grand Park.*

weathered the ravages of time in different ways with varied results. One happy outcome is the sprawling parklands created by areas of erosion-resistant lava. Grand Park is among the largest open meadows in the national park and was dubbed "grand" by park officials.

The backdoor approach to Grand Park likely began as a boot path used by fishermen to access Lake Eleanor. This 20-acre alpine lake and the creek that drains it were named around the turn of the twentieth century by Burgon D. Mesler in honor of his wife, Eleanor. The Mesler family were early settlers in the area, running an inn and other amenities that catered to travelers heading over the Cascades or visiting the park.

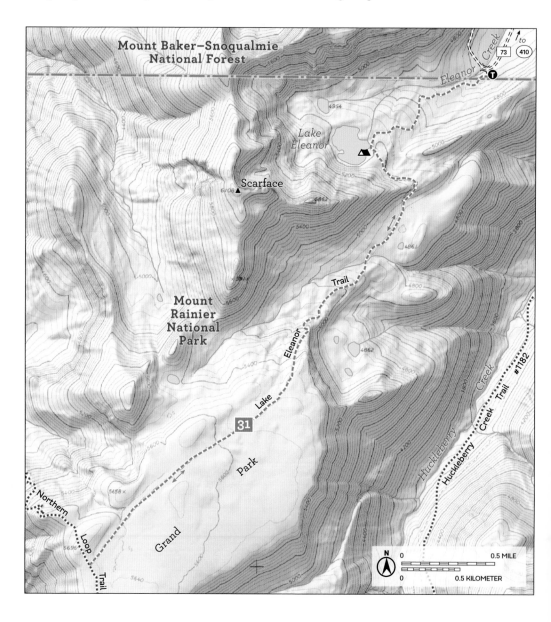

32 FREMONT LOOKOUT

DISTANCE: 5.8 miles
ELEVATION GAIN: 800 feet
HIGH POINT: 7200 feet
DIFFICULTY: Easy
HIKING TIME: 3 to 4 hours
BEST SEASON: Summer
TRAIL TRAFFIC: Heavy foot traffic
PERMIT: National Park Pass

MANAGING AGENCY: Mount Rainier National Park
MAPS: USGS Sunrise; Green Trails Mount Rainier Wonderland No. 269SX
TRAILHEAD GPS: 46.91470°N, 121.64240°W
NOTE: Dogs are prohibited on this trail and elsewhere in Mount Rainier National Park except designated areas.

Follow ridgelines and traverse naked slopes on your way up to a historic fire lookout, with incredible trailside views along the way. The hike starts at 6400 feet, providing relatively easy access to the breathtaking vistas awaiting at the top. As an added bonus, wildflowers blanket portions of the route, and easy access to Berkeley Park promises a sea of blooms and colors.

GETTING THERE: Drive to Sunrise Road, located 36.4 miles east of Enumclaw and 7.1 miles west of Chinook Pass. Turn west onto Sunrise Road and follow it 15.5 miles to Sunrise and the parking area. The trailhead is located at the west end of the lot. Privy available.

From the Sunrise parking area, follow the signs pointing toward Fremont Lookout near the west end of the lot. Follow the paved nature path uphill for a few hundred feet to a well-signed

Cutting through a talus field on Sourdough Ridge toward snowcapped Mount Rainier

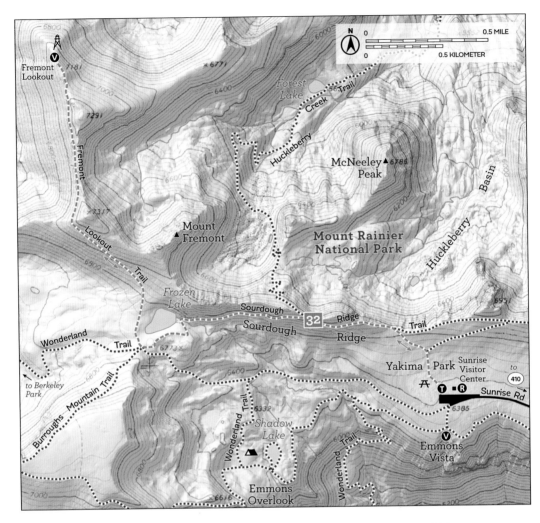

junction and veer right, joining a wide gravel path that gently climbs up through Yakima Park's meadowlands toward Sourdough Ridge. Keep left at the fork to reach the ridgeline, passing colorful trailside wildflowers set against Rainier's bright-white glaciers and snowfields. Because Sunrise is a very popular area, expect crowds on the trails near the parking area; fortunately, the trail is often wide enough for two lanes, which minimizes slowdowns.

After just 0.3 mile, the trail connects with the Sourdough Ridge Trail at a viewpoint showcasing McNeeley Peak and Huckleberry Basin. Head left, navigating your way along the dusty and somewhat rocky trail. Wildflowers spring up along the trail as you pass through small stands of diminutive alpine firs. Further vistas reveal more Mount Rainier close-ups and parkland overlooks, as well as glimpses of farther-flung peaks, such as Mount Baker and Glacier Peak on the clearest of days. Pass the Huckleberry Creek Trail at 0.7 mile before passing behind a prominence and traversing down to Frozen Lake.

At the far end of Frozen Lake, reach a five-way junction at 1.5 miles, where the Sourdough Ridge Trail, the Fremont Lookout Trail, and the Burroughs Mountain Trail all connect with the Wonderland Trail. The lookout is up

FEATURED WILDFLOWER

SPREADING PHLOX
Phlox diffusa

A low-growing plant, spreading phlox is a familiar sight along mid-to-high-elevation trails that traverse dry slopes, which are protected from erosion by the dense mats of vegetation it produces. Numerous tightly packed flowers bloom in a carpet of needle-like leaves from early spring to late summer. Hovering just a few inches above the ground, the flowers, typically pink but sometimes shades of white, blue, or lavender, often markedly contrast with the surrounding gray rock and dusty terrain. In the center of its five overlapping petals, the stamen peeks out just enough to advertise its store of orange pollen within. The name is descriptive: *Phlox* means flame and is a reference to the brightly colored flowers, and *diffusa* suggests diffusion or spreading.

Other Wildflowers on the Trail: Alpine aster, alpine buckwheat, alpine gold daisy, cliff paintbrush, cliff penstemon, Cusick's speedwell, delphinium, elegant Jacob's-ladder, harebell, lanceleaf stonecrop, northern goldenrod, pink mountain-heather, scarlet paintbrush, shrubby cinquefoil, small-flowered paintbrush, small-flowered penstemon, spotted saxifrage, subalpine lupine, western pasqueflower, yarrow

and to the right, following a trail you can easily see scratched in the flanks of Mount Fremont before it disappears around a rib. For those interested in more wildflower exploring, heading straight ahead onto the Wonderland Trail will drop you into the bottom of Berkeley Park via the Northern Loop Trail in less than 1.5 miles.

Head upward on the Fremont Lookout Trail, climbing up steps added by the Washington Trails Association in recent years to ease the steep ascent and minimize trail degradation. Mount Rainier continues to put on a show as you traverse upslope, getting ever-better views of Emmons Glacier clinging to the mountainside. Watch hikers climb up the Burroughs Mountain Trail to the south with the jagged crown of Little Tahoma jutting up above them. As you crest the rib below Mount Fremont's

true summit, the pointed tip of Skyscraper Mountain comes into better view, and you get your first glimpse of the lookout in the distance.

From here, the trail is increasingly loose and rocky as you traverse through talus fields above a rocky bowl. Work your way over scree and boulders, occasionally looking down on the meadows below, watching for the mountain goats that frequent the area. Reach the rock-strewn lookout point at 2.9 miles and do a little exploring. The cabin's catwalks offer spectacular views, but so do nearby perches. Find a spot to take it all in. Here is another opportunity to spy Mount Baker and Glacier Peak to the north along with Mount Stuart. Perhaps more impressive is the bird's-eye view of Grand Park (see Hike 31), looking like a mesa of green amid a sea of mountaintops. To the east look down on McNeeley Peak and

The Fremont Lookout offers a commanding view of Grand Park.

pick out Crystal Mountain and Silver King on the horizon, while to the west, the bare rocky summit of Sluiskin Mountain is easy to pick out, as is the distinctively colored Redstone Peak. Finally, filling the southern horizon is the most spectacular view of Mount Rainier yet, something to be savored at length on your return journey.

HISTORY

Back in 1843, an American explorer named John Frémont witnessed Mount Rainier erupting on one of his multiple expeditions through the Oregon Territory. He recorded the event in his journal, along with reports of fertile farmland and endless forests at the end of a cross-continental journey he thought the average American family could undertake. His journals helped fuel the Manifest Destiny movement, which brought scores of settlers to the Oregon Territory. Decades later, in 1932, a mountain near the volcano he saw erupt was officially

named in his honor. Note that while it's common to find references to "Freemont" in some resources, the added *e* is a typographical error.

At the same time, the National Park Service requested help under the new Emergency Conservation Work Act to build fire lookouts in Mount Rainier National Park. The program provided the manpower to build the trails, haul the materials, and construct eight lookout towers in the park and was the forerunner of the Civilian Conservation Corps. In 1934 the Fremont Lookout was completed, though the roof had to be replaced the following season due to storm damage. Over time, other lookout cabins were lost or removed, with only four remaining today. In 2006, a windstorm tore the roof off the Fremont Lookout and caused extensive damage to the structure. The lookout was popular enough that it was restored and today is frequently visited by hikers and is occasionally staffed for fire detection.

33 TIPSOO LAKE AND NACHES PEAK LOOP

DISTANCE: 3.5 miles
ELEVATION GAIN: 500 feet
HIGH POINT: 5900 feet
DIFFICULTY: Easy
HIKING TIME: 2 to 3 hours
BEST SEASON: Summer to early fall
TRAIL TRAFFIC: Heavy foot traffic
PERMIT: Northwest Forest Pass

MANAGING AGENCY: Mount Baker–Snoqualmie National Forest
MAPS: USGS Chinook Pass, USGS Cougar Lake; Green Trails Mount Rainier Wonderland No. 269SX
TRAILHEAD GPS: 46.86980°N, 121.51960°W
NOTE: Wilderness regulations apply in William O. Douglas and Mount Rainier Wildernesses; see Wilderness Guidelines in Hiking Best Practices.

Explore this very popular landscape, beginning with a picture-perfect meadow-bound lake set against looming Mount Rainier, then escape the crowds on a looping trail that explodes with fiery paintbrush in the summer.

GETTING THERE: From Enumclaw, take State Route 410 east for 42.8 miles to a large parking area on the left just before passing Tipsoo Lake. From Naches, follow SR 410 west for 52 miles to the parking area next to the lake. Privy available.

From the parking area, follow the main boot path down to Tipsoo Lake. The trail branches off in either direction to circle the lake, with Yakima Peak rising above, and offers a peek at the bounty of wildflowers that fill the meadows. This 0.4-mile loop is a perfect hike for little ones:

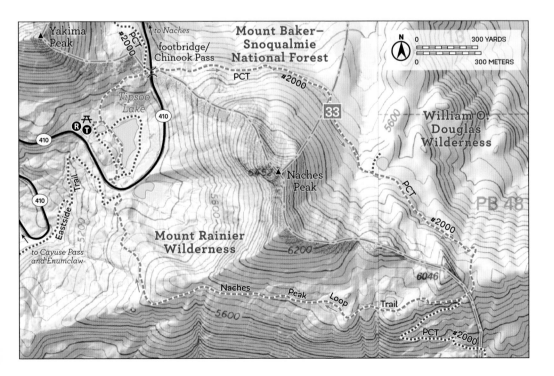

between the water and the flowers, there's plenty to see, and the virtually flat route is short enough for even the youngest hiker.

Whether you loop around the lake now or later, head toward the north end of the lake and traverse up Yakima Peak's open slopes to the log overpass that spans the highway. This clockwise approach to the loop has the advantage of a long westward-looking stretch of trail, which sets showy wildflower meadows against snowy Mount Rainier. Once across the highway, 0.3 mile from the trailhead, the trail joins the Pacific Crest Trail #2000 (PCT), with a long view down the Rainier Fork American River valley with Deadwood Peak and Chinook Peak rising above it. Keep right and continue as it enters a thin forest along the base of Naches Peak. Breaks in the trees offer more views of the river valley as you work your way along the well-trodden trail, crossing into the William O. Douglas Wilderness at 0.9 mile.

Eventually reach the backside of the mountain, filled with tarns and parklands, ideal for exploring and relaxing on a summer's day. The craggy summit of Naches Peak looms high above, tempting adventurous climbers to follow the scramble route to its southern shoulder. Though there are wildflowers at this popular destination, the bigger show is up ahead. Press onward, leaving the crowds behind, and soon cross into the Mount Rainier Wilderness. At the junction with the Naches Peak Loop Trail at 1.8 miles, veer right and climb up a few switchbacks to reach another small basin, complete with a small lakelet. Mount Rainier dominates the skyline above the meadows. The wildflowers here and beyond are vibrant and flourish along the trail, painting the surrounding parklands with deep reds and purples. Stop often to relish this stunning setting.

Continue to follow the narrower and less trafficked trail back toward Tipsoo Lake. Work

This unnamed tarn along the PCT is a popular stopping point.

FEATURED WILDFLOWER

MENZIES' LARKSPUR
Delphinium menziesii

A member of the commonly seen delphinium family, this showy variation known as Menzies' larkspur grows up to 24 inches tall and is found at moderate elevations in areas exposed to direct sunlight, where you are likely to find it surrounded by bees, butterflies, and humming-birds. The leaves are broad, fanlike, and lobed, narrowing toward the top of a finely haired stem. The purple-blue blooms clustered atop each stem are almost friendly in appearance, giving little indication that every part of this plant is highly poisonous to humans, pets, and livestock.

Blooming from late spring to midsummer, the flowers are distinctively shaped, with five sepals arranged in a star around a small cluster of white and purple petals. A single spur protrudes backward from each flower's cen-ter, as if to raise a flag of warning not to consume the plant. The flower is named in honor of Archibald Menzies, a botanist and naturalist who was on the Vancouver Expedition with Captain George Vancouver near the end of the eighteenth century.

Other Wildflowers on the Trail: Avalanche lily, beargrass, broadleaf lupine, Cascade penstemon, Cusick's speedwell, glacier lily, partridgefoot, pink mountain-heather, scarlet paintbrush, small-flowered paintbrush, spreading phlox, spreading stonecrop, spring beauty, western pasqueflower, woolly sunflower, yarrow

your way around the far end of Naches Peak, dropping back toward the highway. At 3.2 miles, cross the highway and return to Tipsoo's shores, perhaps taking the opportunity to wander through the meadows and around the lake one more time before returning to the car.

HISTORY

Back in 1897, Washington State authorized and funded the construction of a wagon road across the Cascades, with the goal of connecting communities in south King County with the town of Naches. The plan was to connect existing county roads along a route that would follow the White River to Silver Creek near Crystal Mountain, then over Bear Gap and down to the American River. The road took years to build and appears on 1909 state highway maps, but the rise of the automobile soon prompted the need for a highway. As a result, the wagon road, then known as State Route 1, was rerouted after much debate, over Cayuse and Chinook Passes.

Construction began in 1927 on either side of the mountains, and the roads met at Chinook Pass in 1931; it became known as the Naches Pass Highway, perhaps a nod to the old wagon road that did go over Naches Pass. As part of the construction, there were plans to make something of a tourist facility at Tipsoo Lake. The result was the Tipsoo Lake Comfort Station, which originally consisted of two restroom facilities built between 1933 and 1934. Only one survives today.

Long before the highway was built, hikers, travelers, and adventurers explored Chinook Pass. Tipsoo Lake was named for its grassy shores, as *tipsu* or *tipso* means "grass" or "grassy

Tipsoo Lake sits below Yakima Peak.

lake" in Chinook Jargon. With the advent of the Naches Pass Highway (now SR 410) more visitors could reach Mount Rainier National Park, and many stopped to sightsee at Tipsoo Lake. Skiers used the area extensively shortly after the road opened. Between 1945 and 1946, portable ski tows were installed to help skiers up the slope, and in 1949 some limited facilities were built—a warming hut, additional parking, limited food service, and a ranger's office. After the 1949 season, the state decided to stop clearing the roads up to Cayuse Pass during the winter, and the ski activity shifted away from the area. Today, picturesque Tipsoo Lake remains an extremely popular area for visitors to explore during their visit to the park.

34 VAN TRUMP PARK

DISTANCE: 6 miles
ELEVATION GAIN: 2900 feet
HIGH POINT: 6500 feet
DIFFICULTY: Hard
HIKING TIME: 4 to 5 hours
BEST SEASON: Summer
TRAIL TRAFFIC: Moderate foot traffic
MANAGING AGENCY: Mount Rainier National Park
PERMIT: National Park Pass

MAPS: USGS Mount Rainier West; Green Trails Mount Rainier Wonderland No. 269SX
TRAILHEAD GPS: 46.77940°N, 121.78240°W
NOTE: Dogs are prohibited on this trail and elsewhere in Mount Rainier National Park except designated areas. Parking is limited; arrive early on a weekend, or try it on a weekday.

Impressive Comet Falls from the wildflower-lined trail to Van Trump Park

FEATURED WILDFLOWER

TALL BLUEBELLS
Mertensia paniculata
Often found near streams or in lower-elevation meadows, tall bluebells is a petite wildflower with dark green, egg-shaped leaves that taper toward the tip. Leaves are larger at the base of the plant and continue up the entire stem. Branches end in many blue, funnel-shaped flower pendants, each with five very shallow and delicate lobes. Blooming from mid-spring to early fall, the plant propagates by seed and is capable of cloning itself by sprouting additional plants along lateral roots. It thrives in disturbed conditions, such as burns or recently logged areas. Historically the leaves of the plant have been used to make medicinal teas, primarily for treating issues with the lungs and respiratory system.

Other Wildflowers on the Trail: American bistort, avalanche lily, beargrass, broadleaf lupine, explorer's gentian, fan-leaf cinquefoil, hookedspur violet, Mount Rainier lousewort, mountain arnica, paintbrush, pink mountain-heather, wandering fleabane, western pasqueflower

Travel alongside rushing creeks and tumbling cascades to reach expansive parklands overflowing with wildflowers as you follow in the footsteps of the first mountaineers to summit Mount Rainier. It's a steep, tough climb, but it's more than worth it; Comet Falls is one of the more impressive waterfall shows in Mount Rainier National Park, and Van Trump Park provides an intimate view of Rainier's glaciers from a sea of flowery meadows.

GETTING THERE: From Elbe, take State Route 706 east toward Mount Rainier National Park. Reach the Nisqually Entrance to the park in 13.7 miles and pay the park fee. From here continue another 10.4 miles to the Comet Falls Trailhead, located at a small parking area on the left side of the road.

From the trailhead, the Comet Falls and Van Trump Park Trail immediately begins climbing from the parking area, entering an ancient forest of mossy fir and cedar above the Nisqually River. Follow the rugged trail for 0.2 mile to reach a sturdy stone bridge, crossing it to the sounds of Van Trump Creek tumbling and crashing nearly 70 feet down over Christine Falls. One of the falls' two tiers is under the bridge, making it all but impossible to see from this vantage point, but peeking over the edge, you can get an idea of the size of this impressive waterfall from the frothing pool below.

Beyond the bridge, the trail turns sharply uphill, climbing steeply through old growth into Van Trump Canyon alongside Van Trump Creek. The narrow canyon reverberates with the sounds of the roaring creek, punctuated by showy cascades rushing over boulders and ledges while you work your way up through tight switchbacks and over avalanche chutes. As you ascend, the white-capped peaks of Adams and Rainier peek over the lip of the canyon, a promise of views to come.

At 1.3 miles cross Van Trump Creek on a log bridge and pause to check out three-tiered Bloucher Falls as it drops 120 feet over a series of steps, though the upper tier is somewhat obscured from the trail. Don't mistake this waterfall for Comet Falls. Push onward to the

Beargrass is common along this trail.

end of the canyon for an impressive show. Here, Van Trump Creek hurtles over the cliffs above, falling more than 300 feet into the bowl below. When the glacier melt is high, the falls are said to resemble a comet streaking across the sky with a misty tail billowing in the wind. Take a moment to linger and let the roar and spray

of the falls wash over you before starting your climb out of the canyon.

Work up a few switchbacks and reach a signed junction at 2.1 miles. The trail to the left leads up to Mildred Point, an impressive viewpoint that takes some work to get to but more than delivers on jaw-dropping views of the

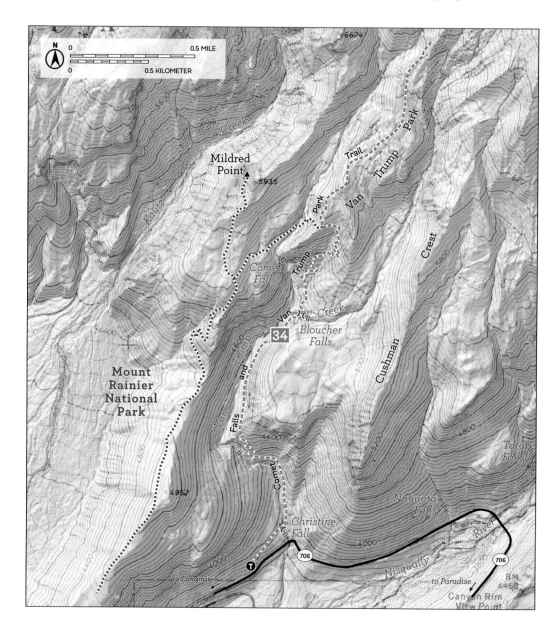

surrounding landscape. It's a worthy addition to the hike for those itching for more trail miles. For now, head to the right toward Van Trump Park, climbing steeply through thinning forest. The flowers and views increase with each step, revealing Mount Adams, Mount St. Helens, and an ever-widening skyline of craggy peaks and forested valleys. Climb up stairs built into steeper sections of trail as Pyramid Peak makes an appearance and Kautz and Van Trump Glaciers loom above. Continue to ascend through slopes blanketed in glacier lilies and paintbrush, delphinium and heather.

At 3 miles, reach the upper reaches of Van Trump Park and a good turnaround point for the day. Or not. You can keep wandering this enchanting flower garden for hours.

HISTORY

In 1867, Philemon Beecher (P. B.) Van Trump traveled to the Washington Territory to start work as the personal secretary of his brother-in-law, Marshall Moore, who was the governor of the territory. Upon arrival he got his first look at Mount Rainier, and he had a spiritual moment. He vowed then and there to do everything in his power to climb to the summit.

In August 1870 he did just that, setting out with General Hazard Stevens, the son of former Washington Territory governor Isaac Stevens; Edmund Coleman, a famed mountaineer and the first person to summit Mount Baker; and a Yakama Tribe guide named Sluiskin. Coleman abandoned the ascent near the base of the mountain, and Sluiskin attempted to convince the other two not to undertake the climb. But Van Trump and Stevens insisted on pressing ahead, following a route that took them through Van Trump Park and cut over to the Gibraltar Ledges route. The night before their ascent, they made camp at a spot near Paradise (see Hike 35), where Sluiskin awaited their return. Though they reached the summit on August 17, that first ascent almost ended in tragedy because the men had left their heavy coats and blankets behind to lighten their loads, thinking that the summit was in easy reach. Luckily, they found shelter from the cold and spent the night in a sulfurous steam-heated cave.

Van Trump would climb Rainier (which he strongly believed should be called Tahoma, the name many American Indian tribes had given the mountain) at least five more times, leading John Muir to the summit in 1888. The following year he brought along his nine-year-old daughter, Christine Louise Van Trump, who suffered from Sydenham's chorea, a crippling condition that made it exceptionally difficult for her to undertake the climb. She made it to about 10,000 feet, impressing many with her strength and determination. Christine Falls along Van Trump Creek is named in her honor. These days, approximately ten thousand people climb Mount Rainier every year, some following trails that began with Van Trump's first ascent more than 150 years ago.

35 PARADISE MEADOWS LOOP

DISTANCE: 4.8 miles
ELEVATION GAIN: 1400 feet
HIGH POINT: 6800 feet
DIFFICULTY: Moderate
HIKING TIME: 3 to 4 hours
BEST SEASON: Summer
TRAIL TRAFFIC: Heavy foot traffic
MANAGING AGENCY: Mount Rainier National Park

MAPS: USGS Mount Rainier East; Green Trails Mount Rainier Wonderland No. 269SX
PERMIT: National Park Pass
TRAILHEAD GPS: 46.78500°N, 121.74170°W
NOTE: Dogs are prohibited on this trail and elsewhere in Mount Rainier National Park except designated areas. Stay on designated trails to protect these very popular and very sensitive meadows.

A marmot surveys the scene in Paradise Meadows.

Explore the aptly named and ever-popular Paradise Meadows, an enormous parkland awash with flowery color and jaw-dropping views. We've outlined a loop trail that provides a decent tour of these wonderous meadows, but there's more than enough additional trail to spend a full day wandering among the wildflowers. Even better, the short paved paths near the parking areas allow hikers of all ages and abilities to access this alpine wonderland.

GETTING THERE: From Elbe, take State Route 706 east toward Mount Rainier National Park. Reach the Nisqually Entrance to the park in 13.7 miles and pay the park fee. From here continue another 17.3 miles to the entrance to Paradise's lower parking area, which allows for longer parking times. Privy available at visitor center.

From the lower parking area, find the Nisqually Vista Trailhead at the far end of the lot. Climb the stone staircase, follow the paved trail to the Dead Horse Creek Trail just beyond the top of the stairs, and veer right. Climb through a short stretch of subalpine trees before entering the meadows, passing the Avalanche Lily Trail at 0.2 mile and the Waterfall Trail soon after at 0.4 mile, where the pavement ends. Stop often to investigate trailside flowers and look up at the sheer bulk of Mount Rainier and its massive glaciers.

Cross Dead Horse Creek and climb up one side of the creek gully on a wide gravel trail. Across the creek is the tree-covered side of Alta Vista, one of many viewpoints in Paradise Meadows. Press upward, with Mount Rainier dominating the skyline, rising grandly above wildflower-covered hillsides. Pass the Moraine Trail at 0.7 mile and the end of the Dead Horse Creek Trail at the 1.1-mile mark, where it joins the Skyline Trail. Turn left and continue to climb through increasingly rocky terrain with innumerable steps built into the trail bed. At 1.2 miles reach the Glacier Vista Trail, providing exceptional views of the Nisqually Glacier. Veer left, and after a short jaunt find the viewpoint. During the summer, much of the lower reaches of the glacier will be covered with rock and debris, but don't be fooled—there's a thick layer of ice just underneath.

Reconnect with the Skyline Trail at the 1.5-mile mark for the steepest section of the hike. Climb through boulder fields as you traverse above the parklands, passing the junction with the Pebble Creek Trail and a sign pointing up to Camp Muir at 1.8 miles before working your way up a ridge with plenty of steps to help you keep your footing. Reach the ridgetop and Panorama Point at 2.1 miles and savor the commanding views. Paradise Meadows spreads out before you, with the jagged peaks of the Tatoosh Range rising across the Paradise River

valley. Farther afield, Mount Adams and Mount St. Helens are usually easy to pick out. On the best days, Mount Hood makes an appearance as well.

When you've had your fill, continue onward. The quicker route is to cut across the snowfield, but if you'd prefer to heed the warning signs when snow is present, the Upper Skyline Trail continues up the ridge and around the snowfield. Either way, soon find yourself working your way around the upper end of the Edith Creek basin before switchbacking down toward greener meadows. At 2.9 miles reach the Golden Gate Trail. Turn right and continue your descent, switchbacking alongside a rocky, tumbling creek. For those looking for a little extra, the Van Trump–Stevens Monument, marking the start of the first ascent of Mount Rainier (see Hike 34), is 0.6 mile farther down the Skyline Trail, found just after crossing the Paradise River.

FEATURED WILDFLOWER

PINK MOUNTAIN-HEATHER
Phyllodoce empetriformis

The tough stems of pink mountain-heather, a low shrub, are woody and leafless at the base and branch upward 6 to 12 inches, at which point they are covered with thick, shiny green, pine-needlelike leaves all the way to a cluster of blossoms. Pink flowers bloom all summer and are shaped like plump bells hanging down from red pedicels covered in fine yellow hairs. Dense spreading patches of this evergreen plant are found at mid to high elevations in meadows, forests, and talus.

Other Wildflowers on the Trail: Alpine aster, alpine buckwheat, alpine speedwell, American bistort, avalanche lily, beargrass, birdsfoot trefoil, bracted lousewort, broadleaf arnica, Cusick's speedwell, elegant Jacob's-ladder, false hellebore, Jeffrey's shooting star, Lewis's monkeyflower, magenta paintbrush, partridgefoot, pearly everlasting, selfheal, shrubby cinquefoil, Sitka valerian, spreading phlox, subalpine lupine, subalpine spirea, wandering fleabane, western pasqueflower, yellow mountain-heather

Soon reach the bottom of the creek basin, where the trail levels out. Now back in the parklands, keep your eyes peeled for wildlife— marmots and deer are common in the meadows. Wander through nearly a mile of wildflowers before reaching the end of the Golden Gate

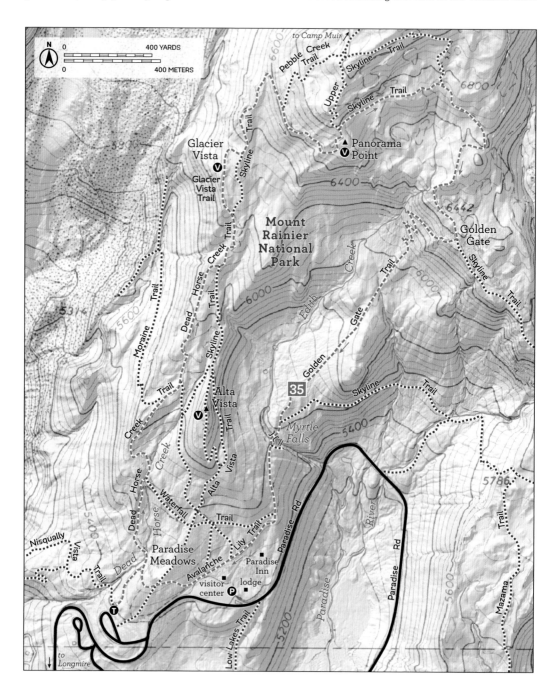

Pinnacle Peak and Mount Adams off in the distance from the upper reaches of Paradise Meadows

Trail at 3.9 miles, where it reconnects with the Skyline Trail. Veer right and soon cross Edith Creek on a sturdy log bridge, watching as the creek disappears over a sharp drop. This is Myrtle Falls, which can be viewed by following a short spur trail just beyond the bridge.

Now back on pavement again, pass the Waterfall Trail at 4.1 miles and connect with the Avalanche Lily Trail at the 4.3-mile mark. Veer right and follow the trail as it passes behind the bustling Paradise visitor center. The Alta Vista Trail cuts across your path at the 4.5-mile mark, but ignore this and press on another 0.1 mile to arrive at the Dead Horse Creek Trail and close the loop. Head left to return to the parking area and call it a day. Or don't—there's a lot more to explore!

HISTORY

While American Indians knew this area as "the land of peace," the name Paradise originated with the Longmire family. Back in the 1850s, James Longmire and his family were homesteaders on the Yelm Prairie who had a long fascination with Mount Rainier. In 1870, Longmire guided Philemon Beecher (P. B.)

Van Trump and Hazard Stevens to the Mount Rainier foothills and connected them with Sluiskin to help guide them farther up the mountain (see Hike 34). In 1883, Longmire summited Mount Rainier himself, and along the way discovered mineral springs that were valued for medicinal purposes during that era. He quickly filed a mineral claim and soon built a trail to the springs as well as a cabin. Over the years the Longmires spent their summers expanding their claim, building more cabins and eventually the Longmire Hotel and health spa.

During one of those first summers on the mountain, Longmire's wife, Virinda, rode up to the high meadowlands above the springs and supposedly said, "O, what a paradise!" Later accounts suggest that it was the entire family that dubbed it Paradise. More likely than not, the enterprising family sought any way to entice folks to visit their hotel and mineral springs, and the name Paradise certainly fits that bill. Whatever the origin, the Longmires were among the earliest boosters of the park, and Paradise is a lasting legacy of the decades they spent on the mountainside.

36 SOUTH COLDWATER TRAIL

DISTANCE: 6.6 miles
ELEVATION GAIN: 1300 feet in; 100 feet out
HIGH POINT: 3900 feet
DIFFICULTY: Moderate
HIKING TIME: 3 to 4 hours
BEST SEASON: Late spring to early summer
TRAIL TRAFFIC: Light foot traffic
MANAGING AGENCY: Mount St. Helens National Volcanic Monument

PERMIT: Northwest Forest Pass
MAPS: USGS Spirit Lake West, USGS Elk Rock; Green Trails Mount St. Helens National Volcanic Monument No. 332S
TRAILHEAD GPS: 46.28560°N, 122.25400°W
NOTE: This trail falls within a restricted area in Mount St. Helens National Volcanic Monument, where dogs and other pets are prohibited.

The 1980 eruption of Mount St. Helens utterly transformed the surrounding landscape on a massive scale. Few places offer a better perspective on those changes than a tour of ash-covered Coldwater Ridge. Hike along what remains of the old logging roadbed and through a ghost forest above a lake that did not exist before the volcano erupted to find views of hollowed-out Mount St. Helens and vast swaths of still-scarred terrain.

GETTING THERE: Take I-5 to exit 49 for State Route 504 toward Castle Rock and Toutle. Turn onto SR 504 east and proceed for 46 miles to the South Coldwater Trailhead, located on the left side of the road. Privy available.

Wildflowers dot the slopes above Clearwater Lake.

FEATURED WILDFLOWER

FOXGLOVE
Digitalis purpurea

Foxglove, a familiar and distinctive roadside wildflower, was imported from Europe and is now often found in gardens and urban areas throughout the US. It quickly colonizes open and disturbed areas, much like fireweed (see Hike 12). The plant forms a base of large, fuzzy, oblong leaves. The flower stalk grows 3 to 6 feet high from the center, forming a dramatic array of bright, speckled, bell-shaped blossoms up one side of the stalk, with flowers opening first near the base. Blooming from late spring to midsummer, flowers are generally purple-pink but may also be white or pale pink. Popular with bees and hummingbirds, this plant is highly toxic to humans and pets. Its leaves were once the primary source for certain cardiac medications, though most of those medications are made synthetically today.

Other Wildflowers on the Trail: Avalanche lily, birdsfoot trefoil, broadleaf lupine, bush penstemon, candy flower, common gypsyweed, fireweed, oxeye daisy, pearly everlasting, prairie lupine, scarlet paintbrush, sheep sorrel, small-flowered paintbrush, tansy ragwort, tiger lily, Virginia strawberry, western pasqueflower, white clover

Start your tour from the parking area, following the South Coldwater Trail #230A as it begins climbing the ridge. Quickly crest a small rise and proceed up the backside of the ridge, entering a young forest dominated by alder and willow. After a quiet climb through the trees, leave the canopy at 0.75 mile and take your first steps into open country. Here wildflowers carpet slopes still pocketed with ash. At 1.4 miles arrive at the ridgeline and a big jumble of rusted cables and twisted metal. This is an old log yarder used to drag logs upslope to be loaded into trucks. From the rig, you also get your first big view of Mount St. Helens, looking as though a third of the mountain was scooped out and discarded. In reality, the eruption's lateral blast sent Mount St. Helens's north face roaring toward Coldwater Ridge, burying ridges and valleys beneath boiling lahars.

When you're ready, push onward down the ridge along an old logging roadbed and past the occasional tree while taking in lovely views of Coldwater Lake below. Alternate between stands of trees and open slope along the wildflower-lined trail. Coldwater Peak can be seen in the distance along with Blastzone Butte. Not long before the junction with the Coldwater Trail #230, pass what remains of a bulldozer, another pre-eruption relic.

At 3.3 miles reach the junction and a good turnaround point. Hikers looking for a little more can head right on the Coldwater Trail to reach Coldwater Peak and the site of a former fire lookout with views of St. Helens Lake and Spirit Lake, roughly 3.5 miles down the trail. To the left, the Coldwater Trail drops down to Coldwater Lake and the Lakes Trail, providing access to a number of alpine lakes and backpacking destinations. Wander this altered landscape until you've gotten your fill, then retrace your steps back through lake-filled views to the car.

HISTORY

Back in the 1930s, only a couple of decades after it was founded, the Forest Service worked furiously to build modern fire lookouts on hundreds of peaks and precipices across Washington. Coldwater Peak was among those lofty high points that were selected as lookout sites, and in 1935 a Civilian Conservation Corps crew blazed a trail and built a cabin on Coldwater's rocky peak. That trail was simply called the Coldwater Trail, and it provided access to the lookout until it was decommissioned and removed in 1968.

Over the next few years, logging roads were built to harvest timber on Coldwater Ridge, in some places following the route of the old lookout trail. By 1980 logging operations on the ridge were in full swing, with crews working steadily to clear the timber. Logging crews were off in the early morning hours of Sunday, May 18, when an earthquake destabilized the north slope of Mount St. Helens and the mountain blew apart, unleashing an incomprehensible amount of force and avalanche debris that instantly transformed the landscape. It flattened entire forests and tossed logging equipment around like toys—derelicts still seen along the trail today.

The eruption spewed a hot mix of ash, melted ice, and debris down the Toutle River valley and blocked Coldwater Creek. Trapped behind a debris dam, the water backed up for 5 miles, filling the glacier-carved valley. The newborn lake grew so rapidly that the Army Corps of Engineers calculated it would overflow the debris dam before 1982 and could cause dangerous flooding. To prevent damaging overflow, the corps built a spillway to control the draining of the new lake. The lake eventually stabilized and active monitoring of its levels ended in 1998.

Coldwater Peak no longer hosts a lookout scanning the horizon for smoke, but the mountain is now home to volcano-monitoring equipment, which keeps watch over the ever-restless mountain.

37 JOHNSTON RIDGE

DISTANCE: 7.4 miles
ELEVATION GAIN: 700 feet in; 400 feet out
HIGH POINT: 4600 feet
DIFFICULTY: Moderate
HIKING TIME: 4 to 5 hours
BEST SEASON: Summer to early fall
TRAIL TRAFFIC: Heavy foot traffic near
observatory; moderate near Harry's Ridge
MANAGING AGENCY: Mount St. Helens National
Volcanic Monument

PERMIT: Northwest Forest Pass: To hike this trail,
you must purchase a monument pass at the
observatory.
MAPS: USGS Spirit Lake West; Green Trails Mount
St. Helens National Volcanic Monument No. 332S
TRAILHEAD GPS: 46.27800°N, 122.21480°W
NOTE: This trail falls within a restricted area in
Mount St. Helens National Volcanic Monument,
where dogs and other pets are prohibited.

Trek along a ridgetop thick with wildflowers and featuring views of Mount St. Helens on your way up to Harry's Ridge, where you can survey Spirit Lake and a landscape still recovering from the 1980 eruption. Wildflowers thrive here, their blooms adding much-needed color to the dry and dusty ridge. This hike offers a unique overview of a scarred and transformed landscape along well-graded trail that is approachable for most hikers.

GETTING THERE: Take I-5 to exit 49 for State Route 504 toward Castle Rock and Toutle. Turn onto SR 504 east and proceed for 51.7 miles to the Johnston Ridge Observatory parking area and the end of the road. Privy available in observatory.

FEATURED WILDFLOWER

CARDWELL'S PENSTEMON
Penstemon cardwellii
Found on rocky, open slopes like those around Mount St. Helens, Cardwell's penstemon is a low shrub that produces flowers from late spring to midsummer. Narrow, bell-shaped flowers in purple and blue-violet cluster together in a broad carpet no more than 12 inches high and generally shorter. The blooms have flared mouths that curl and feather, giving this flower an alternate name: beardtongue. The flowers attract butterflies and nocturnal moths, and the leaves, which are oblong with rounded tips in sets of alternating pairs, stay green year-round. The plant was named for Dr. James R. Cardwell, who researched wildflowers in Oregon in the late nineteenth century.

Other Wildflowers on the Trail: Avalanche lily, bluebells, broadleaf arnica, broadleaf lupine, fireweed, gentian, meadow hawkweed, oxeye daisy, partridgefoot, pearly everlasting, prairie lupine, scarlet paintbrush, spreading stonecrop, Virginia strawberry, yarrow

Wildflowers thrive in this recovering landscape.

From the parking area, begin the path along the paved Eruption Trail that can be taken from the observatory or the east end of the parking area. The short loop has interpretive signs, views, and plenty of company. At the east end of the loop, find the Boundary Trail #1 leading off the pavement and onto a wide gravel grade heading out toward the edge of the ridge.

Mount St. Helens fills the horizon and will be front and center for the entirety of this hike along the open ridge. Only a few small trees have managed to take hold along a ridge that was once covered with a thick forest of old growth. Where trees were, now find a ridge blanketed in brilliant paintbrush and bluebells. As you progress, take a look across the hummock-filled plain between the ridge and the crumpled face of St. Helens. The Toutle River cuts a swath through the ash and sediment, and decades of erosion have carved gullies and small canyons, sculpting new terrain. Push farther down the trail, past interesting interpretive signs, soon finding that you have the trail mostly to yourself.

At 1.5 miles reach a junction with what was once the most treacherous portion of the trail, known as the Devil's Elbow. The narrow, perilous path was retired in 2016, when the current trail was cut with help from the Washington Trails Association. The new traverse sticks to the ridgeline and is both safer and faster than the old route, which should be avoided.

Continue straight, climbing over exposed rock to reach the other end of the Devil's Elbow at 1.9 miles; this end of the Elbow is still open and leads out to a viewpoint for those looking for a short side trip. Not much farther down the trail reach the junction with the Truman Trail #207 at the 2-mile mark.

Push onward along the Boundary Trail toward the colorful slopes of Harry's Ridge. Catch glimpses of Spirit Lake in the distance as the trail veers north, continuing its flower-filled tour beneath the ridge. Soon find yourself working your way over rockier terrain alongside hardy scrub and huckleberry. At 2.9 miles, reach the junction with the Harry's Ridge Trail #1E, heading up and to the right. The "Harry" and "Truman" trail names in this area honor a Harry Truman who lived along Spirit Lake and famously refused to leave his lodge when ordered to evacuate; he was killed in the eruption.

The spur trail climbs directly but gently up the back of Harry's Ridge, offering widening views with each passing step. At 3.7 miles reach the high point and spectacular views obstructed only by a small volcano-monitoring station. Mount St. Helens dominates the skyline, with volcanic neighbors Mount Hood in the distance, just east of the lava dome, and Mount Adams anchoring the eastern horizon. To the north find Coldwater Peak, the Dome, and Mount Margaret. Spirit Lake spreads out below, its deep-blue waters filled with hundreds of bleached-white logs that have been floating in the lake for decades, another legacy of the eruption. Winds constantly push the logs from one shore to another in a dance that will go on for years to come.

HISTORY

Back in 1905, the Forest Service was created and the process of reorganizing the US government's timber reserves began. In 1907 the massive Mount Rainier Forest Reserve was renamed Rainier National Forest, and the following year the southern portion of the forest was separated and organized as the Columbia National Forest. The boundary between these

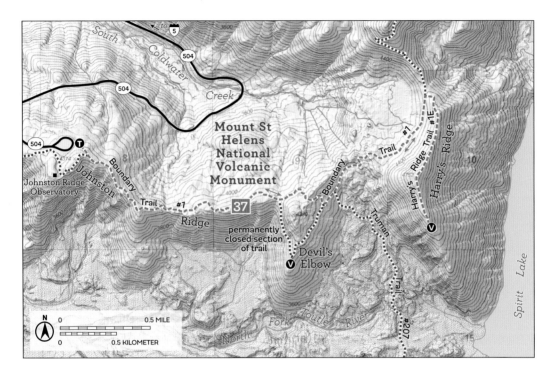

new administrative forests stretched between Mount St. Helens and Mount Adams.

This boundary roughly followed the contours of trails that American Indians had used as trade routes for untold generations. The Forest Service connected and expanded them into a pack trail that was used by rangers on horseback patrols and would become the backbone of a growing trail system. Found on maps as early as 1911, the trail continued to be popular until the eruption of Mount St. Helens in 1980 destroyed large portions of it.

In the months prior to the eruption, Mount St. Helens experienced a series of minor earthquakes and eruptions. During this time, a volcanologist named David Johnston worked tirelessly to keep the public away from a volcano he was convinced was on the verge of erupting. On the morning of May 18, he was manning a US Geological Survey observation point named Coldwater II, located 6 miles north of Mount St. Helens. As an earthquake shook the ground beneath his feet, Johnston watched the north face of the mountain collapse and slide toward him. With all that earth removed, the pressure within the volcano exploded in a lateral blast that sent pyroclastic flows hurtling toward him at supersonic speeds. It took less than a minute to reach him, and in those moments, he was the first to report the eruption, famously radioing, "Vancouver! Vancouver! This is it!" before the blast hit the ridge. It was quickly followed by a landslide of ash and debris. Pieces of his camper were found in 1993, but his body was never recovered.

By resisting intense public pressure to reopen Mount St. Helens to recreation, David Johnston likely prevented the deaths of thousands of people. To honor the volcanologist, the ridge where he had camped was named Johnston Ridge. The location of his camp was cordoned off and the Johnston Ridge Observatory was eventually built there, opening in 1997. Damaged portions of the Boundary Trail in the blast zone were fully repaired by the early 1990s, and today, the trail officially known as Boundary Trail #1 travels 52.7 miles from Johnston Ridge to Council Lake at the foot of Mount Adams.

38 NORWAY PASS AND MOUNT MARGARET

DISTANCE: 11 miles
ELEVATION GAIN: 2200 feet in; 100 feet out
HIGH POINT: 5800 feet
DIFFICULTY: Moderate
HIKING TIME: 6 to 7 hours
BEST SEASON: Late spring to summer
TRAIL TRAFFIC: Light foot traffic
PERMIT: Northwest Forest Pass

MANAGING AGENCY: Mount St. Helens National Volcanic Monument
MAPS: USGS Spirit Lake East; Green Trails Mount St. Helens National Volcanic Monument No. 332S
TRAILHEAD GPS: 46.30450°N, 122.08210°W
NOTE: Most of this trail falls within a restricted area in Mount St. Helens National Volcanic Monument, where dogs and other pets are prohibited.

Climb along a historic trail through an eruption-ravaged landscape to reach the towering heights of Mount Margaret and its volcano-filled views. Along the way, wildflowers flourish in a gray landscape, bringing dazzling colors to mountainsides dominated by ghost-white timber and ashen soil.

GETTING THERE: From Randle, head south on State Route 131, bearing right in 1 mile onto Forest Road 25 toward Mount St. Helens and Cougar. Continue 18.8 miles to FR 99, veering right toward the Windy Ridge viewpoint. Follow FR 99 for 9 miles to FR 26. Turn right and continue to the Norway Pass Trailhead on the left side of the road. Privy available.

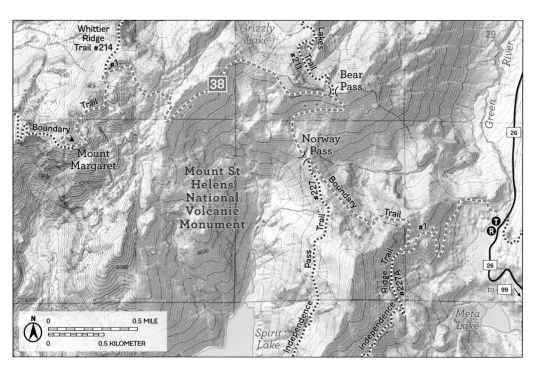

OPPOSITE: *Paintbrush brightens these ashen slopes with the crater of Mount St. Helens filling the horizon.*

FEATURED WILDFLOWER

SUBALPINE MARIPOSA LILY

Calochortus subalpinus

Found almost exclusively in Washington and Oregon, the fetching subalpine mariposa lily is made distinctive by numerous long, yellow hairs ringing the interior of its petals that give it an almost fuzzy appearance. Grass-like leaves sprout from the base of the plant, supporting a central floral stem that grows from 4 to 8 inches high and can host several blooms from early to midsummer. Each flower consists of a triad of woolly petals complemented by an outer ring of greenish sepals that can be seen between the petals. Usually bright white, this lily can also be found in a delicate mauve with dark purple speckles near its center. Adapted to thrive in loose volcanic soils, subalpine mariposa lily can be found in the area's dry meadows and open forests.

Other Wildflowers on the Trail: American bistort, arrow-leaf groundsel, avalanche lily, broadleaf lupine, candy flower, Cardwell's penstemon, Cascade aster, false bugbane, false hellebore, fan-leaf cinquefoil, fireweed, goatsbeard, meadow hawkweed, orange agoseris, pearly everlasting, pussytoes, scarlet paintbrush, small-flowered paintbrush, small-flowered penstemon, spreading phlox, spreading stonecrop, subalpine spirea, tiger lily, Virginia strawberry, wandering fleabane, western columbine, white mountain-heather, white rhododendron, woolly sunflower, yarrow

Begin your climb from the trailhead, following the dusty Boundary Trail #1 as it crosses the Green River and begins steeply climbing up ash-covered slopes through the bones of a blast-flattened forest. The acres of sun-bleached logs and stumps are slowly disappearing beneath a mix of enterprising firs and pines rubbing elbows with alders and willows. Soon switchback above Meta Lake along a wildflower-lined trail with Mount Adams as a backdrop on the horizon. Pass the junction with the Independence Ridge Trail #227A at 1.2 miles and keep right, continuing over a rib and pressing upward toward Norway Pass.

Once over the rib, the trees thicken and huckleberries crowd the trail as the boot-pounded route begins a climbing traverse above a creek basin and leads toward the ridgetop. Crest the ridge at 2.2 miles to find Mount St. Helens waiting, its broken cone dominating the skyline above log-clogged Spirit Lake. To the east find Mount Adams, while ahead the ridges of Mount Margaret and Mount Whittier beckon. Here is Norway Pass and the junction with Independence Pass Trail #227. With excellent views of lakes, volcanoes, and eruption-scoured mountainsides, it's easy to see why this is a popular turnaround point. Press onward and upward for bigger views and even more wildflowers.

Beyond Norway Pass, the trail continues up through fallen forest, passing fallen log after fallen log before leaving the ridgeline to round the top of the creek basin. Switchback up to another ridge, passing the junction with the Lakes Trail #211 at Bear Pass at 2.9 miles. Continue straight ahead, soon attaining another ridgeline that offers views of Mount Rainier rising above the sliver of Grizzly Lake, which you can just glimpse above the tree line. Not far beyond, enter sloping meadowlands bursting with wildflowers, a trend that will only continue as you press upward. Alternate between flower-dotted parklands and stretches that are more ash and exposed rock than dirt. Work your way up and along various ridges and high points as you drop and then climb your way toward Mount Margaret. Pass the Whittier Ridge Trail #214 at the 4.7-mile mark, staying left and enjoying enchanting views of a landscape that feels increasingly parklike.

At 5.3 miles, find the Mount Margaret Trail #1F spur to the summit. Head up the last 0.2 mile to the top for spectacular 360-degree views. Find four volcanoes on three horizons: Rainier, Adams, St. Helens, and Hood. Here, too, is nearby Coldwater Peak and the Dome to the southwest. That's Mount Whittier immediately to the north, with innumerable peaks in the distance. Spirit Lake shimmers along with its smaller neighbor, St. Helens Lake. Survey a landscape still very much recovering from a cataclysmic eruption. Settle in to enjoy this hard-earned vantage point.

HISTORY

While the Boundary Trail #1 has its own history (see Hike 37), portions of this route can be traced back to the region's mining days, when ore was hauled out of the Norway and Swedish claims along mining trails and roads and shipped down to Portland to be processed. Norway Pass inherited its name from the Norway claim and is part of that mining legacy.

Back in 1891, a pair of farmers turned novice prospectors were fishing around Spirit Lake when they stumbled across some mineral formations that suggested gold, silver, and other valuable minerals were in the area. They quickly staked as many claims as they could before returning to the Portland area and spreading the news of their discovery. The promise of mineral wealth kicked off a small gold rush, drawing scores of miners and prospectors to the Green River valley. That same year, the Green River Mining District was created to manage all the new claims and was then quickly renamed the Mount St. Helens Mining District.

Wildflower meadows along the Boundary Trail with Spirit Lake and Mount St. Helens in the distance

Looking across Spirit Lake to Mount St. Helens from Norway Pass

In 1896, the Norway vein was discovered, and over the next four years, 330 feet of tunnel were dug, pulling a few tons of copper out of the ground. In 1900, the mine was taken over by the Mount St. Helens Consolidated Mining Company, run by Dr. Henry Waldo Coe of Portland. Coe also picked up the adjacent Swedish claim farther down the Norway vein and immediately set to work expanding the claim into a full-fledged mining operation.

Between 1900 and 1910, Coe spent $700,000 trying to make the Swedish mine into a profitable copper mine. Unfortunately for Coe, while the Swedish mine produced more ore than any mine in the Mount St. Helens Mining District, the quality of the copper was poor and investors pulled out. By 1916, almost all mining activity had ceased. In 1969, Duval Corporation purchased most of the historical claims and spent much of 1970 drilling more than one hundred exploratory holes in the area. Again, it was found that the ore quality was too poor to turn a profit. After the eruption, the mining claims languished until 2010, when Ascot USA acquired mineral rights to some of the historical claims. In 2018, Ascot was granted permission to drill another sixty-three roadside exploratory holes. As of late 2019, environmental groups led by the Cascade Forest Conservancy have filed a lawsuit with the hope of preventing the drilling.

39 TONGUE MOUNTAIN

DISTANCE: 3 miles
ELEVATION GAIN: 1000 feet
HIGH POINT: 4600 feet
DIFFICULTY: Moderate
HIKING TIME: 2 to 3 hours
BEST SEASON: Late spring to early summer
TRAIL TRAFFIC: Light foot, mountain bike, and ORV traffic

PERMIT: None
MANAGING AGENCY: Gifford Pinchot National Forest
MAPS: USGS Tower Rock; Green Trails McCoy Peak No. 333
TRAILHEAD GPS: 46.39680°N, 121.76510°W
NOTE: Portions are multiuse; expect bikes and motorized vehicles along Trail #294.

Wildflowers and cliffs near the top of Tongue Mountain on a foggy day

FEATURED WILDFLOWER

WESTERN COLUMBINE
Aquilegia formosa

The color and shape of western columbine inspire comparisons to rocket ships or fireworks. Often found catapulting above bushy greenery along trails, these wildflowers can grow more than 3 feet high. The adaptable plant prefers moist slopes and embankments but will grow in drier soils as well. Its fanlike, lobed leaves are basal, which means found near the base of the plant. Branching stems hold multiple flowers, and each nodding blossom produces five spurs that extend upward as deep red tubular shafts with bulbous, nectar-filled tips and a ring of bright yellow around the base. A red skirt of long sepals bursts horizontally outward, below which a blaze of yellow stamens shoots earthward, as if propelling the blooms skyward. Moths, butterflies, and hummingbirds enjoy the nectar and pollen of these visually dazzling flowers, which bloom from late spring to late summer.

Other Wildflowers on the Trail: Beargrass, bunchberry, cliff penstemon, Columbia windflower, dwarf mountain fleabane, fireweed, harsh paintbrush, lupine, mountain arnica, silverback luina, small-flowered paintbrush, small-flowered penstemon, spotted saxifrage, spreading phlox, spreading stonecrop, tiger lily, trillium, Virginia strawberry, wandering fleabane, western wallflower, white campion, yarrow

Follow this short but steep route up to the site of a long-gone fire lookout, beginning in lush forest and ending on a barren precipice. Along the way, pass a wide variety of wildflowers that thrive in these diverse environments.

GETTING THERE: From Randle, head south on State Route 131 for 1 mile to Forest Road 23 (Cispus Road), veering left toward Cispus Learning Center and Trout Lake. Continue on FR 23 for 8.1 miles to signed Cispus Road (FR 28), taking a right toward the Cispus Learning Center. Continue 0.9 mile to FR 29, veering left toward Boundary Trail No. 1 and leaving the pavement. Continue 3.8 miles to FR 2904. Turn left and follow FR 2904 for 4 miles to the trailhead on the left side of the road.

From the trailhead, the Tongue Mountain Trail #294 begins along a wide tire-gouged track leading through young forest. The first section of the hike undulates over small hummocks for nearly a mile, past slender trunks of lichen-covered hemlocks and fir surrounded by a dense understory of vine maple. Find water-loving blooms crowding the trail along this stretch, thriving in small patches between the ferns.

Breeze along the trail to the 0.9-mile mark and the junction with the hiker-only Tongue Mountain Lookout Trail #294A and step over the logs meant to discourage bikes and vehicles from venturing up the mountainside. From here, trade the wide and easy trail for a

OPPOSITE: *The forested shoulders of Tongue Mountain*

narrow and steep boot path. Switchback up the slope, pushing up toward the tree line. Soon, trees yield to brushy slopes, which in turn yield to flowery meadows. Pause to enjoy the trailside color and hunt for the western columbine. Here you will also catch your first glimpse of Mount St. Helens in the distance before continuing the climb toward the summit beneath Tongue Mountain's exposed cliff walls.

The trail becomes increasingly rough near the top. Use caution as you navigate a crumbling old trail bed full of loose rocks, that make it easy to lose your footing. Soon reach a saddle below the summit, where cliffs drop steeply off the east side of the mountain down into the Cispus River valley. From here the trail becomes increasingly steep, with sections of loose scree that can be challenging for some hikers. Continue slowly, stopping often to inspect the wide array of wildflowers that have made a foothold in this rocky terrain. Reach the summit at 1.5 miles, where you'll be treated to expansive vistas full of snowcapped volcanoes—Mount St. Helens and Mount Adams to the south and Mount Rainier to the north. Pick out nearby neighbors like Juniper Peak and Langille Peak to the south while taking in the vast expanse of forest stretching to the horizons.

HISTORY

Long before European explorers were plying the Strait of Juan de Fuca searching for the Northwest Passage, the Sahaptin-speaking Taidnapam Tribe (sometimes referred to as the Upper Cowlitz) controlled this area, establishing permanent villages as well as temporary camps for hunting and fishing. One of the tribe's favorite hunting grounds for mountain goats was near a rocky crag known as "tongue place." Today we call it Tongue Mountain.

In 1902 and again in 1918, massive wildfires tore through the Cispus River valley, burning nearly 100,000 acres. The fires left ridges and mountaintops covered with bleached snags that acted as lightning rods, igniting more fires. In an effort to reduce the risk of more lightning-sparked wildfires, Forest Service crews and eventually the Civilian Conservation Corps (CCC) worked to cut down the snags starting in 1929, work they continued for more than a decade. While the CCC cleared fire-damaged trees, they also built a fire lookout cabin on Tongue Mountain in 1934, but the structure did not last long; it was abandoned in 1947 and reportedly gone by 1948.

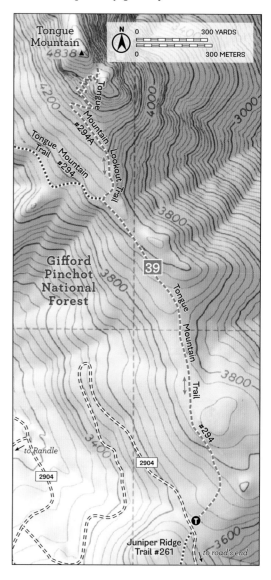

40 SNOWGRASS FLAT

DISTANCE: 10.2 miles
ELEVATION GAIN: 1800 feet
HIGH POINT: 6400 feet
DIFFICULTY: Moderate
HIKING TIME: 6 to 7 hours
BEST SEASON: Summer
TRAIL TRAFFIC: Heavy foot traffic
MANAGING AGENCY: Gifford Pinchot National Forest
PERMIT: Northwest Forest Pass

MAPS: USGS Hamilton Buttes, USGS Walupt Lake; Green Trails Packwood No. 302, Green Trails White Pass No. 303, Green Trails Blue Lake No. 334, Green Trails Walupt Lake No. 335
TRAILHEAD GPS: 46.46400°N, 121.51890°W
NOTE: Trailhead parking fills up early for the most popular hike in the Goat Rocks Wilderness. Wilderness regulations apply; see Wilderness Guidelines in Hiking Best Practices.

Tour the Goat Rocks Wilderness, trekking through creek basins and up ridgelines on a wildflower-lined trail to reach a sprawling parkland at the foot of an ancient volcano. With relatively easy access to fairy-tale meadows and astounding views, it's no surprise that this is the most popular trail in this wilderness. All that foot traffic has taken a toll on Snowgrass Flat—tread softly on this fragile landscape.

GETTING THERE: From US Highway 12, 13.3 miles east of Randle and 2.7 miles west of Packwood, turn south onto Forest Road 21 toward Walupt Lake and Chambers Lake. Stay on FR 21 for 14.1 miles, at which point the road splits. Veer left onto FR 2150 and continue 2 miles to the FR 045 spur (FR 2150-045) on the right. Turn right and find parking as close to the trailhead at the far end of the loop as possible. If the parking area is full, return to FR 2150 and continue another 0.4 mile to the Berry Patch Trailhead and road's end, where the Snowgrass Trail #96 begins.

FEATURED WILDFLOWER

WANDERING FLEABANE
Erigeron peregrinus
A member of the daisy family, wandering fleabane produces dozens of blooms from a single plant, with each flower atop its own stem that grows roughly 6 to 18 inches high. Blooming all summer, multipetaled flowers appear in shades of white, pink, blue, and purple, with the yellow-orange center many people associate with daisies. The plant covers broad swaths of mountain slopes and peeks out from piles of rock. Leaves are lancelike or oblong, narrowing up the stem. Both the leaves and stems can be covered in short, soft hairs.

Other Wildflowers on the Trail: Avalanche lily, bunchberry, Columbia windflower, cotton-grass, elephant's head, fan-leaf cinquefoil, foamflower, gentian, glacier lily, Jeffrey's shooting star, Lewis's monkeyflower, pink mountain-heather, queen's cup, Sitka valerian, small-flowered paintbrush, spreading phlox, tall bluebells, western columbine, western pasqueflower

From the FR 045 spur trailhead, the Snowgrass Trail #96A begins gently, quickly moving into the Goat Rocks Wilderness at 0.1 mile and reaching the Snowgrass Trail #96 not far beyond (if you started from the Berry Patch Trailhead, then you're already on this trail). Keep right, joining the main trail and meandering through a thin subalpine forest of diminutive firs, pines, and cedar intermingled with flower-speckled meadows. The trail is largely flat as it zips along the lower reaches of Goat Ridge toward the pointed peaks of Goat Rocks while Mount Adams keeps you company on the horizon.

Soon leave Goat Ridge and trek out across Goat Creek basin, crossing the creek on a sturdy bridge and traveling through a tarn- and meadow-dotted stretch before beginning the climb up out of the basin. Switchback up the basin walls through thinning forest and occasional talus fields, briefly approaching Snowgrass Creek as you climb. Push up to the top of Goat Creek basin, where the trail levels out and soon arrives at the junction with the Bypass Trail #97 at 3.8 miles, which connects to the Pacific Crest Trail #2000 (PCT) and leads to Cispus Pass. Keep left here on the Snowgrass

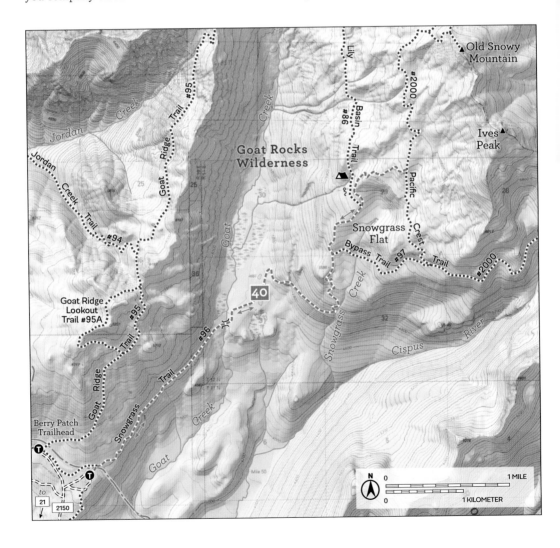

Old Snowy Mountain and Ives Peak rise above Snowgrass Flat.

Trail, following it through increasingly expansive parklands that are home to a dizzying array of wildflowers.

At 4.4 miles reach another junction, this time with the Lily Basin Trail #86. Keep right and leave the trees behind. Mount Adams is on full display as are the bright trailside flowers competing for your attention, and Mount St. Helens makes an appearance as well. Cross a few creeks to reach the edge of a vast parkland, undoubtably dotted with tents and other visitors. This is Snowgrass Flat. Above, what remains of a long-extinct volcano: the barren and snow-patched slope of Old Snowy Mountain and Ives Peak rise imposingly above these green slopes. And wildflowers are everywhere. Reach the junction with the PCT at 5.1 miles and the turnaround point, but there is no need to stop. Take the time to wander and wonder at this magical, flower-filled landscape before making the return trip.

HISTORY

For thousands of years, the Taidnapam people (also known as the Upper Cowlitz) hunted, fished, and traded throughout this area. They established a network of trails linking villages to camps for hunting and gathering food, as well as to maintain contact with neighboring tribes. One such camp was an important berry-gathering site along a trade and travel route known as the Klickitat Trail, which connected the Cowlitz Valley and the Yakima Valley via Cispus Pass. That site is now known simply as Berry Patch, a lingering vestige of the Taidnapam.

Today's Snowgrass Trail is part of the old Klickitat Trail system, following the Taidnapam traders' route up to Snowgrass Flat. Named for the snowgrass prevalent in the area—a generic term for mountain grasses favored by sheep and stock—the flat likely got its name from sheepherders who grazed their flocks in the area around the turn of the last century.

The PCT winds through wildflower-covered Snowgrass Flat toward Old Snowy Mountain.

41 KILLEN CREEK MEADOW

DISTANCE: 8 miles
ELEVATION GAIN: 2300 feet
HIGH POINT: 6900 feet
DIFFICULTY: Moderate
HIKING TIME: 5 to 6 hours
BEST SEASON: Summer
TRAIL TRAFFIC: Moderate to heavy foot traffic
MANAGING AGENCY: Gifford Pinchot National Forest

PERMIT: Northwest Forest Pass
MAPS: USGS Green Mountain; Green Trails Mount Adams No. 367S
TRAILHEAD GPS: 46.28840°N, 121.55240°W
NOTE: Cascade Volcanoes Pass required to hike above 7000 feet. Wilderness regulations apply in Mount Adams Wilderness; see Wilderness Guidelines in Hiking Best Practices.

Follow this popular trail through dense forest to a flower-filled parkland before climbing steeply up to a climber's camp on the rubble-strewn flanks of Mount Adams. Wildflowers are found along the entire hike, from dense blooms carpeting trailside meadows and crowding streambeds to hardy heathers clinging to windswept vistas above.

GETTING THERE: From Randle, head south on State Route 131 for 1 mile to Forest Road 23 (Cispus Road), veering left toward Cispus Learning Center and Trout Lake. Continue on FR 23 for 22.3 miles to FR 2329 (the pavement ends after a little more than 16 miles on FR 23). Turn left onto FR 2329 toward Takhlakh Lake, continuing 5.8 miles to the Killen Creek Trailhead and parking area on the right side of the road.

FEATURED WILDFLOWER

FAN-LEAF CINQUEFOIL
Potentilla flabellifolia
Deceptively similar to the common buttercup, the fan-leaf cinquefoil features layers of deep green leaves that complement the vivid yellow blooms of this mid-to-high-altitude meadow flower. Its fanlike leaves are deeply serrated, and occur in clusters of three. Look underneath a blossom to find a ring of pointed green bracts above a ring of rounded green sepals. The plant blooms all summer and is often found growing in loose clusters among grasses and other flowers in moist soil on mountain slopes and in meadowlands.

Other Wildflowers on the Trail: Alpine laurel, avalanche lily, beargrass, broadleaf lupine, elephant's head, fireweed, gentian, glacier lily, harsh paintbrush, Jeffrey's shooting star, leatherleaf saxifrage, Lewis's monkeyflower, magenta paintbrush, marsh marigold, northern bog violet, pearly everlasting, roundleaf violet, Sitka valerian, spreading phlox, subalpine lupine, wandering fleabane, white mountain-heather

A trailside meadow covered in avalanche lilies

From the trailhead, follow the Killen Creek Trail #113 as it leads directly into the Mount Adams Wilderness in a dense, pine-dominated forest. Much of the first 2 miles of the hike is confined to the trees, occasionally broken by small but increasingly frequent meadows and boggy streams, where flowers like the fan-leaf cinquefoil thrive. As you progress, the trail steepens, with log staircases built into the trail bed to minimize trail erosion.

At 2.3 miles reach the first big meadowlands and cross the East Fork Adams Creek. Pause at the creek to admire the floral show and look for Jeffrey's shooting star, which is common here. Here, too, Mount Adams makes its first appearance, with the glacier-clad mountain rising grandly above a field of wildflowers. From here the trail follows an ancient lava flow up the mountainside, navigating talus fields and jagged outcroppings along the way. The trees thin as you climb, opening up bigger and better views while making more room for flowery parklands.

Keep pressing upward, arriving at the end of the Killen Creek Trail as it connects to the Pacific Crest Trail #2000 (PCT) at the 3.2-mile mark. The High Camp Trail #10 begins here, marked by a sign and large cairn, leading straight up the mountain toward Adams Glacier. The trail now becomes much steeper and much rougher. The trees and parklands fade, and soon you'll find yourself carefully traversing sections of loose rock through a glacier-scoured landscape. Stop often to look back on the meadows spreading out below with Mount Rainier hovering on the horizon. Eventually the trail deposits you at High Camp, a relatively flat meadowy area, sparsely patched with vegetation at 4 miles.

Here are grand views. Adams Glacier looms above, helping to fuel the creeks, streams, and small waterfalls trickling down the mountainside. Mount Rainier and Goat Rocks are in attendance, as is Mount St. Helens. Gaze at the hummocked parkland below, a legacy of long-ago eruptions. Wander and explore this boulder-filled moonscape, maybe climb farther up the mountain to a small icy lake, or just find the best view and see how many mountaintops you can count. Take your time to soak up this rugged landscape before packing up and heading back toward the trailhead.

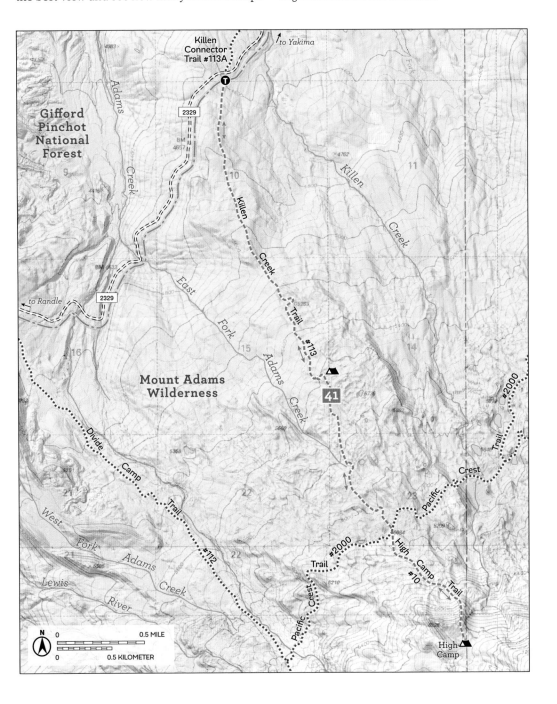

Killen Creek Meadow near the PCT junction

HISTORY

Back in 1911, an intrepid group of mountaineers geared up for an ascent of Mount Adams. They established a camp in a meadowland just below the tree line before their final push up the mountain, a site that would be used repeatedly in years to come. They referred to the meadow as Killing Creek Meadow, after the nearby creek. The creek had been named for the ghostly forests of burnt timber in the area. Sheepherders who had been grazing their flocks around Mount Adams since the late 1880s began to guide their flocks to the meadow to graze for the summer, and by the 1920s "Killing" had become "Killen."

Older trail maps show the lower portions of the trail running along Killen Creek, which is likely where the trail got its name. At some point, the trail was rerouted, likely to ease the climb. Today, the Killen Creek Trail no longer approaches its namesake creek, though the upper sections of the trail still follow a route first blazed by those shepherds of old.

42 DOG MOUNTAIN

DISTANCE: 6.6 miles
ELEVATION GAIN: 2800 feet
HIGH POINT: 2900 feet
DIFFICULTY: Moderate
HIKING TIME: 4 to 5 hours
BEST SEASON: Late spring to summer
TRAIL TRAFFIC: Heavy foot traffic
MANAGING AGENCY: Gifford Pinchot National Forest
PERMIT: Northwest Forest Pass; see note

MAPS: USGS Mount Defiance, OR; Green Trails Columbia Gorge West No. 428S
TRAILHEAD GPS: 45.69920°N, 121.70800°W
NOTE: Each hiker must also secure a Dog Mountain permit, via recreation.gov, on weekends from April through June. The large parking area fills up during wildflower season; a shuttle departs from the Skamania County Fairgrounds every half hour during permit season. Watch for poison oak in lower reaches of trail.

Dog Mountain is both very popular and very steep. The meadows that cover its upper reaches turn vibrant during wildflower season, drawing flower aficionados from across the state. Unsurprisingly, this former lookout site also presides over stunning vistas. Given the extremely accessible trailhead just off the highway, expect to find a full parking lot during wildflower season; consider taking the shuttle on weekends during peak bloom.

GETTING THERE: From the town of Stevenson, drive east on State Route 14 for 10 miles. Just past milepost 53, the well-signed gravel parking area for Dog Mountain Trailhead will be on the left. Some overflow parking can be found a few hundred feet to the west in front of Grant Lake. Alternatively, a shuttle provides access to this extremely popular trailhead from the Skamania County Fairgrounds on weekends from April to June. Privy available.

The Dog Mountain Trail #147 begins steeply, climbing toward deep forest and quickly leaving the sounds of the highway behind. Switchback past imposing pines and a mixed understory as you work your way up the shoulders of the mountain. After a thigh-burning 0.6 mile, reach a junction. Either path leads toward the summit, but the route to the right yields more views of the surrounding landscape. It's in these lower portions of the trail that you can find the diminutive and somewhat elusive calypso orchid. Keep your eyes peeled as you push upward for another mile, passing increasingly tantalizing glimpses of the Columbia

FEATURED WILDFLOWER

CALYPSO ORCHID
Calypso bulbosa var. *occidentalis*
Often called fairy slipper or occasionally deer orchid, the small calypso orchid can be found in coniferous forests from low to high elevations where there is plenty of moisture. The plant consists of a single stem that grows from 2 to 10 inches tall. One large oval leaf grows at the base of the stem and often withers when the plant is in bloom. Blooming from early spring to early summer, the light pink to purple flower looks vaguely slipper-like. The lowest petal is pouch shaped with a white apron and dark purple spots; another petal forms a hood over the pouch, while several other lance-like petals point upward from behind.

Other Wildflowers on the Trail: Ballhead waterleaf, chocolate lily, cliff penstemon, Fendler's pennycress, glacier lily, harsh paintbrush, hookedspur violet, kittentails, miner's lettuce, nineleaf biscuitroot, pioneer violet, prairie lupine, Puget balsamroot, Sierra pea, small-flowered prairie-star, small-flowered blue-eyed Mary, trillium, upland larkspur, Virginia strawberry, western buttercup, woodland star, yellow bell

River below before emerging from the forest into the first of many wildflower-filled meadows. From this viewpoint you get your first big views of the summit above, the Columbia below, and Wind Mountain, the prominence just to the west—an ancient cinder cone and lingering reminder of the area's volcanic past.

Press upward for another 0.5 mile to another junction. The path to the left will take you back down to the trailhead. Keep right and up, climbing through a brief section of forest before once again emerging into meadowlands and arriving at the Dog Mountain Lookout site at 2.5 miles from the trailhead, once home to a lookout cabin. Sometimes referred to as Puppy Dog Lookout because of the Puppy triangulation stations located here, the site offers commanding views of the landscape that on good days include three volcanoes: Adams, Hood, and St. Helens.

From this lookout site it's 0.4 mile to Dog Mountain's summit along the main trail (a slightly longer, less traveled trail leads up into the trees here—both lead to the same place). The rocky route through fields of balsamroot and other wildflowers is fully exposed, providing an amazing backdrop for the last leg of this climb. It can also be quite windy, so be prepared to weather the wind gusts that the Columbia River Gorge is famous for. A short spur trail leads the last few hundred feet to the top, where a small grove of trees provides a little shelter from the wind. The views do not get any better from this vantage point, so take a moment to enjoy your accomplishment before heading back down the spur to the main trail.

Instead of retracing your steps back to the lookout site, head right and start the longer but gentler route back to the trailhead. The trail has a few ups and downs as it traverses fields of balsamroot before returning to the shelter of the forest. Continue another 0.9 mile to the junction with the Augspurger Trail #4407. Veer left and downhill to return to the trailhead in another 2.7 miles.

OPPOSITE: *Wildflower meadows near the summit of Dog Mountain*

Intrepid hikers can continue out to Augspurger Mountain, which has similar meadows of wildflowers and is much less visited. However, the end of the Augspurger Trail is another 4 miles past the junction with the Dog Mountain Trail. If you're not up for adding 8 full miles to your day, consider returning to the trailhead and driving another 2 miles farther east along SR 14 to the Dog Creek Falls observation site. Here you can peek at a 25-foot cascade hidden just a few hundred feet off the highway.

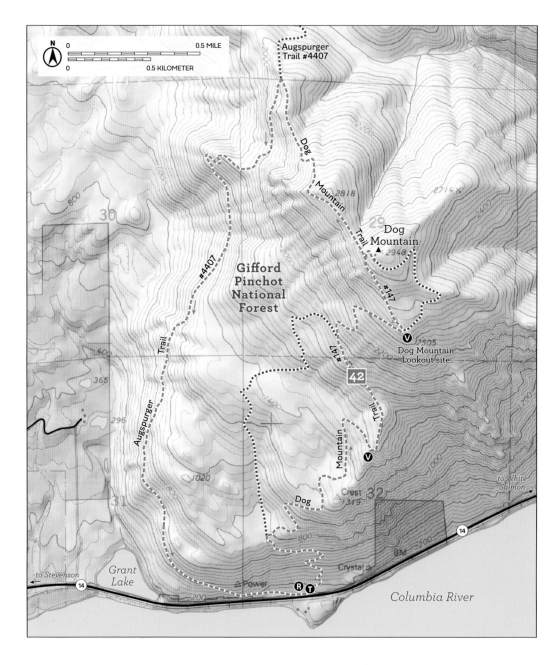

The Columbia River Gorge from the lookout site atop Dog Mountain

HISTORY

The Dog Mountain Lookout cabin was first built in 1931. The L-4 cabin lasted until 1953, when it was replaced by another L-4-style cabin that was used as a fire lookout until 1967, when it became obsolete. The trail to the summit was first blazed in order to access the lookout site.

Nearby Augspurger Mountain was named in honor of Stanley R. Augspurger, who performed timber surveys in the Pacific Northwest as a field assistant in the US Forest Service before joining the US Army's 20th Engineers (Forestry). He was subsequently killed during World War I when German U-boats sent the SS *Tuscania* to the bottom of the Irish Sea.

43 COLUMBIA HILLS

DISTANCE: 6.4 miles
ELEVATION GAIN: 800 feet in; 100 feet out
HIGH POINT: 1200 feet
DIFFICULTY: Easy
HIKING TIME: 3 to 4 hours
BEST SEASON: Spring to early summer

TRAIL TRAFFIC: Heavy foot traffic
MANAGING AGENCY: Washington State Parks
PERMIT: Discover Pass
MAPS: USGS Stacker Butte; Green Trails
Columbia Gorge East No. 432S
TRAILHEAD GPS: 45.65720°N, 121.08690°W

FEATURED WILDFLOWER

COLUMBIA GORGE BROADLEAF LUPINE
Lupinus latifolius var. thompsonianus

With more than two hundred species worldwide, lupine is a common and easily identifiable wildflower. The broadleaf lupine may be especially familiar to hikers, as it resides at lower elevations. The Columbia River Gorge is home to a specific variation of broadleaf lupine, aptly named the Columbia Gorge broadleaf lupine, which can be found nestled in the Columbia Hills along with a number of other lupine species.

From late spring to midsummer, blooms of light blue to violet blossom from a single stem, 1 to 3 feet high, in dense cones called racemes. Leaves grow in tiers up the stem in distinctive wheels of six to ten oblong leaves. The main differentiation between the common broadleaf lupine and the Columbia Gorge variety is that the latter has an abundance of fine white-to-reddish hairs on its flowers and stem.

Other Wildflowers on the Trail: Arrowleaf balsamroot, blanket flower, California poppy, cushion fleabane, grass widow, Howell's triteleia, Menzies' fiddleneck, nineleaf biscuitroot, Scouler's hawkweed, showy phlox, smooth woodland star, yarrow

Every spring the shoulders of Dalles Mountain put on a spectacular flower show, with fields of balsamroot and lupine painting the mountainside with vibrant yellows and purples. One of the best places to enjoy the show is the Columbia Hills Historical State Park, which has miles of trails snaking through the wildflowers in the Dalles Mountain Ranch trail system. Although there is a moderate amount of elevation gain, the trails are wide and well maintained, making it easy to navigate this gorgeous, family-friendly hike.

GETTING THERE: From The Dalles, Oregon, head north on US Highway 197, crossing the Columbia River into Washington, and proceed for 3.7 miles to the junction with State Route 14. Veer right toward Kennewick. In 3.6 miles find the Crawford Oaks Trailhead on the left. Privy available.

From the Crawford Oaks Trailhead, begin by following an access road as it begins gently climbing up the hillside. Almost immediately you'll reach the Ice Age Floods viewpoint and its interpretive signs, along with a lovely view of Horsethief Butte and the Columbia River. As you continue, you'll hear the rushing of Eightmile Creek, and just off the trail you can catch a glimpse of the creek cascading over some cliffs in a small waterfall. The road parallels the creek until the 1-mile mark, when the road crosses the creek and reaches a junction. Here you enter wildflower country, with grassy hills just teeming with blooms throughout the spring and summer.

At the junction, you have the choice of heading down Vista Loop to the right or heading

OPPOSITE: *Balsamroot and lupine are prolific along the Vista Loop, where the Columbia River, The Dalles, and Mount Hood are all on display.*

Columbia Hills is a great family-friendly hike.

left on Military Road, which is the oldest section of trail in the park, built in 1856 to provide stagecoach access to the next nearest military fort, Fort Simcoe, some 67 miles down the road. While either way will work, heading left helps maximize the time you'll spend savoring the views. Follow Military Road for 0.3 mile to the Eightmile Alternate Trail. Veer left and once again follow Eightmile Creek as you climb toward the historic Crawford Ranch and an alternate trailhead and parking area. The trail soon becomes the Vista Loop, offering a sea of wildflowers with stunning vistas dominated by Mount Hood, Mount Adams, and the Columbia River. Pass Military Road at the 3.7-mile mark and savor the setting as you slowly descend, keeping to the Vista Loop until you reconnect with the access road at the Military Road–Vista Loop junction. From here retrace your steps along the gravel road back to the parking area.

For those with an interest in the history of the area or looking to make a day of it, you can get some extra trail time by touring the Crawford Ranch, which has plenty of rusty farm equipment, abandoned buildings, and even a cemetery to explore. And for those looking for some more elevation gain, it's possible to follow the Dalles Mountain Road about 4 miles up to 3200-foot Stacker Butte, or stop along the way to visit Oak Spring, about 3 miles along the road.

HISTORY

Back in 1866, William T. Murphy filed the first claim of what would eventually become the Dalles Mountain Ranch. In 1877, William and Julia Crawford filed for a homestead in the area, and in 1905, their son John built the house that still stands on the property. The Crawfords eventually lost the ranch in the Great Depression, and subsequent owners added acreage to the property until Pat and Darlene Bleakney bought the 6000-acre ranch in 1975. The Bleakneys renamed the property the Dalles Mountain Ranch.

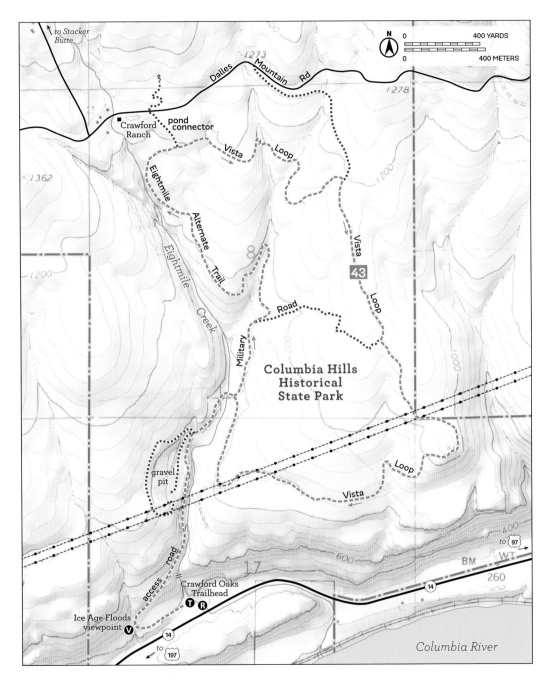

In 1993 they donated the land to the state to both operate as a park and preserve some plant species that are unique to the area. For decades intrepid hikers would simply wander through the open scrubland, enjoying the views and amazing wildflower displays. That changed in 2014, when the current trail system opened, providing miles of well-graded trail to explore.

EASTERN WASHINGTON

44 UMTANUM CREEK CANYON

DISTANCE: 3.6 miles
ELEVATION GAIN: 200 feet
HIGH POINT: 1600 feet
DIFFICULTY: Easy
HIKING TIME: 2 to 3 hours
BEST SEASON: Spring to early summer

TRAIL TRAFFIC: Moderate foot traffic
MANAGING AGENCY: Bureau of Land
Management: Yakima River Canyon
PERMIT: BLM parking fee
MAPS: USGS Wymer, USGS Ellensburg
TRAILHEAD GPS: 46.85550°N, 120.48280°W

Explore the bottom of a steep-walled canyon, following Umtanum Creek along a flower-lined trail through a long-abandoned homestead. The nearly flat trail offers plenty of boot paths and social trails for a little extra rambling, making it an excellent choice for hikers of any skill level. More adventurous hikers can climb the ridges in pursuit of desert blooms.

GETTING THERE: Take I-90 to exit 109 for Canyon Road and Ellensburg. Turn south onto Canyon Road (State Route 821) and continue 12 miles to the Umtanum Recreation Site on the right side of the road. The trailhead is near the west end of the lot. Privy available.

From the parking area, cross the Yakima River on a long, swinging suspension bridge. Once on the other side, carefully cross the railroad tracks, finding a signboard marking the beginning of the trails at 0.2 mile. Ignore the trails heading up Umtanum Ridge; instead head out straight toward the canyon through desert scrub. Follow what remains of the old homestead road, soon

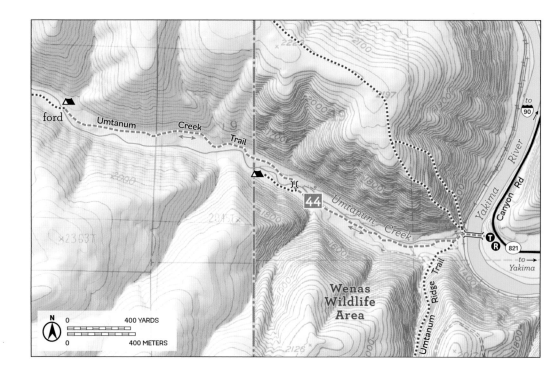

Crossing the Yakima River near the mouth of Umtanum Creek Canyon

passing apple and walnut trees and old fence posts. As you progress, watch the canyon walls for bighorn sheep that frequent the canyon.

Wildflowers are common along the route, often better near the creek. Take your time, and do not hesitate to wander down an inviting boot path to do some exploring and wildflower hunting. Reach a fork at 0.9 mile, in the vicinity of the buildings seen on old USGS maps, an area now used for campsites. Keep right here, crossing the bridge and heading through a small stand of trees. Beyond is open country, with little to block your views of the rugged canyon. Hike through a few boulder fields and by the occasional tree to the 1.7-mile mark and another camping area. Not far beyond, at 1.8 miles, is yet another camp and a good turnaround point and lunch spot.

If you want to go farther, you'll need to ford the creek—not typically difficult in the summer. The upper reaches of the trail are rockier and rougher but offer more opportunities to see wildlife. For more flowers, explore the ridges above.

HISTORY

Umtanum means "contentment" in the Sahaptin language of the Yakama people. The name is a reference to the deer and game that were drawn to the area due to the early snowmelt. In the 1850s, railroad surveyors came through and mapped out a route to Ellensburg along the Yakima River. They marked a site for a station in the area, dubbing it "Em-te-num," their best guess at how to spell the Sahaptin word. By the time the railroad was built in 1886, the name was

---

FEATURED WILDFLOWER

YELLOW SALSIFY
Tragopogon dubius

Hit the trail early on a sunny day to catch these bright yellow blooms, which close in midafternoon. Yellow salsify's leaves are grasslike with a slight blue-green tinge. Growing between 1 and 2 feet tall, stems are similarly blue-green, each producing a single flower: a burst of tightly packed yellow petals and brown stamens ringed by longer, broader yellow petals, in turn ringed by a layer of thin, pointed sepals.

The face of this flower follows the sun, and it may not open at all on a cloudy day. Flowers bloom from late spring to late summer; later in the season, look for their large, round seed puffs that resemble those of oversized dandelions. This wildflower is also known as wild oyster plant.

Other Wildflowers on the Trail: American vetch, bitterbrush, bugloss fiddleneck, Carey's balsamroot, Columbia prickly pear, desert parsley, desert yellow fleabane, Harrison yellow rose, hoary cress, Hood's phlox, Jim Hill mustard, narrowleaf mule's ears, northern buckwheat, parsnip-flower buckwheat, prairie lupine, red osier dogwood, Rocky Mountain iris, shaggy fleabane, showy penstemon, slender hawksbeard, small bluebells, sticky geranium, wax currant, western horsemint, white campion, white sweetclover, Wood's rose

Wildflowers dot the scrublands near Umtanum Creek Canyon.

Umptanum, but the nearby creek was Umtanum. Over the years the maps have been updated so that both are Umtanum.

The railroad brought new settlers, and a homestead was established along Umtanum Creek around the turn of the twentieth century. Land patents show that Galusha A. Bailey and his wife, Olive, owned the area at one point. Galusha was also the postmaster for the short-lived Umtanum Post Office, which operated from 1906 to 1911. Today, you can still find remnants of that homestead, largely in the form of fruit and nut trees, though traces of the old farmhouse can also be found.

45 RATTLESNAKE SLOPE

DISTANCE: 5 miles
ELEVATION GAIN: 700 feet
HIGH POINT: 1100 feet
DIFFICULTY: Easy
HIKING TIME: 2 to 3 hours
BEST SEASON: Spring to summer

PERMIT: Discover Pass
TRAIL TRAFFIC: Light foot and mountain bike traffic
MANAGING AGENCY: Washington Department of Fish and Wildlife
MAPS: USGS Benton City
TRAILHEAD GPS: 46.34310°N, 119.47500°W

FEATURED WILDFLOWER

HOWELL'S TRITELEIA
Triteleia grandiflora var. howellii

Howell's triteleia is a wildflower found only in the Pacific Northwest and parts of western Canada, where it has been classified as endangered since 2003 due to habitat destruction and competition with invasive species. Blooming from mid-spring to early summer, the blossoms range from white to purple and occur in a cluster at the top of a thin, smooth stem that grows 8 to 10 inches high. Grasslike leaves grow upward from the base of the plant. Just under the surface of the soil, the stem of this flower widens into a squat, bulbous organ called a *corm*, which stores nutrition that helps the plant survive harsh environmental conditions, not uncommon in the dry scrubland where it resides. The plant was named in honor of Thomas J. Howell, an Oregon botanist who put together some of the earliest collections of Washington and Oregon plants.

Other Wildflowers on the Trail: Bugloss fiddleneck, Canby's angelica, Carey's balsamroot, Columbia milkvetch, Hood's phlox, longleaf phlox, orange globe mallow, prairie lupine, upland larkspur, yarrow

---

This short hike explores the Rattlesnake Slope Wildlife Area, complete with wildflowers and the option for further treks though this unique landscape. The wildflowers that thrive in this desert prairie have a special kind of beauty, as their brilliant blooms splash color across the harsh scrubland.

GETTING THERE: From Yakima, head east on State Route 24 for 38.4 miles to SR 240. Take a right and drive 20.5 miles to SR 225, signed for Benton City. Turn right and proceed 4.1 miles to a large gravel parking area on the right, just beyond the shooting range.

From the parking area, follow the only trail as it gently climbs into the hills. Soon reach a junction at a fence corner that divides the wildlife area from the Rattlesnake Mountain Shooting Facility at a little over 0.3 mile. The route to the right dips down into the bottom of the canyon, while the route to the left (not shown on map) keeps to the upper reaches of the canyon. The trails eventually reconnect, making either route workable, though the path to the left puts on the better wildflower show.

Whichever route you chose, soon pass under the buzzing powerlines while working your way over seasonal streambeds. Balsamroot and lupine are common along the slopes here, and sharp-eyed hikers might spy Howell's triteleia as well. As you work your way up the canyon, note the exposed rock; most of it is dark basalt, a legacy of ancient volcanism. Keep your eyes peeled for erratics—large granite boulders that are much lighter in color, making them easy to pick out from the scrubland. These are a much more recent addition to the landscape, deposited here by Ice Age floods around fifteen thousand years ago.

Eventually the trail levels out, leaves the canyon, and enters a sprawling prairie stretching out toward the base of Rattlesnake Mountain. Wander through the scrub, passing lupines and balsamroot to an old jeep track. Take a moment to enjoy the views of Richland in the distance and the rolling slopes of Rattlesnake Mountain, as well as Red Mountain and Candy Mountain lined up in the distance. Do a little exploring to see what other flowers you can find nearby before retracing your steps back down to the parking lot.

While this tour of Rattlesnake Slope does not have much of a payoff at the end of the hike, the landscape is so engaging that you hardly mind that the trail ends somewhat abruptly in the middle of a desert prairie. Wildflowers are abundant, and you are unlikely to have a great

deal of company, as this area tends to be overlooked. Note that the neighboring gun ranges can be noisy on a busy weekend, though the sound of gunfire eventually disappears as you press deeper into the scrubland.

Hikers hungry for more trail time can follow the jeep track toward Rattlesnake Mountain, passing two roads that eventually lead back to the parking lot along the way (not shown on the map in this book). If you are looking to scale Rattlesnake Mountain, you can navigate a network of overgrown roads up to the top, though reaching the summit can add 10 or

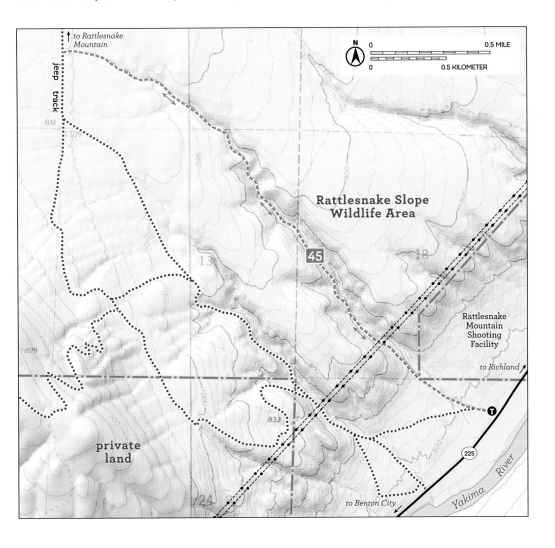

The hilly scrubland of Rattlesnake Slope Wildlife Area

more miles to the hike. Make sure you are prepared for the long journey with enough gear, supplies, and a map of the terrain.

HISTORY

The Rattlesnake Slope Wildlife Area was created in 1973 as part of an effort to preserve its unique landscape. Largely undeveloped, the 3661-acre preserve offers excellent opportunities to explore the scrubland, its mixed habitats, and the wildflowers that thrive here. A series of wildfires between 2000 and 2003 wiped out much of the native shrub-steppe habitat that once dominated the area, allowing a variety of species to come in and colonize. Today, partially because of the fires, Rattlesnake Slope is awash in flowers in the spring, helping make it a popular wildflower destination.

46 HANFORD REACH AND WHITE BLUFFS

DISTANCE: 6 miles
ELEVATION GAIN: 200 feet
HIGH POINT: 1000 feet
DIFFICULTY: Easy
HIKING TIME: 2 to 3 hours
BEST SEASON: Spring to late summer

TRAIL TRAFFIC: Light foot traffic
MANAGING AGENCY: Hanford Reach National Monument
PERMIT: Discover Pass
MAPS: USGS Locke Island
TRAILHEAD GPS: 46.67710°N, 119.44460°W

This short jaunt is an excellent introduction to the Hanford Reach National Monument, home to a surprising variety of wildflowers and flowering plants. At the same time, the shifting sand dunes amid this expansive landscape dominated by the rolling Columbia River are a treat to visit. Beyond the natural beauty, the trail wanders through areas that were once part of the bustling community of White Bluffs.

GETTING THERE: From Yakima, head east on State Route 24 for 38.4 miles to the junction with SR 240. Take a left to stay on SR 24 toward Othello, crossing the Columbia River and veering right soon after, again following signs for Othello. Continue on SR 24 for another 19 miles to an unsigned gravel road. Turn right and drive 4 miles to a four-way intersection. Turn right and in 1.3 miles find a parking area at the trailhead before reaching the larger parking area near the boat launch.

From the gravel parking area, the White Bluffs Trail cuts through a grassy field and climbs to a ledge above the river. The Columbia flows beneath you and around Locke Island a short way upriver. On the other side of the river, powerlines and roads crisscross an otherwise

FEATURED WILDFLOWER

VEINY DOCK
Rumex venosus
Commonly found in low to mid elevations in sandy scrubland, veiny dock is also sometimes called winged dock or wild begonia. Often avoided by livestock, this wildflower is common in range areas. It spreads via a woody rootstock or rhizome and can create thick colonies over wide areas. The plant grows upward of 18 inches tall with oval, somewhat leathery leaves that have a pointed tip and obvious veins. Flowers bloom from early summer to early fall and grow in upright spikes, usually red to pink.

Veiny dock is technically edible, though it must be boiled a considerable time to remove the bitter taste. Even then, the plant contains high levels of oxalic acid, which can cause some negative side effects when consumed in large quantities.

Other Wildflowers on the Trail: Bitterbrush, Carey's balsamroot, clasping pepperweed, Grey's desert parsley, Hood's phlox, larkspur, longleaf phlox, low pussytoes, northern buckwheat, sand dune lupine, threadleaf phacelia, western goldenrod, western wallflower, White Bluffs bladderpod

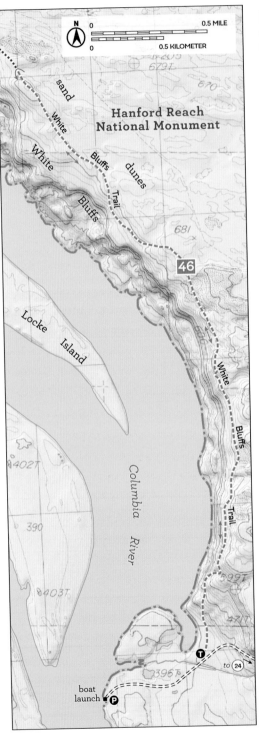

barren landscape populated by only a few scattered industrial-looking buildings—what remains of Hanford's nuclear reactors.

Work your way through patches of sage-brush and veiny dock, navigating the ups and downs of the riverside trail. Soon the dunes come into view, though they are farther away than they seem. Keep an eye out for the purples of phacelia and larkspur among the yellows of wallflower and balsamroot. Several varieties of phlox also line the trail. Reach the dunes at 3 miles from the trailhead. Wind-swept and constantly in flux, the dunes can be a little tricky to hike on, but it's not a difficult trek to go the additional mile to the far end of the sand.

Abundant wildflowers, engaging landscapes, and a healthy dose of history—this easy hike packs a lot into a few miles. It's a great option for youngsters or anyone looking for a short hike through this unique environment.

HISTORY

Named for the chalk-white cliffs prominent along the trail, the town of White Bluffs was one of the first settlements along the Columbia in Washington Territory. Today's boat launch was once a busy ferry terminal that shuttled people and cattle across the river. By the 1850s, steamboats regularly visited White Bluffs from Portland, Oregon. Though the town was first settled near the area where the trailhead is now, the settlement expanded across the water, and with the coming of the railroad in 1913, the community's businesses shifted entirely to the other side of the river. In 1943 the US government condemned White Bluffs so that the land could be used for the Hanford project, and nearly everything was razed to the ground within a few weeks.

During the Cold War a number of nuclear reactors were built at Hanford to process and create weapons-grade plutonium. While most of the reactors have been shut down, a few remain in operation, though now they are used as part of the ongoing cleanup and containment of the site's nuclear waste.

ABOVE: *Patches of veiny dock grow on the sandy bluffs above the Columbia River.*
BELOW: *Hiking the bluffs with views west over the Columbia River*

47 ANCIENT LAKES AND POTHOLES COULEE

DISTANCE: 5 miles
ELEVATION GAIN: 200 feet
HIGH POINT: 1000 feet
DIFFICULTY: Easy
HIKING TIME: 2 to 3 hours
BEST SEASON: Spring to late summer
TRAIL TRAFFIC: Moderate to heavy foot and mountain bike traffic

MANAGING AGENCY: Washington Department of Fish and Wildlife
PERMIT: Discover Pass
MAPS: USGS Babcock Ridge
TRAILHEAD GPS: 47.16040°N, 119.98060°W
NOTE: If you're staying overnight, bring your own water. The lake water is not safe for human consumption.

Potholes Coulee was carved by the Ice Age flooding caused by the sudden drainage of glacial Lake Missoula around fifteen thousand years ago. While the sheer scale of these floods can be difficult to grasp, Potholes Coulee provides a dramatic visual for the volume of water that inundated this area. The rushing waters scoured out the ravine, known as a coulee, leaving a thin rib of basalt dividing the 2-mile-wide coulee into two alcoves. It's not hard to imagine water plunging over the cliffs above and rushing toward the Columbia River.

GETTING THERE: From I-90, take exit 149 for State Route 281 north to Quincy and Wenatchee. Turn north on SR 281 for 5.6 miles, and turn left on White Trail Road, following it 7.8 miles through a couple of curves to Road 9 NW. Take a left onto the gravel road and continue 5.9 miles as Road 9 NW drops down toward the river and becomes Ancient Lake Road. Find the parking area at the end of the road.

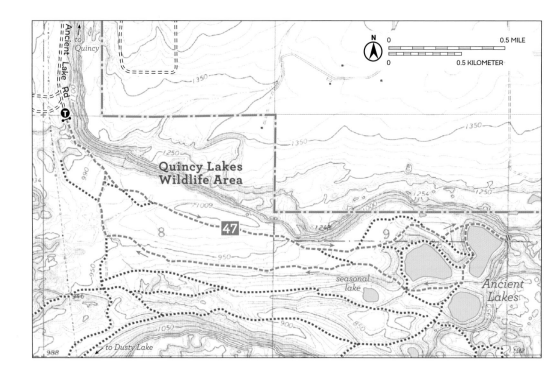

On top of the cliffs overlooking the Ancient Lakes

Begin your tour by following a gated jeep track that leads into Potholes Coulee and runs just below the exposed cliffs that make up the north wall of the coulee. Follow the dusty road for 0.3 mile to an unmarked trail leading into the coulee and toward Ancient Lakes. (From here the road continues another 4.5 miles along the Columbia River, past access to Dusty Lake, and out to the Gorge Amphitheatre.) Veer left into the grass-lands, enjoying wild roses and other wildflowers while marveling at the rugged landscape.

Follow the trail for a little over 1 mile to a junction with access to the shores of the first of a handful of Ancient Lakes. Continue past the lake to the north to reach the top of a low rise that provides one of the better views of the cou-lee, including your first glimpse of the waterfall tumbling down from the cliffs above. Wild-flowers are abundant here, so take a moment to enjoy your surroundings before continuing down to the upper lake. Reach a junction and veer left toward the rocky lakeshore. If you're

Approaching the first of the Ancient Lakes

feeling adventurous, you can pick your way along the lakeshore to the base of the waterfall, though the route is more boulder than trail.

Retrace your steps to the low rise and the junction and take the path to the left around the west side of the lake. Follow it as it hugs the lakeshore and arrives at a junction between three of the Ancient Lakes. Head right and to the west, back toward the river. In a few tenths of a mile, reach a junction that provides access to one of the lakes. Keep left and continue working your way back through the scabland

FEATURED WILDFLOWER

HOOKER'S ONION
Allium acuminatum

Also known as tapertip onion, Hooker's onion is a wild onion typically found in dry, rocky areas. A thick floral stalk grows up to 12 inches high and supports clusters of bright pink to light purple flowers, though it occasionally sports white flowers. Flowers bloom from mid-spring to early summer and consist of six tepals arranged in two tiers, with tepals tapering to a sharp point, thus inspiring the "tapertip" descriptor. The plant grows a few grasslike leaves that wither by the time it blooms.

It was named in honor of William Jackson Hooker, a botanist who cataloged hundreds of Pacific Northwest plants that collectors sent him in England during the first half of the nineteenth century. His son, Joseph Dalton Hooker, a renowned botanist himself, continued his father's work with a visit to the Pacific Northwest in 1877. Wildflowers that refer to Hooker refer to one or both of these botanists.

Other Wildflowers on the Trail: Carey's balsamroot, cut-leaf thelypody, mariposa lily, purple cushion fleabane, purple sage, rock buckwheat, Thompson's paintbrush, thymeleaf buckwheat, Wood's rose, yarrow

to the main road. Head right to close the loop and return to the car.

The abundant wildflowers and dramatic geology attract many hikers to this area, and the vastness of the coulee means there is plenty of room for everyone. Easy enough for even the tiniest of hiking boots, Ancient Lakes is a great option for a family day hike.

Although we've described a tidy loop for exploring this area, a maze of trails crisscrosses the coulee floor, allowing hikers to ramble at will. Several trails lead up the basalt cliffs, which provide the best vantage point for taking in the full extent of Potholes Coulee. A visit to Dusty Lake adds roughly 3 miles to the day; the lake can be accessed by continuing down the main road, past the cliffs that divide the coulee. Eventually you'll reach an obvious junction that heads down the middle of the coulee to Dusty Lake.

HISTORY
The name Ancient Lakes comes from the fact that after the Ice Age floods, a lake filled the bottom of the coulee; but having no natural inflow beyond precipitation or subsequent flooding, it quickly dried up. The lakes that sit in that lake bed today are the result of irrigation runoff that has been occurring since the 1940s. As a result, the water is not safe for human consumption, even after filtering or treating it. Be prepared to carry in all your own water.

48 STEAMBOAT ROCK

DISTANCE: 3.9 miles
ELEVATION GAIN: 700 feet
HIGH POINT: 2300 feet
DIFFICULTY: Easy
HIKING TIME: 2 to 3 hours
BEST SEASON: Early spring to early summer
TRAIL TRAFFIC: Moderate foot traffic

MANAGING AGENCY: Washington State Parks
PERMIT: Discover Pass
MAPS: Steamboat Rock State Park website
TRAILHEAD GPS: 47.86400°N, 119.12170°W
NOTE: Rattlesnakes are common on the summit of Steamboat Rock, so pay close attention to your environment as you hike.

Climb to the top of a massive basalt mesa to vistas that provide a bird's-eye view of the area's fascinating geological history. Loop through scablands brimming with wildflowers in season and find vantage points that reveal the colossal scale of the Ice Age floods that carved this landscape.

GETTING THERE: Take State Route 155 to the Steamboat Rock State Park entrance, 17.8 miles north of Coulee City and 10.1 miles south of Grand Coulee. Turn west onto the park road and follow it 3 miles to the parking area. The trailhead is across the road on the west end of the lot. Privy available.

From the parking area, follow a dusty path toward Steamboat Rock. Wander through the sagebrush along the base of the butte for 0.4 mile to a rough trail leading uphill. The first section is a steep climb on scree and loose rock that very quickly leads to a hillside with more stable footing. The 0.25-mile climb ends at an intersection in a low point that divides

FEATURED WILDFLOWER

SAGEBRUSH VIOLET
Viola trinervata

This charming violet prefers the cooler months of spring and early summer in which to display its array of five petals: two deep purple to burgundy and three light lavender to lilac. In addition, the flowers sport a distinctive pattern of dark veins and dots highlighted with a burst of yellow. Leaves are small, fleshy, and sharp-tipped, with prominent veins. Found on rocky hillsides and sagebrush flats that receive seasonal rains, sagebrush violet sits low to the ground—no more than 3 inches high—in rounded bunches that share an underground root system.

Other Wildflowers on the Trail: Arrowleaf balsamroot, Columbia prickly pear, dark-throated shooting star, desert yellow fleabane, nineleaf biscuitroot, small-flowered prairie star, sulfur lupine, Thompson's paintbrush

The views of the Columbia River from Steamboat Rock are expansive.

Steamboat Rock. This low point is actually a coulee, the legacy of a stream that ran here before Ice Age floods tore through and made Steamboat Rock into an island.

Head right, climbing out of the sloped coulee and onto the flat-topped summit at the 0.8-mile mark. Just beyond, reach the intersection for the loop trail, with one trail leading straight out toward the edge of the rock and the other to the left cutting across the interior, where wildflowers are more prevalent. Take the loop in either direction, though the clockwise approach delivers some stunning vistas and leaves the wildflowers for the end, after you've had your fill of beautiful views. To the east, find the Devils Punch Bowl and camping areas below and the vast, flat stretch of farmlands receding into the distance. To the north, gaze upon the peaks of the south end of the Okanogan Highlands; the

most prominent on the horizon is Moses Mountain. To the west, the Cascade Range fills the horizon above Banks Lake.

Explore the loop, using caution near the edge, as loose rock can make for unstable footing. As you progress, you'll pass orphaned boulders—glacial erratics—a legacy of the last ice age. Follow footpaths and game trails out to viewpoints and prominences, and watch for wildlife. This sprawling scabland often hosts deer or coyote, and it's common to spy raptors riding thermals above. Rattlesnakes are often encountered here as well, so pay a little extra attention to the ground as you walk. Complete the loop and head back to the coulee, retracing your steps back to the trail leading to the parking area.

From here you can opt to explore the south end of Steamboat Rock. While it is possible to make another short loop, there are a jumble

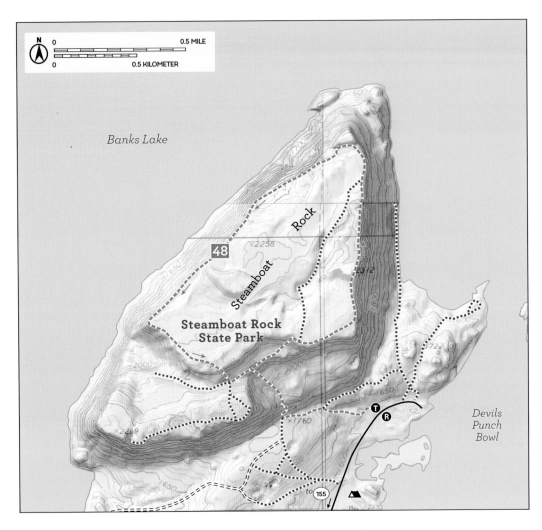

of trails to follow and not all of them connect together. Wander until you get your fill, keeping in mind that the trail you're on may dead-end. Vantage points here offer better views of Banks Lake and the far reaches of the Grand Coulee. When you're ready, make your way back to the coulee intersection and descend the scree-covered trail to the car.

HISTORY

Back when lobes of Ice Age glaciers extended south from what is now Canada, the Okanogan lobe pushed down to the vicinity of Grand Coulee. The advancing ice blocked off the natural route of the Columbia River, turning it sharply south along the edge of the glacier, first down Moses Coulee and later down the Grand Coulee. At the same time, ice dams formed, creating glacial lakes that periodically burst forth to scour the land. Much of Eastern Washington was sculpted by a series of titanic Ice Age floods.

Steamboat Rock and the Grand Coulee were carved out this way, the result of waterfall erosion. At one time, Steamboat Rock was the lip of a massive waterfall that plunged 800 feet to the coulee bottom. While softer rock was quickly washed away, Steamboat Rock, a massive chunk of basalt, refused to yield and was left orphaned in the riverbed.

Eventually the ice retreated and the Columbia River returned to its old riverbed and left Grand Coulee dry. Early European settlers likened the rock to a battleship or a steamboat marooned on land. In 1951 water returned to the coulee when the Grand Coulee Dam was built, and Banks Lake was created as a reservoir. Now surrounded on three sides by water, Steamboat Rock became a state park in 1972 and has been one of the most popular parks in Washington ever since. In 2009, the Ice Age Floods National Geologic Trail was created and integrated into the National Park System, with Steamboat Rock as one of the many stopping points on the trek from Missoula, Montana, to Astoria, Oregon.

On the approach to Steamboat Rock

49 LITTLE SPOKANE RIVER NATURAL AREA

DISTANCE: 7.7 miles
ELEVATION GAIN: 1000 feet
HIGH POINT: 2450 feet
DIFFICULTY: Moderate
HIKING TIME: 4 to 6 hours
BEST SEASON: Spring to early summer
TRAIL TRAFFIC: Moderate foot traffic

MANAGING AGENCY: Washington State Parks
PERMIT: Discover Pass
MAPS: USGS Dartford
TRAILHEAD GPS: 47.78270°N, 117.49660°W
NOTE: Dogs are prohibited in the Little Spokane
River Natural Area.

Follow this loop through a vibrant natural area, where wildlife sightings are common and wildflowers brighten the trail during the spring and summer. As you explore, wander along riversides, climb to viewpoints on rocky outcroppings, and follow decommissioned logging roads through a recovering burn. Here, too, are the Painted Rocks, a reminder of the people who roamed this land long before our boots hit the trail.

GETTING THERE: From I-90 in Spokane, take exit 280 (exit 280A westbound) for Maple and Walnut Streets, and turn north onto Walnut Street. Continue on Walnut Street as it turns into Maple Street for 4.4 miles to Francis Avenue. Turn left and continue 1.1 miles, staying in the right-hand lane to merge onto Indian Trail Road. Follow the road for 5.5 miles (road changes to Rutter Parkway after 4.7 miles) to the Indian Painted Rocks Trailhead on the left side of the road. Privy available.

Yellow flag iris has colonized this marsh along the Little Spokane River.

FEATURED WILDFLOWER

YELLOW FLAG IRIS
Iris pseudacorus

An invasive Eurasian species, yellow flag iris prefers marshes and wetlands. Reaching up to 3 feet tall, the plant consists of swordlike leaves surrounding a rigid flower stalk. From mid-spring to early summer, one or more blooms sprout from the top of the stalk, each with three large sepals that droop toward the ground, leading the eye to a crown of feathered yellow petals reaching skyward, akin to a flag waving in the wind. For that reason, the plant is also commonly called water flag. Known for its high nectar production, this bright yellow bloom is popular with bees, humming-birds, and butterflies.

Yellow flag iris produces seeds that are carried away by water to root downstream. It may also propagate when sections of roots are washed away to land in new soil. In this way, the plant can aggres-sively colonize an area and crowd out native species.

Other Wildflowers on the Trail: American vetch, arrowleaf balsamroot, common bugloss, Dalmatian toad-flax, Hooker's onion, hound's tongue, Jim Hill mustard, large-flower triteleia, longleaf phlox, mallow ninebark, nineleaf biscuitroot, showy penstemon, silky lupine, silverleaf phacelia, spreading dogbane, sticky purple geranium, western butterweed, Wood's rose, yarrow, yellow salsify

From the trailhead, begin the loop by following the Little Spokane River Trail as it leads out toward the river. A few steps down the trail, note the path leading toward a large rock and a small metal fence. These are the Painted Rocks, displaying pictographs painted by members of the Spokane Tribe more than 250 years ago. After you take a moment to consider the glyphs and symbols, head down the trail near the edge of the Little Spokane River and its vibrant marshes. Slip between pines and alders on nearly flat trail, getting glimpses of the water from breaks in the trees. Yellow flag iris crowds out native species and lights up the marshes with brilliant-yellow blooms in late spring. Waterfowl, including great blue herons, wood ducks, and mallards, is commonly seen here as well.

Glide along the trail, quickly covering the 1.7 miles to River Park Lane, a paved private road leading to homes higher up on the bluff. Turn right and uphill a short distance to the beginning of the Knothead Trail, which follows an old jeep track up the mountainside. Keep pushing upward, sticking to the main road-trail and ignoring the ORV tracks that lead off into the trees.

At 2.2 miles, cross River Park Lane again, following the track for a short while before trail signs point you onto a newer trail. The new trail is part of the 2014 effort to reroute the trail away from private property. Continue up to a currently unmarked trail at 2.9 miles, a recently blazed addition to the natural area that leads out to a series of overlooks. Turn right and get ready to do some exploring.

Eventually a loop is planned for the overlooks, but for now this section is an out-and-back. The views open and the wildflowers proliferate as you progress through the edges

The snaking Little Spokane River from one of the clifftop viewpoints

of a 2015 burn area. Keep an eye out for deer and wild turkey, common in this area. Watch, too, for rattlesnakes, which sometimes sun themselves on the rocks here.

Reach the first overlook at 3.3 miles, offering lovely views of the Little Spokane River valley and the meandering river below. Raptors are often seen riding thermals here. Press on another 0.3 mile down the trail for more views, where you can spy Mount Spokane in the distance to the northeast and Lookout Mountain just to the north. A thin boot path here leads up to another, still higher viewpoint with similar views. After you take some time to enjoy the views, head back to the junction, clocking in at 4.3 miles.

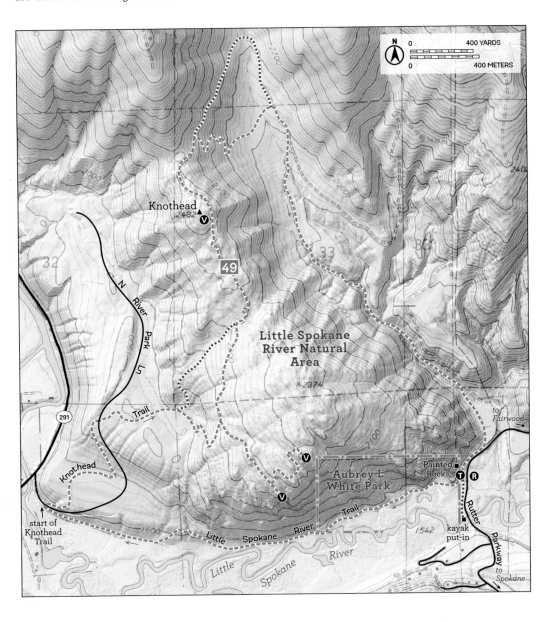

From the junction, head right to continue on the Knothead Trail. The trail rejoins the jeep track as it climbs up along a ridgeline through semi-open forest that offers occasional views of the surrounding landscape. At 5.1 miles, reach a small rise as the trail levels out. This is Knothead; follow a faint boot path up to a rocky viewpoint, where you can make out Long Lake in the distance to the northwest and a slice of glittering Spokane to the south.

From Knothead, the descent begins. Leave the jeep track and follow a narrow trail as it switchbacks sharply and steeply down through the pines to the bottom of a creek basin, where it rejoins an old road. Continue downhill, entering the 2015 burn again and leveling out as you approach Rutter Parkway. Just before the logging road merges with pavement, veer off the roadbed and follow a trail a short distance to the parking area, closing the loop at 7.7 miles.

HISTORY

Back around 1750, one or more members of the Spokane Tribe mixed some crushed red rock with a little animal fat and drew figures and symbols on a rock near the Little Spokane River. The naturally sheltered rock absorbed the paint and preserved it, and since its discovery by fur trappers, it has been largely protected as an important historical site. The fence, a relatively recent addition, was built to curb vandalism.

The Little Spokane River Natural Area was designated in 1987, but the work to make the park a reality began back in 1973 and was spearheaded by the Spokane County Parks Department, who worked with local landowners to purchase 811 acres of the natural area over the course of thirteen years. By 1985, the county transferred ownership to the Washington State Parks Department, and it was eventually merged into Riverside State Park. In 2000, the Van Horn, Edburg, and Bass Conservation Area was created, adding 701 acres to the natural area. Trails are still being developed in the area, with many of them following the traces of the old logging roads that crisscrossed the slopes.

50 DISHMAN HILLS CONSERVATION AREA

DISTANCE: 5 miles
ELEVATION GAIN: 1200 feet
HIGH POINT: 3600 feet
DIFFICULTY: Moderate
HIKING TIME: 3 to 4 hours
BEST SEASON: Spring to early summer

TRAIL TRAFFIC: Moderate foot and mountain bike traffic
MANAGING AGENCY: Spokane County Parks
PERMIT: None
MAPS: USGS Spokane SE
TRAILHEAD GPS: 47.60180°N, 117.28170°W

Climb up through cool forests to reach cliffs and crags popular with hikers and climbers alike. Scramble up to your own private perch to enjoy the views before looping back down through open ridgelines brimming with wildflowers.

GETTING THERE: From I-90 just east of Spokane, take exit 287 for Argonne Road. Turn south and proceed 1.2 miles to a major intersection, where Argonne Road becomes Dishman-Mica Road. Continue straight ahead for another 2.3 miles to Schafer Road. Turn right, continuing 0.9 mile to 44th Avenue. Turn right on 44th Avenue for 0.2 mile to Farr Road. Take a left, following Farr Road for 0.3 mile to Holman Road. Turn right and continue on Holman Road for 0.7 mile to the Iller Creek Trailhead at a sharp turn where the road becomes E. Rockcrest Lane.

Flowers brighten this trail in the Dishman Hills.

From the trailhead, the loop begins along the Iller Creek Loop Trail, entering a mixed forest of alder and hemlock. Ignore the trail to your left leading up the mountainside; this is your return

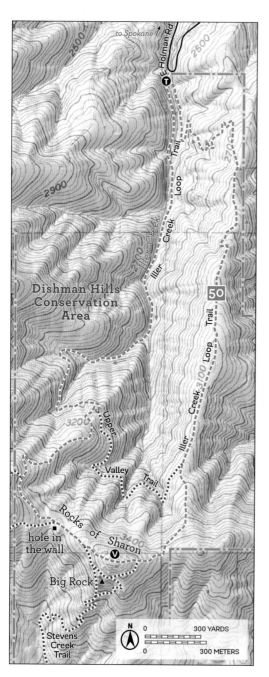

trail. For now, continue straight ahead, following the boot-pounded former roadbed as it saddles up alongside Iller Creek. More boisterous during rainier seasons, the creek may have slowed to a trickle during the summer months. Glide along the shady, nearly flat trail, sticking to the wide path and avoiding boot paths that lead off into the trees. Pass benches and other rest stops as you duck through darkened glades and emerge into wider openings. Keep an eye out for water-loving wildflowers along this section. Eventually the trail starts to climb, working its way up the sides of the creek basin.

At the top of a rise, reach the junction with the Upper Valley Trail at 1.6 miles. This trail is a cutoff that traverses the creek basin and avoids the climb up to the Rocks of Sharon. It's a great option if you're looking for a shorter day. Otherwise, keep right and continue climbing up the forest that begins to be dominated by pines and hemlock as you leave the alders and willows behind. At 2.1 miles the trail connects with the remnants of an old jeep track. Don't be tempted off course—the track leads out to radio towers on nearby Krell Hill. Turn left and push onward through younger forest that soon reveals the stone monoliths of the Rocks of Sharon.

Arrive at a junction at the 2.3-mile mark. The signpost points straight ahead for the Iller Creek Trail, but the boot path to the right is a worthy side trip. Not only will you find excellent viewpoints, but also here is the "hole in the wall," which is, quite literally, a hole in a large monolith. Once you've explored, return to the loop trail, proceeding through much more open forest with a meadowy understory perfect for wildflowers. At 2.4 miles pass another tempting side trail down to Big Rock, the king of this tribe of basalt outcroppings. Explore, or continue on another 0.1 mile to the top of the Rocks of Sharon.

From here, find sweeping views of the Palouse, with pastures and farmland stretching into the distant southern horizon. Find the Selkirk Mountains filling the skyline to the east. Krell Hill's radio towers dot the hillsides to the west. Keep your eyes and ears open for marmots that are often found sunning themselves on these rocks. It's hard to imagine a better

FEATURED WILDFLOWER

SHOWY JACOB'S-LADDER
Polemonium pulcherrimum

A member of the phlox family, showy Jacob's-ladder blooms throughout the summer and grows in clumps, with compound, fernlike leaf structures that are said to resemble a ladder. The small oval leaflets become smaller toward the tip of the leaf. The plant has several flower stems, 8 to 12 inches tall, each of which sprouts several bell-like flowers with overlapping, rounded petals that vary in color from light blue to periwinkle and taper to a bright yellow center. Generally found in talus fields and other dry, rocky settings, the plant gives off a skunky odor that is sometimes stronger in the evening.

Other Wildflowers on the Trail: Balsamroot, baneberry, calypso orchid, chocolate lily, desert parsley, false Solomon's seal, heartleaf arnica, longleaf phlox, mallow ninebark, meadow larkspur, nineleaf biscuitroot, paleyellow ragwort, pioneer violet, Piper's anemone, rock clematis, silky lupine, small-flowered blue-eyed Mary, small-flowered prairie-star, starry false lily of the valley, Utah honeysuckle, Virginia strawberry, Wood's rose

picnic spot, so find your favorite vista and settle in to enjoy the view.

When you're ready, return to the loop trail, which drops steeply along loose, rocky trail. At 2.6 miles pass another junction that provides access to Big Rock. Stay on the loop trail as it drops back into the trees and passes the other side of the Upper Valley Trail at 3 miles. The forest is fairly open here, with low shrubs allowing partial views of the Iller Creek basin as well as glimpses of the surrounding landscape to the east. Eventually reach the edge of the 1991 burn to reveal big views of suburban Spokane with Mount Spokane in the distance. Drop down along a flower-lined trail, passing a few side trails that are best ignored. Eventually reach a series of steep switchbacks that lead you back down into the Iller Creek basin. As you near the bottom, the trail splits—either way leads back down to the trailhead to close the loop at 5 miles.

HISTORY

For generations, people have been exploring this area, which is just a few miles away from bustling downtown Spokane and surrounded by outlying communities. The summit's distinctive rock formations, so beloved by climbers, have also long intrigued local residents. They named the largest of the formations Big Rock, and the group is sometimes collectively known as Big Rocks. Back in 1905, the Great Northern Railway operated a line that ran under the south end of those jutting rocks. The closest station, Sharon, became popular with hikers and picnickers, who would climb up the slopes to enjoy the view. As a result, the collection of rocks became known as the Rocks of Sharon.

In 1966 a high school science teacher named Tom Rogers founded the Dishman Hills Natural Area Association to preserve hundreds of acres in Spokane Valley. Later renamed the Dishman Hills Conservancy, it has preserved more than 2500 acres. In 2011, after years of effort, the conservancy acquired 966 acres that included the Rocks of Sharon. Since that time, the area has become a refuge for wildlife and a popular recreation destination.

ACKNOWLEDGMENTS

This book would not have been possible without the tireless support of our families, our friends, and the hikingwithmybrother.com community, all of whom have collectively tolerated years of us frantically crisscrossing the state to hike trails during the short wildflower season. The journey of writing this book (in conjunction with our other title, *Alpine Lakes Wilderness: The Complete Hiking Guide*, Mountaineers Books) has been so long that, along the way, we each got married, and a child was born. That little girl, who has never known a day when her father wasn't working on a guidebook, will be six by the time this book hits shelves.

We have more people to thank than we could possibly list. We have had so much support and encouragement from the Mountaineers team, especially Kate Rogers and Laura Shauger, who have helped us take our ideas from better to best. Special thanks to our sister Emily Barnes, a freelance editor who worked with Mountaineers Books on the final draft of this book, making it a family effort. Our families and close friends all played a part in making sure we could devote the time and energy into this project, especially Alysha Yagoda, Hillary Witte, Meg Manthos, and Nathan's daughter, Myrna Barnes, who has since forgiven Daddy for being away so often and has started her own hiking adventures. Thanks, too, to those who braved the trails with us, including Bryan Page and Kolbe Kegel.

The view from the Rocks of Sharon in the Dishman Hills (Hike 50)
OPPOSITE: *South Navarre Peak from the Summer Blossom Trail (Hike 18)*

APPENDIX: MANAGING AGENCIES

Bureau of Land Management:
Yakima River Canyon
www.blm.gov/visit/yakima-river-canyon

Wenatchee Field Office
915 Walla Walla Avenue
Wenatchee, WA 98801
(509) 665-2100

Gifford Pinchot National Forest
www.fs.usda.gov/giffordpinchot

Cowlitz Valley Ranger District
10024 US Highway 12
PO Box 670
Randle, WA 98377
(360) 497-1100

Mount Adams Ranger District
2455 Highway 141
Trout Lake, WA 98650
(509) 395-3400

Mount St. Helens National
Volcanic Monument
42218 NE Yale Bridge Road
Amboy, WA 98601
(360) 449-7800

Hanford Reach National Monument
www.fws.gov/refuge/Hanford_Reach

US Fish and Wildlife Service
(manages the monument)
64 Maple Street
Burbank, WA 99323
(509) 546-8300

Mount Baker–Snoqualmie National Forest
www.fs.usda.gov/mbs

Darrington Ranger District
1405 Emens Avenue North
Darrington, WA 98241
(360) 436-1155

Mount Baker Ranger District
810 State Route 20
Sedro-Woolley, WA 98284
(360) 856-5700, ext. 515

Skykomish Ranger District
74920 NE Stevens Pass Highway
PO Box 305
Skykomish, WA 98288
(360) 677-2414

Snoqualmie Ranger District
902 SE North Bend Way, Building 1
North Bend, WA 98045
(425) 888-1421

Mount Rainier National Park
www.nps.gov/mora

OPPOSITE: *A wildflower-filled meadow bursting with rich color on Tiffany Mountain (Hike 17)*

Mount Rainier Administration Office
55210 238th Avenue East
Ashford, WA 98304
(360) 569-2211

North Cascades National Park
www.nps.gov/noca

Park Offices
810 State Route 20
Sedro-Woolley, WA 98284
(360) 854-7200

Okanogan-Wenatchee National Forest
www.fs.usda.gov/okawen

Cle Elum Ranger District
803 West Second Street
Cle Elum, WA 98922
(509) 852-1100

Methow Valley Ranger District
24 West Chewuch Road
Winthrop, WA 98862
(509) 996-4000

Wenatchee River Ranger District
600 Sherbourne Street
Leavenworth, WA 98826
(509) 548-2550

Olympic National Forest
www.fs.usda.gov/olympic

Forks Ranger District
437 Tillicum Lane
Forks, WA 98331
(360) 374-6522

Hood Canal Ranger District
295142 Highway 101 South
PO Box 280
Quilcene, WA 98376
(360) 765-2200

Olympic National Park
www.nps.gov/olym

Olympic National Park Visitor Center
3002 Mount Angeles Road
Port Angeles, WA 98362
(360) 565-3130

Spokane County Parks
www.spokanecounty.org/1383/Parks

Parks, Recreation & Golf
404 North Havana Street
Spokane, WA 99202
(509) 477-4730

Washington Department of Fish and Wildlife
www.wdfw.wa.gov

Natural Resources Building
1111 Washington Street SE
Olympia, WA 98501
(360) 902-2200

Washington State Department of Natural Resources
www.dnr.wa.gov/DiscoverPass

Natural Resources Building
1111 Washington Street SE
Olympia, WA 98501
(360) 902-1000

Washington State Parks
https://parks.state.wa.us

1111 Israel Road SW
Tumwater, WA 98501-6512
(360) 902-8844

Ebey's Landing State Park
(jointly managed by the National Park Service
and Washington State Parks)
www.nps.gov/ebla/planyourvisit/maps.htm

REFERENCES

BOOKS

Fagan, Damian. *Pacific Northwest Wildflowers: A Guide to Common Wildflowers of Washington, Oregon, Northern California, Western Idaho, Southeast Alaska, and British Columbia.* Guilford, CT: Globe Pequot Press, 2006.

Hitchman, Robert. *Place Names of Washington.* Tacoma: Washington State Historical Society, 1985.

Parratt, Smitty. *Gods & Goblins: A Field Guide to Place Names of Olympic National Park.* 2nd ed. Forks, WA: Poseidon Peak Publishing, 2009.

Spring, Ira, Arthur Kruckeberg, Karen Sykes, and Craig Romano. *Best Wildflower Hikes: Washington.* Seattle: Mountaineers Books, 2004.

WEBSITES

The Mountaineers Annual, www.mountaineers.org/about/history/the-mountaineer-annuals

Washington Native Plant Society Plant Lists, www.wnps.org/plant-lists

Washington Trails Association, www.wta.org

Wildflower Search, www.wildflowersearch.org

The camas-filled prairie of Mima Mounds (Hike 8)

INDEX

Bold indicates hikes and featured flower boxes.

OPPOSITE: *Iceberg Lake and Mount Baker from the Chain Lakes Trail (Hike 11)*

ABOUT THE AUTHORS

Born and raised in the Pacific Northwest, the Barnes brothers cultivated their enthusiasm for the outdoors at a young age by way of trips to the Columbia River Gorge, Bend, Mount Rainier, Mount St. Helens, and countless hikes through the region's forests. A few years after college, they needed a new challenge and decided to tackle Mount Rainier. After months of training, they reached Columbia Crest on September 7, 2008.

In the weeks that followed, Nathan and Jeremy resolved to keep up their training regimen of weekly hikes to stay in shape. Idle trail talk led them to set a goal: Explore all the hikes in Harvey Manning and Ira Spring's *55 Hikes Around Snoqualmie Pass* (Mountaineers Books). Before long, they decided it would be fun to track their progress, and hikingwithmybrother.com was born. Nathan researches the background on their hikes and writes most of the content, while Jeremy takes almost all the photographs, creates the maps, and manages most of the technical aspects of the website.

Over the last decade, the brothers' approach to recommending hikes has evolved into a distinctive style that showcases aspects of the hike they find most valuable while detailing the pitfalls, capturing the essence of each hike in pictures, and providing a little extra background on the history of the trail. Long ago they moved beyond the confines of Snoqualmie Pass, and they continue to add more hikes to the website from around the state.

Along the way, Nathan and Jeremy have met a lot of hikers and outdoors lovers, as well as partnered with *Backpacker Magazine*, the *Seattle Times*, Washington State Parks, the Washington Trails Association, and Mountaineers Books. In 2019 they released their first book published by Mountaineers Books, *Alpine Lakes Wilderness: The Complete Hiking Guide*. Today they continue to hike as often as their careers and families allow, no longer simply for exercise, but also for everyone who follows hikingwithmybrother.com and enjoys up-to-date trail reports, out-of-the-way destinations, and adventuresome hikes. Feel free to reach out to them at hikingwithmybrother @gmail.com.

MOUNTAINEERS BOOKS including its two imprints, Skipstone and Braided River, is a leading publisher of quality outdoor recreation, sustainability, and conservation titles. As a 501(c)(3) nonprofit, we are committed to supporting the environmental and educational goals of our organization by providing expert information on human-powered adventure, sustainable practices at home and on the trail, and preservation of wilderness.

Our publications are made possible through the generosity of donors, and through sales of 700 titles on outdoor recreation, sustainable lifestyle, and conservation. To donate, purchase books, or learn more, visit us online::

MOUNTAINEERS BOOKS

1001 SW Klickitat Way, Suite 201 • Seattle, WA 98134
800-553-4453 • mbooks@mountaineersbooks.org • mountaineersbooks.org

An independent nonprofit publisher since 1960

Mountaineers Books is proud to support the Leave No Trace Center for Outdoor Ethics, whose mission is to promote and inspire responsible outdoor recreation through education, research, and partnerships. The Leave No Trace program is focused specifically on human-powered (nonmotorized) recreation. For more information, visit www.lnt.org.

YOU MAY ALSO LIKE:

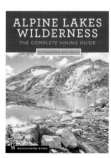

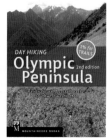